THE Baseball Research JOURNAL

Editor
Jim Charlton

Designer
Glenn LeDoux

Cover Illustration
Jeff Suntala

Our thanks to these peer reviewers
and designated readers:

Dick Beverage

Lyle Spatz

Charlie Pavitt

Phil Birnbaum

Ted Turocy

Ed Hartig

Keith Carlson

Bill Nowlin

Tom Ruane

Clifford Blau

Gabriel Schechter

Marty Appel

Scott Flatow

ISBN 1-933599-00-6

Contents

Dave Stieb photographs on back cover courtesy of the Toronto Blue Jays

THE BASEBALL RESEARCH JOURNAL #34. Published by The Society for American Baseball Research, Inc., 812 Huron Rd., Suite 719, Cleveland, OH 44115. Postage paid at Kent, OH. Copyright ©2005, The Society for American Baseball Research, Inc. All rights reserved. Reproduction in whole or in part without written permission is prohibited. Distributed by the University of Nebraska Press, Lincoln, NE 68588.

Editor's Note

The last issue of *The Baseball Research Journal* featured lengthy articles by George Michael, on mystery photos, and Phil Lowry, on marathon games of 20 innings or more. The essays were so well received that the two authors have returned for another bow. This time Phil gives us marathon games of six hours or more, while George invites readers to help him identify photographs that have eluded even his keen detective skills.

Tom Ruane offers two thoughtful pieces: one on clutch hitting, the elusive grail of researchers, and the other on a question we've all asked ourselves; do some players reach base on errors more than others? Some surprising names emerge.

Phil Birnbaum also has two articles here, including another question many of us have asked: Do traded players turn out to be lemons? While we can all think of names to support each side of that argument, Phil goes the sabermetric route to try and answer it definitively. Phil's other article "Which Great Teams were Just Lucky?" is the inspiration for the delightful cover sketch by artist Jeff Suntala.

Father Gabe Costa heads a trio of writers who chart the dependable falloff of home run production by sluggers as they age. It happens to all sluggers, except, as the article shows, three contemporary hitters. Cy Morong punctures the published story that Greg Maddux served up a homerun to Jeff Bagwell to set him up for a pitch months later. Maddux is a future Hall of Famer, but even he is not that good. Keith Olbermann details a fascinating change in scoring games that occurred more than a hundred years ago.

Trying to acquire photographs for articles can often be a frustrating and time-consuming occupation. In some cases, no photo exists. This happened with Phil Lowry's marathon essay, where, apparently, photographers were too tired to raise their cameras and snap pictures. It also is the case with Scott Schleifstein's poignant article on a 1972 A's—White Sox game. No photo exists of a heartfelt gesture by three A's players.

Jim Charlton
December 2005

Normalized Winning Percentage, Revisited
Big Unit Stands Tall, for Now

In the 1996 *Baseball Research Journal*, I presented something I call "Normalized Winning Percentage," or NWP. After a decade's passage of time, and the emergence of a new all-time leader and number two man, it seems a good time to revisit this statistic.

NWP projects how a pitcher might perform on a .500-team, thus putting all hurlers, past and present, on an even plane of comparison. The concept starts out by comparing a pitcher's won-lost record to that of his team, neutralizing the impacts of a team's offense and defense on its pitchers' records. This idea is hardly new: Ted Oliver used it in his *Kings of the Mound* in 1944; David Neft and Richard Cohen used it in *The Sports Encyclopedia: Baseball* in 1973; Merritt Clifton used it in *Relative Baseball* in 1979; and Pete Palmer used it in *The Hidden Game of Baseball* in 1984. Each of these men analyzed the data differently, but each overlooked one basic problem: a pitcher on a poor team has more room for improvement than one on a good team. In other words, it's easier for Walter Johnson to exceed his team's win percentage by 100 points than it is for Whitey Ford.

Consider the performances of Steve Carlton in 1972 and Greg Maddux in 1995. Carlton had a 27–10 (.730) record for the last-place Phillies, who were a woeful 32–87 (.269) in games Lefty did not get a decision. Carlton's percentage therefore exceeded his team's by a whopping 461 points—*out of a possible 731*. On the other hand, it is hard to imagine anyone pitching any better than Maddux did when he went 19–2 with an ERA (1.63), more than 2.5 runs better than the league's. Yet Maddux's winning percentage was "only" 328 points above that of his Braves (71–52, .577, without Mad Dog's decisions). Moreover, even if Maddux had been a perfect 21–0, he would have fallen short of Carlton's 461-point cushion. The point here is not to diminish Carlton's achievement, but to illustrate the potential inequity in this type of comparison.

NWP basically measures how much a pitcher has exceeded his team's performance, divided by how much he *could* have done so, and scaling the result as if he had pitched for an average (.500) team. Thus, a hurler who posts a .520 percentage for a .400 team gets credit for the same NWP score (.600) as a .600 pitcher on a .500 team, or a .680 pitcher on a .600 team—because each has

exceeded his team's percentage by 20% of the potential room for improvement.

For a pitcher whose win percentage exceeds his team's, the formula for NWP is as follows: average percentage plus [(pitcher percentage minus team percentage) times (perfect percentage minus average percentage) divided by (perfect percentage minus team percentage)]. Rather cumbersome but, since "average percentage" is always equal to .500 and "perfect percentage" is always equal to 1.000, we can simplify the formula as follows:

$$\text{NWP} = .500 + \frac{(\text{Pitcher \%} - \text{Team \%})}{2 \times (1.000 - \text{Team \%})}$$

Incidentally, for a pitcher whose percentage is *lower* than his team's, the converse-NWP formula is applicable: .500 minus [(team percentage minus pitcher percentage) divided by (team percentage doubled)].

To put the NWP formula into practice, let's take a look at Johan Santana's performance for the 2005 Twins. Santana compiled a 16–7 (.696) log, while his team was 83–79 overall. Subtracting his decisions, the Twins had a 67–72 record for a .482 percentage. Santana's NWP is calculated as follows:

$$\text{NWP} = .500 + \frac{(.696 - .482)}{2 \times (1.000 - .482)}, \text{ or } .500 + (.214 \div 1.036)$$

Santana's resultant NWP (.706) was fifth best in the majors last year, only a little below his Cy Young Award performance of '04; a list of the 2005 leaders accompanies this article.

I developed the concept for NWP in the early 1980s. The formula has undergone several minor refinements over the years, and undoubtedly has room for more. Perhaps NWP's biggest weakness is that it assumes all pitching staffs to be created equal, so that an average pitcher on a poor staff can appear better than an excellent pitcher on a great staff. While this creates some aberrant single-season results, things usually tend to even out over a pitcher's career.

NWP can be, and has been, incorporated into what analyst Pete Palmer calls "wins above team" (WAT), the number of victories a pitcher contributes over what an "average" pitcher might. Palmer revised his formula to include mine in *Total Baseball* and *The ESPN Baseball Encyclopedia*. The formula for WAT (for pitchers with higher percentages than their teams) is as follows:

BILL DEANE's work has earned him the 1989 SABR-Macmillan Baseball Research Award, the 2001 SABR Salute, and the 2003 Cliff Kachline Award.

$$WAT = \text{Pitcher decisions} \times \frac{\text{Pitcher \% } - \text{ Team \%}}{2 \times (1.000 - \text{Team \%})}$$

Incidentally, NWP gives Carlton's 1972 season a score of .815, while Maddux's 1995 campaign checks in at .887. But because Carlton maintained his excellence over a greater number of decisions, he beats out Maddux in WAT, 11.7 to 8.1.

A list of the top 20 career NWPs (minimum 200 wins since 1900) follows. Each of the pitchers who is eligible is in the Hall of Fame. As a group, their careers are quite evenly distributed over the 106-year span, as opposed to conventional measures of pitching, which suggest that all of the best hurlers toed the rubber before Warren Harding was president.

Since joining the 200-win club, Randy Johnson (.673) and Roger Clemens (.650) have supplanted Lefty Grove (.643) for the best career normalized winning percentages. The Big Unit and the Rocket also rank in the top five all-time in Wins Above Team. No fewer than five of the top 20 NWP pitchers—including some surprises—were active in 2005. Three others—including Curt Schilling (192 wins, .606 NWP) and Kenny Rogers (190, .597)—stand good chances of joining them soon, once they reach the 200-win barrier.

And Pedro Martinez, with 197 wins and a .686 NWP, should become the Daddy of them all.

LEADERS IN NORMALIZED WINNING PERCENTAGE, WITH WINS ABOVE TEAM

(Active players in italics. Compiled by Bill Deane, with assistance from Pete Palmer)

All-Time Leaders (Minimum 200 Wins since 1900)

Pitcher	W	L	WAT	NWP
Randy Johnson	*263*	*136*	*69.2*	*.673*
Roger Clemens	*341*	*172*	*76.7*	*.650*
Lefty Grove	300	141	62.9	.643
Grover Alexander	373	208	81.6	.640
Whitey Ford	236	106	44.4	.630
Walter Johnson	417	279	90.0	.629
Cy Young	511	316	99.7	.621
Christy Mathewson	373	188	64.9	.616
Tom Seaver	311	205	58.9	.614
Mike Mussina	*224*	*127*	*36.8*	*.605*
Juan Marichal	243	142	38.7	.601
Bob Feller	266	162	36.8	.586
Greg Maddux	*318*	*189*	*43.4*	*.586*
Carl Hubbell	253	154	34.6	.585
Joe McGinnity	246	142	32.4	.584
Kevin Brown	*211*	*144*	*29.6*	*.583*
Warren Spahn	363	245	45.8	.575
Ted Lyons	260	230	36.2	.574
Bob Gibson	251	174	31.0	.573
Jim Palmer	268	152	30.2	.572

Note: Although Young and McGinnity started their careers before 1900, they are included because each won at least 200 games after that year; their statistics include pre-1900 records. Statistics for active pitchers are complete through 2005.

2005 Leaders (Minimum 15 Wins or 20 Decisions)

Pitcher, CLUB (LG)	W	L	%	TmW	TmL	Adj. %	NWP	WAT
Chris Carpenter, SL (N)	21	5	.808	100	62	.581	.771	7.04
Cliff Lee, CLE (A)	18	5	.783	93	69	.540	.764	6.07
Carlos Zambrano, CHI (N)	14	6	.700	79	83	.458	.723	4.47
Jamie Moyer, SEA (A)	13	7	.650	69	93	.394	.711	4.22
Johan Santana, MIN (A)	16	7	.696	83	79	.482	.706	4.74
Dontrelle Willis, FLA (N)	22	10	.688	83	79	.469	.706	4.22
Bartolo Colon, LA (A)	21	8	.724	95	67	.556	.689	5.48
Kenny Rogers, TEX (A)	14	8	.636	79	83	.464	.661	3.53
Jake Peavy, SD (N)	13	7	.650	82	80	.486	.660	3.19
Josh Beckett, FLA (N)	15	8	.652	83	79	.489	.660	3.67
Pedro Martinez NY (N)	15	8	.652	83	79	.489	.660	3.67

Has Greg Maddux Employed the "Bagwell Gambit" in His Career?

In a *Newsweek* article George Will called Greg Maddux "the most artistic pitcher of the lively-ball era." As an example of Maddux's knowledge of the hitters, Will wrote the following:

Leading 8–0 in a regular season game against the Astros, Maddux threw what he had said he would never throw to Jeff Bagwell—a fastball in. Bagwell did what Maddux wanted him to do: he homered. So two weeks later, when Maddux was facing Bagwell in a close game, Bagwell was looking for a fastball in, and Maddux fanned him on a change-up away.

This is what I call the "Bagwell gambit," allowing a batter to get a hit in a lopsided game to get him looking for a certain pitch in a close game later on (and then get him out on some other pitch). Before looking into the question of whether or not Maddux really makes a habit of doing this, I first examine what happened when Bagwell has homered against Maddux and if it led to a key strikeout in a later game.

Bagwell has hit seven home runs against Maddux. Here they are, in chronological order, with a description of what happened in that game and then their next meeting.

1. May 28, 1995:eighth inning with none on and ATL ahead, 2–0. This was the only hit Maddux gave up. The final score was 3–1, ATL. NEXT MEETING: June 3, 1995: Maddux struck out Bagwell twice, but Bagwell hits a key home run off Maddux (see home run #2).

2. June 3, 1995:fifth inning with none on and the score tied, 0–0. The final score was 2–1, HOU. NEXT MEETING: July 7, 1996. ATL won, 9–1 (and led 4–0 after three innings). Bagwell struck out once.

3. September 18, 1996: sixth inning with none on and ATL ahead, 6–0. The final score was 6–1, ATL. NEXT MEETING: April 2, 1997. HOU won, 4–3. Bagwell had one hit and struck out once.

CYRIL MORONG, a lifelong White Sox fan, teaches economics at San Antonio College, San Antonio, Texas.

4. September 2, 1998: second inning with none on and ATL ahead, 1–0. The final score was 4–2, HOU. NEXT MEETING: June 16, 1999. ATL won, 3–1. Bagwell is 0–4 with two strikeouts against Maddux.

5. August 11, 1999: third inning with one on and ATL ahead, 5–1. The final score was 8–5, ATL. NEXT MEETING: September 2, 2000. ATL wins, 8–6. Bagwell is 1–3 with one strikeout and one walk against Maddux.

6. May 26, 2004: third inning with one on and HOU ahead, 1–0. The final score was 7–3, HOU. NEXT MEETING: May 31, 2004. CHI wins, 3–1. Bagwell is 1–4 with no strikeouts.

7. April 29, 2005: third inning with none on and CHI ahead, 2–1. The final score was 3–2, CHI. NEXT MEETING: October 2, 2005. Bagwell reached base on a fielder's choice as a pinch-hitter in his only appearance against Maddux.

There is no case that fits exactly what Will described. The only home run allowed to Bagwell in a lopsided game might have been #3. The other six home runs don't appear to be ones that Maddux would have intentionally allowed to set up Bagwell for a later date, since the score was close or it was early in the game. Certainly no home run allowed with the score 8–0 followed by a strikeout two weeks later.

In playoff meetings, Bagwell was only 2 for 10 against Maddux. One playoff game was in 1997, when Bagwell went 0–4 with two strikeouts. But Bagwell did not homer off Maddux that year during the regular season. Bagwell was 1–4 in a playoff game on October 5, 1999, that Maddux started. But the Astros beat the Braves, 6–1. Bagwell was 1–2 against Maddux on October 9, 2001, but with no strikeouts. Bagwell did not homer off Maddux during the 2001 regular season.

In general, Bagwell did very well against Maddux with an AVG-OBP-SLG of .309-.367-.593. This compares very favorably to Bagwell's overall numbers of .297-.408-.541. He has had a better OPS against Maddux (.959) than against all other pitchers (.949). Even using a weighted average, with OBP being considered 50% more important than SLG, Bagwell has done just about as well against Maddux as other pitchers. Multiplying OBP by 1.5 and then adding it to SLG would give Bagwell 1.143 against Maddux and 1.153 against other pitchers. Bagwell struck out just about once in every five ABs in his career while it was once in every 5.67 ABs against Maddux. Per plate appearance Maddux did strike out Bagwell more often than other pitchers, but not by much, once in every 5.73 PAs vs. once in every 5.92 PAs. In general, Maddux has had no dominance over Bagwell. In fact, Bagwell did not homer off him until 1995, four years after he came into the league, covering 36 ABs. This means that Bagwell hit seven home runs against Maddux in his last 45 ABs, quite a high ratio. It seems that Bagwell is figuring out Maddux, not vice-versa.

But what about in general? Has Maddux made a habit of using the "Bagwell gambit" to trick hitters in crucial situations? I looked at how he did in close and late situations (CL) compared to how he did in non-close and late situations over the years 1991–2000 (these are situations when the game is in the seventh inning or later and the batting team is leading by one run, tied, or has the potential tying run on base, at bat or on deck). Since hitters generally don't do as well in CL as they normally do because they are likely to face relief aces who often have the platoon advantage, it would not be fair to Maddux to judge him based on whether or not he does better in CL than NONCL. So I also looked at how other pitchers fared, in particular, the other nine pitchers in the top ten in innings pitched from 1991 to 2000.

Table 1 shows how these pitchers did when it was close and late and not close and late.

Table 1

Pitcher	NONCL OPS	CL OPS	Diff.
Chuck Finley	0.729	0.638	-0.091
Tom Glavine	0.665	0.600	-0.065
Andy Benes	0.714	0.684	-0.030
Roger Clemens	0.639	0.609	-0.029
Mike Mussina	0.687	0.671	-0.016
Randy Johnson	0.619	0.631	0.012
Greg Maddux	0.580	0.606	0.026
Scott Erickson	0.750	0.789	0.039
Kevin Brown	0.634	0.680	0.046
David Cone	0.659	0.725	0.066

Maddux does worse in CL than NONCL (his OPS increases .026) while some other pitchers actually do better. If Maddux has a pattern of setting up hitters to expect a certain pitch in key situations, it is not evident here, since CL is just the time when he would want to take advantage of the "Bagwell gambit." In fact, other pitchers seem to improve in CL. That would indicate that they, even more than Maddux, *might* have been setting up the hitters to look for a certain pitch.

It is possible that Maddux's OPS in CL is raised by intentional walks, which I have not accounted for here (OBP included only hits, walks, and ABs). But his AVG and SLG also increase, although just 4 and 6 points, respectively. Five pitchers saw their AVG fall and five saw their SLG fall.

In fairness to Maddux, he did face more hitters in CL than these other pitchers. Table 2 shows how many PAs they each had

in CL and NONCL and the percentage in CL.

Table 2

Pitcher	Total PA	CLPA	%CL
Greg Maddux	9335	1089	0.117
Randy Johnson	8428	933	0.111
Kevin Brown	9147	949	0.104
Roger Clemens	8745	850	0.097
Tom Glavine	9213	844	0.092
Mike Mussina	8081	729	0.090
Chuck Finley	8943	785	0.088
David Cone	8052	699	0.087
Andy Benes	8456	641	0.076
Scott Erickson	8438	588	0.070

But even so, if Maddux were really setting up the hitters with the "Bagwell gambit," we would see him do better in CL, if only in comparison to other pitchers.

Another time when we might see the "Bagwell gambit" manifest itself would be in the post-season, particularly the Divisional Series (DS) and League Championship Series (LCS), when Maddux would face hitters he has faced before (in World Series action, he is less likely to have seen the opposing batters before). The hitters in the playoffs are likely to be better than average, so we would expect any pitcher's ERA to go up then. So I looked at how the top ten pitchers in ERA relative to the league average from 1989 to 2003 (covering the time period in which Maddux appeared in the playoffs) did in DS and LCS games in comparison to their regular season ERAs. Table 3 summarizes this.

Table 3

Pitcher	IP	PL-ERA	ERA	Diff.
Schilling	66.2	2.03	3.36	-1.33
Mussina	101.2	3.19	3.85	-0.66
Smoltz	149.0	2.78	3.12	-0.34
Brown	56.1	3.36	2.86	0.50
Clemens	133.1	4.05	3.36	0.69
Maddux	151.1	3.51	2.75	0.76
Glavine	143.0	4.03	3.15	0.88
Johnson	90.2	3.47	2.56	0.91
Cone	81.2	4.41	3.43	0.98
Martinez	72.1	3.73	2.38	1.35

PL-ERA is each pitcher's composite ERA from the DS and LCS. ERA is their composite regular season ERA from years in which they also pitched in the playoffs. Maddux's performance does not appear to be unusual here. His ERA goes up in the playoffs when facing NL hitters he has faced before. Not a big surprise since these hitters will be better than average. But some pitchers' ERAs actually go down. In fairness to Maddux, he has pitched the most innings here. But Smoltz has almost as many IP and his ERA actually went down (and Glavine's performance is very close to Maddux's). If Maddux was setting up hitters to look for certain

Jeff Bagwell

Greg Maddux

pitches, it again does not appear that he was fooling them (at least not any more than he normally fools hitters).[1]

In all, the evidence does not seem to support the idea that Maddux employs the "Bagwell gambit." If so, we would see unusual improvement in his performance in close and late situations and in NL playoff games. But we do not. Every manager would certainly have loved to have Maddux pitching when it was close and late or in the playoffs. But not because he has the hitters expecting a certain pitch that they hit before. They would have loved to have him because he was a great pitcher in general.

Notes

1. In World Series play, Maddux has an ERA of 2.09. But that is against hitters he had less experience facing. His ERAs in the 1995 and 1996 series, before inter-league play began, were 2.25 and 1.72, respectively. He pitched very well against those hitters yet had little opportunity to set them up with the "Bagwell gambit."

Sources

George Will. "The Artistry of Mr. Maddux," *Newsweek* magazine, April 25, 2005, p. 84.
ESPN Website
Yahoo Sports Web site
Retrosheet Web site
STATS, Inc. Player Profiles books

I Don't Care If I Ever Get Back:
Marathons Lasting Six or More Hours

For more than 40 years I have exhaustively researched marathon games by time and by innings played at all levels of professional and amateur baseball. Last year the *Baseball Research Journal* published part of that research: marathons lasting 20 or more innings. Continuing that effort, I now present the research on games lasting six hours or more.

My marathon research into longest games has resulted in rewriting five records in four different record books. Since 1919, the major league record for shortest full-length game by time, the first game of a doubleheader September 28, 1919, at the Polo Grounds between the Phils and Giants, had been recorded as 51 minutes. However, in my research I discovered the record correctly belongs to the 50-minute game played April 12, 1911, also at the Polo Grounds between the same two teams.

Before my research, the NCAA record was 22 innings. However, I uncovered a 23-inning NCAA game in Lafayette, Louisiana March 27, 1971 between McNeese State and SW Louisiana. The NAIA record was also 22 innings, set in 2005, but I discovered a second 22-inning NAIA game played in Arkadelphia, Arkansas April 28, 1970 between Harding and Henderson State. The NCAA record for most innings in a doubleheader was 29, but the McNeese State-SW Louisiana 23-inning game was the opener of a 30-inning DH.

Since 1976, the National Federation of State High School Association's (NFSHSA) record for most innings had been recorded as 28 innings. However, this research discovered that the record correctly belongs to two 24-inning games, played on April 23, 1970, in Miami Beach, FL, between Miami HS and Hialeah HS, and May 18/25, 2004 in Norridge, IL, between Evergreen Park HS and Ridgewood HS.

A rough guess for the number of baseball games that have ever been played is 16 million (see 2004 *BRJ*). So far I have discovered only 106 games lasting six hours or more. This indicates one game in roughly every 149,000 takes six hours or more.

The Longest Game

The longest that baseball has been continuously played in one game was 31 hours, 30 minutes, for a planned marathon at Campanelli Stadium in Brockton, MA, on April 16–17, 2005. Team

In 1986, **PHIL LOWRY** argued passionately for asymmetrical ballparks in his book *Green Cathedrals*, stating that symmetrical toilet bowl, cookie-cutter, ashtray stadia were destroying the soul of the game. If you know of any marathons missing from Phil's list, let him know at plowry1176@aol.com.

Marciano beat Team Hagler 88–79 in a 100-inning game to raise funds for ALS research.

A 19th-century game played under Massachusetts Rules established a record time of game which has never been equaled. However, this record must be considered differently from other records, since one inning was defined not by three outs, but rather by one out. On September 25, 1860, at the Agricultural Grounds in Worcester, MA, the Upton Excelsiors and Medway Unions began a game that would take 172 innings over seven days! Play continued through September 26, 27, 28; October 1, 4, and 5 until finally it was called a complete game with the score Upton 50, Medway 29 after a time of game of 21 hours, 50 minutes. Total elapsed time also set an all-time record of more than 25 hours, including a dinner delay, lunch delay, and four rain delays.

Hard-to-Understand Marathon #1
10:00 in Piedras Negras, Mexico

Our first "mystery" is this 10-hour long July 18, 1926 game. The July 20 *Eagle Pass Guide* (TX) states the San Luisito team from Eagle Pass defeated Piedras Negras 29–19 Sunday in a "scrap" which began at 9:00 a.m. and was called due to darkness in the sixth inning at 7:00 p.m. The July 24 *San Antonio Express* (TX) and the July 25 *Lima Sunday News* (OH) say the game lasted from 9:00 a.m. to 7:00 p.m., and San Luista defeated Piedras Legras Negras from across the border 129-–119, with shortstop Mircles committing 24 errors in the 3rd inning (and only 30 or 31 for the entire game).

The August 20 *Lincoln Star* (NE) and August 25 *Los Angeles Times* (CA) state the Mexican team won 129–119, with one player making 24 errors in the third inning. And the June 18, 1938 *Lowell Sun* (MA) says San Luista defeated visiting Piedras Legras of Mexico 129–119 in a game beginning at 10:00 a.m. with the losing team making 23 errors in the 3rd inning.

The Mexican town of Piedras Negras (Black Rock) is just across the Rio Grande from Eagle Pass, Texas. San Luisito (not San Luista) is a neighborhood in Eagle Pass. But who won? Was the score 29–19 or 129–119? Did the shortstop make 24 errors, or did the entire team make 23 errors in the 3rd? And most importantly, why did it take 10 hours to play only 5½ innings? We may never know. Some answers will remain forever shrouded in the fog of the past.

First Lieutenant Abner Doubleday of the U.S. Army Field Artillery was stationed in Eagle Pass at Fort Duncan in 1854–55.

His wife, who was petrified of mice, arranged for a mice-protection net to be built around their bed..

Hard-to-Understand Marathon #2
8:30 in Pottsville, PA

Our second "mystery" is how a game between two unnamed Pottsville teams on July 8, 1902, could have taken eight and a half hours to play. The final score was 38–36. The local paper relates that the game began at 9:00 a.m., and finished at 5:30 p.m., with no break for dinner.

So OK, it was high-scoring. But how could it have taken almost an hour to play each inning? Assuming the game took nine innings, which we don't know for sure, it would have taken 57 minutes per inning. That is high, but not a record. The Piedras Negras game took 109 minutes per inning.

But that's nothing if we count elapsed time. The Tigers and Yankees struggled through two long rain delays at Yankee Stadium in the first game of a scheduled doubleheader on August 9, 1991, and took 5 hours, 41 minutes, to play just two innings before the umpires finally called it at 10:16 p.m. This works out to 170.5 minutes, or almost three hours per inning! A critical fact to remember: the Tigers led 1–0 when the game was called off.

Longest Minor League Marathon
8:25 in Pawtucket, RI

At 4:07 a.m. on Easter morning, April 19, 1981, just 51 minutes before sunrise, 17 freezing and very fortunate souls huddled in the 28-degree pre-dawn chill of Pawtucket, RI's McCoy Stadium. Their beloved Paw Sox had just failed to break a 2–2 tie with the Rochester Red Wings in the bottom of the 32nd. When the umpires suspended the game, these brave 17 fans looked back on eight hours and seven minutes of baseball, preceded by a half-hour power-failure delay.

The game resumed on June 23 with McCoy packed to capacity, and the mercury all the way up to 80. The Paw Sox won, 3–2, in the 33rd on Dave Koza's bases-loaded single. The final totals of eight hours, 55 minutes, elapsed time and eight hours, 25 minutes, game time are modern baseball records.

Longest Japanese Marathon—8:19 in Mito

When play began on September 20, 1983, in the title game of the 38th annual Emperor's Cup Nan-shiki Tournament in Mito, Japan, nobody had the least idea what lay ahead! The game between Light Manufacturing of Tokyo and Tanaka Hospital of Miyazaki began at 8:50 a.m. The local Mito Band was to be ready at 11:00 a.m. to play at the post-game award ceremony.

The game finally ended at 5:15 p.m. after Light Manufacturing scored in the top of the 45th to win 2–1 after 8 hours, 19 minutes, of baseball. Including a six-minute delay in the 26th, the game lasted 8 hours, 25 minutes. The Mito Band finally got to play after waiting for over six hours.

Longest American League Marathon
8:06 in Comiskey Park

At old Comiskey Park on May 8–9, 1984, the White Sox downed the Brewers, 7–6, in 25 innings and 8 hours, 6 minutes, the major league record for game time. Suspended after 17 innings at 1:05 a.m. by the AL curfew, the game was won the next evening in the 25th by Harold Baines' homer which just barely cleared the bullpen fence in center.

The White Sox scored two in the ninth, and three in the 21st to keep the game tied, and would have won in the 23rd except that Dave Stegman was ruled out for coach's interference. Third-base coach Jim Leyland helped Stegman to his feet after he tripped rounding third.

Hard-to-Understand Marathon #3
8:00 in Carrollton, KY

This is our third "mystery" marathon. Ghent defeated Carrollton, 179–70, on July 4, 1868. The game began at 9:00 a.m. and was called off in the sixth inning due to darkness at 10:00 p.m. The time of game was only eight hours, though, because the players and the umpire took a five-hour break for dinner.

Questions are numerous. Why did it take eight hours to play less than six innings? That's almost an hour and a half per inning. How could they play until 10:00 p.m. without lights? Why did they take five hours to eat dinner? That's almost 15 minutes per bite. Did they use Massachusetts Rules? Why did they score so many runs? And why is the only source of information on this game Mr. Stonecroft's personal notes from a Carrollton newspaper?

Longest Two-Year College Marathon
7:30 in Bradenton, FL

On April 4, 1987, at Wynn Field, the Hillsborough Hawks defeated the Manatee Lancers 6–4. The original crowd of 200 had dwindled to just 45 loyal fans when the end came at 9:30 p.m.

Longest National League Marathon
7:23 in Shea Stadium

In the nightcap of a doubleheader on May 31, 1964, the Giants beat the Mets, 8–6, in 23 innings as Willie Mays played center field *and* shortstop for the Giants. 8,000 Mets fans from the original crowd of 57,037 stayed until the bitter end at 11:25 p.m.

Longest High School Marathon
7:15 in Byron/Plainview, MN

On June 22 and July 6, 2003, the Byron Braves defeated the Plainview Bucks, 4–3, in 21 innings. The game began in Byron and was suspended due to darkness after 5 hours and 15 innings. Two weeks later, the game was concluded in Plainview.

Longest Four-Year College Marathon
6:43 in Houston, TX

On February 21, 1999, at Cougar Field, the Baylor Bears beat the Houston Cougars, 8–2, in 22 innings. Given the large number of four-year college games, we should expect a longer marathon someday soon.

Longest Minor League Playoff
6:25 in Nashville, TN

It was 3:50 a.m. when the Omaha Royals finally defeated the hometown Sounds, 8–7, in 20 innings on the evening/morning of September 7/8, 1990, in an American Association playoff game. The crowd of 14,482 shrank to only 500 during a long 106-minute rain delay in the bottom of the 11th, and 300 loyal fans remained until the very end.

Longest American Legion Marathon
6:06 in Midwest City, OK

In July 1973, Post 170 of Midwest City defeated Post 170 of Choctaw 2–1 in 24 innings at Regional Park. Of the original 50 fans, only 15 remained until the end at 2:06 a.m.

Longest Major League Playoff
5:50 in Minute Maid Park

Down 6–1 to Atlanta on October 9, 2005, the Astros rallied to win 7–6 with an eighth-inning grand slam by Lance Berkman and Brad Ausmus' game-tying homer with two outs in the bottom of the ninth that hit just inches above the yellow home run stripe on the left-field wall. Chris Burke's walk-off homer in the bottom of the 18th ended the game. The game broke by one minute the old 5:49 record set when the Red Sox and David Ortiz defeated the Yankees 5–4 in 14 innings on October 18, 2004.

A Different Type of "Marathon" at the Ballpark

On May 31, 1952, starting with the first pitch and ending with the last pitch of a Carolina League doubleheader between Greensboro and Danville at Greensboro's War Memorial Stadium, marathon runner HardRock Simpson delighted 2,678 fans by running 99 times around the 1,140-foot-long dirt racetrack surrounding the ball field, for a total of 21.4 miles.

Longest Doubleheader
9:52 in Shea Stadium

The longest doubleheader took almost ten hours to play May 31, 1964, as the Giants swept the Mets, 5–3 in the opener and 8–6 in the nightcap in 23 innings. New York's WOR-TV broadcast all 32 innings, in the process attracting the highest number of viewers in the station's history. Elapsed time was 10:20, from 1:05 p.m. to 11:25 p.m., which is *not* a record. The Phils and Padres split in 12:05 on the evening/morning of July 2/3, 1993, beginning at 4:35 p.m., struggling through three rain delays, and ending at 4:40 a.m.

Longest Tripleheader
10:20 in Lubbock, TX

On March 6, 2004, Harvard beat Air Force, 25–20, before dropping a pair to Texas Tech, 18–6 and 30–8. Elapsed time was 11:15, from 12:32 p.m. to 11:47 p.m., which is *not* a record. Georgia Tech's Ramblin' Wreck swept NC, Florida State, and NC State in 11:20 on May 25, 2003, in the ACC tournament, beginning at 9:34 a.m. and finishing at 8:54 p.m.

Longest Quadrupleheader
9:08 in Buffalo, NY

On March 29, 1998, Siena beat Canisius, 6–3, and then Canisius swept three games, 9–4, 9–6, and 11–-10. All games were scheduled for seven innings. In the last game, Siena scored three in the top of the seventh to take a four-run lead, but Canisius stormed back with four to tie, and won it in the eighth, so the entire day took 29 innings. Elapsed time was 10:08, from 11:54 a.m. to 10:02 p.m., which is also a record.

Longest Elapsed Time Game
10:02 in Holyoke, MA

Counting rain delays, the longest NL game is 8 hours 28 minutes on July 2, 1993 at the Vet when the Phils and Padres nine-inning opener ended at 1:03 a.m. after three long rain delays. The nightcap ended at 4:40 a.m. The longest AL game is 9:01, September 19, 2000 at Camden Yards when the A's and O's nine-inning day game ended at 10:36 p.m. after two rain delays. The PA announcer said the night game would begin "shortly", but five minutes later announced it was postponed. The longest minor league game is 9:56 at Yogi Berra Stadium in Little Falls, NJ on August 14, 2000 when the Catskill Cougars and NJ Jackals game was delayed by rain for 7 hours 6 minutes. The longest game ever is 10:02 on May 24, 1978 at Holyoke, MA when Delaware emerged victorious over Harvard with a 6-inning 1-0 NCAA tourney win after an 8 hour 12 minute rain delay.

Summary: Piedras Negras, Pawtucket, and Enya

So can lightning strike more than once in the same place, in the same ballpark, in the same city? Yes, it can! Five marathons lasting six hours or more have been played in New York, four in Chicago, and three each in San Antonio and Cleveland. Two each have been played in eight major league ballparks - the Astrodome, Cleveland Stadium, Comiskey Park (I), DC/RFK Stadium, San Diego Stadium, Shea Stadium, Wrigley Field, and Yankee Stadium (II); and also in four minor league ballparks—Al Lang Field in St. Petersburg, Ed Smith Stadium in Sarasota, Keefe Stadium in San Antonio, and Municipal Stadium in Greenville, SC. The most at any one site is three (two at Yankee Stadium (II) and one at Yankee Stadium (I).

Baseball fans, who continue to be fascinated by marathon games, are probably of two minds: one part says, "Gee, it would have been great to be at the Pawtucket game in 1981 that lasted 8 hours and 25 minutes," while the other half is saying, "I'm glad I could just read about it." Will a game ever break that record or the others listed here? As Enya sings: Only time will tell.

Appendix: List of Every Marathon of Six or More Hours

Time	Location	Date	League	Outcome and Notes
10:00	Piedras Negras, Mexico	7/18/1926	Amateur	San Luisito 29 Piedras Negras 19 in 5 1/2 innings
8:30	Pottsville, PA	7/8/1902	Amateur	Team A 38 Team B 36
8:25	McCoy Stadium, Pawtucket, RI	4/18 & 6/23/1981	International League	power failure delay 0:30 at start, Pawtucket Paw Sox 3 Rochester Red Wings 2 in 33 innings
8:19	Ibaraki-Mito Kenei Kyujyo, Mito, Japan	9/20/1983	Amateur Industrial Emperor's Cup Nan-shiki Tournament	Tokyo Raito Kogyo 2 Miyazaki Tanaka Byouin 1 in 45 innings, umpire snack break delay 0:06 top 26th, players refused 0:30 break top 26th
8:16	Athletic Stadium, Burlington, NC	6/24/1988	Appalachian League	Bluefield Orioles 3 Burlington Indians 2 in 27 innings
8:06	Comiskey Park (I), Chicago, IL	5/8 & 5/9/1984	American League	White Sox 7 Brewers 6 in 25 innings
8:00	Carrollton Commons, Carrollton, KY	7/4/1868	Amateur	Ghent 179 Carrollton 70 in 7 innings, dinner delay 5:00
7:37	Waterloo Stadium, Waterloo & Riverview Stadium, Clinton, IA	7/6 & 8/17/1989	Midwest League	Waterloo Diamonds 4 Clinton Giants 3 in 25 innings
7:30	Wynn Field, Bradenton, FL	4/4/1987	NJCAA	Hillsborough Hawks 6 Manatee Lancers 4 in 32 innings
7:23	Shea Stadium, New York, NY	5/31/1964	National League	Giants 8 Mets 6 in 23 innings in 2nd game
7:23	Keefe Stadium, San Antonio, TX	7/14 & 7/16/1988	Texas League	San Antonio Missions 1 Jackson Mets 0 in 26 innings
7:15	High School Field, Byron & Eckstein Field, Plainview, MN	6/22 & 7/6/2003	High School League	Byron Braves 4 Plainview Bucks 3 in 21 innings
7:14	Estadio Emilio Ibarra, Los Mochis, Mexico	11/26/1988	Mexican Pacific League	Los Mochis Caneros (Sugar Cane Growers) 4 Mazatlan Venados (Deer) 2 in 21 innings
7:14	Astrodome, Houston, TX	6/3/1989	National League	Astros 5 Dodgers 4 in 22 innings
7:13	Memorial Stadium, Everett, WA & Civic Stadium, Eugene, OR	8/18 & 8/24/1989	Northwest League	Eugene Emeralds 6 Everett Giants 5 in 25 innings
7:07	MacArthur Stadium, Syracuse, NY	6/19 & 6/20 & 6/21/1985	International League	Pawtucket Paw Sox 3 Syracuse Chiefs 1 in 27 innings, rain delay 0:13 top 23rd, 2nd rain delay 0:50 bottom 24th
7:07	Al Lang Field (II), St. Petersburg, FL	4/14/1994	Florida State League	St. Petersburg Cardinals 8 Lakeland Tigers 7 in 20 innings
7:04	Shea Stadium, New York, NY	9/11/1974	National League	Cardinals 4 Mets 3 in 25 innings, Commissioner Bowie Kuhn stayed for the entire game
7:02	Estadio Teodoro Mariscal, Mazatlan, Mexico	10/26/1993	Mexican Pacific League	Mazatlan Venados (Deer) 2 Guasave Algodoneros (Cotton Pickers) 1 in 22 innings
7:00	Tiger Stadium, Detroit, MI	6/24/1962	American League	Yankees 9 Tigers 7 in 22 innings

7:00	Recreation Park, Visalia, CA	6/19 & 6/20/1971	California League	Visalia Mets 11 Bakersfield Dodgers 9 in 22 innings, suspended after 15 innings and called a tie, but league president reversed this ruling and ordered game to be continued
7:00	Legion Field, Downers Grove, IL	4/28 & 5/3 & 5/8 & 5/12/1995	High School League	Downers Grove North Trojans 12 Elmhurst York Dukes 11 in 23 innings
6:59	Al Lang Field (I), St. Petersburg, FL	6/14/1966	Florida State League	Miami Marlins 4 St. Pete Cardinals 3 in 29 innings
6:44	Capital City Park, Columbia, SC	7/4/2003	South Atlantic League	Asheville Tourists 7 Capital City Bombers 5 in 19 innings
6:43	Cougar Field, Houston, TX	2/21/1999	NCAA	Baylor Bears 8 Houston Cougars 2 in 22 innings
6:41	Estadio Tetelo Vargas, San Pedro de Marcoris, DR	10/19/2002	Dominican Winter League	Orientales Estrellas (Oriental Stars) 4 Escogido Leones Rojos (Red Lions) 3 in 20 innings
6:40	Wolff Stadium, San Antonio, TX	8/14/2004	Texas League	Midland RockHounds 7 San Antonio Missions 5 in 21 innings
6:39	Smith-Wills Stadium, Jackson, MS	7/6/1982	Texas League	Tulsa Drillers 11 Jackson Mets 7 in 23 innings
6:39	Municipal Stadium, Phoenix, AZ	6/23/1990	Pacific Coast League	Calgary Cannons 12 Phoenix Firebirds 9 in 20 innings
6:38	D.C. Stadium, Washington, D.C.	6/12/1967	American League	Senators 6 White Sox 5 in 22 innings
6:38	Estadio Tomaz Oroz, Guaymas, Mexico	12/30/1984	Mexican Pacific League	Guaymas Ostioneros (Oyster Growers) 6 Obregon Yaquis 4 in 15 innings
6:37	All-Sports Stadium, Oklahoma City, OK	5/28 & 5/29/1970	American Association	Indianapolis Indians 10 Oklahoma City 89'ers 7 in 23 innings
6:37	Hoover Met Stadium, Hoover, AL	6/2/1989	Southern League	Birmingham Barons 5 Huntsville Stars 4 in 18 innings
6:37	Dust Devils Stadium, Pasco, WA	8/16 & 8/17/2004	Northwest League	Spokane Indians 2 Tri-City Dust Devils 1 in 23 innings
6:36	Jacobs Field, Cleveland, OH	5/7/1995	American League	Indians 10 Twins 9 in 17 innings
6:35	Ballpark in Arlington, Arlington, TX	8/25/2001	American League	Rangers 8 Red Sox 7 in 18 innings
6:35	Scott Park, Toledo, OH	5/19/2002	NCAA	Central Michigan Chippewas 16 Toledo Rockets 15 in 18 innings
6:34	Falcon Park, Auburn, NY	7/7 & 8/14/2005	New York-Penn League	Auburn Doubledays 6 Batavia Muckdogs 5 in 22 innings
6:32	Tim McCarver Stadium, Memphis, TN	6/17 & 6/18/1991	Southern League	Huntsville Stars 9 Memphis Chicks 7 in 20 innings
6:30	Estadio Nacional, Managua, Nicaragua	7/10/1949	First Division Amateur League	Navarro Cubs 4 Escuelas Internacionales 3 in 26 innings
6:30	Kentucky Wesleyan Field, Owensboro, KY	4/20/1964	NCAA	Kentucky Wesleyan Panthers 8 Oakland City Mighty Oaks 7 in 22 innings, 2nd game postponed
6:30	Estadio Cordoba, Cordoba, Mexico	4/28/1977	Mexican League	Aguascalientes Rieleros (Railroadmen) 6 Cordoba Cafeteros (Coffee Growers) 2 in 23 innings

6:30	Cleveland Stadium, Cleveland, OH	4/11/1992	American League	Red Sox 7 Indians 5 in 19 innings
6:30	Estadio Roberto Clemente, Carolina, PR	11/4/2001	Puerto Rican Winter League	Carolina Giantes (Giants) 2 Caguas Criollos (Natives) 1 in 22 innings
6:29	Ed Smith Stadium, Sarasota & Dunedin Stadium at Grant Field, Dunedin, FL	4/24 and 5/17/1989	Florida State League	Dunedin Blue Jays 8 Sarasota White Sox 3 in 21 innings
6:29	Ed Smith Stadium, Sarasota, FL	5/5/2001	Florida State League	Vero Beach Dodgers 11 Sarasota Red Sox 7 in 19 innings
6:28	Royals Stadium, Kansas City, MO	6/6/1991	American League	Royals 4 Rangers 3 in 18 innings
6:28	Myers Field, Manhattan, KS	4/9/2004	NCAA	Texas Longhorns 10 Kansas State Wildcats 6 in 20 innings
6:26	Koshien Kyujyo, Osaka, Japan	9/11/1992	Japanese Central League	Yakult Swallows 3 Hanshin Tigers 3 in 15 innings, rhubarb delay 0:37
6:26	Municipal Stadium, Greenville, SC	8/6 and 8/7/1998	Southern League	Greenville Braves 10 Huntsville Stars 7 in 23 innings
6:25	Greer Stadium, Nashville, TN	9/7/1990	American Association	Omaha Royals 8 Nashville Sounds 7 in 20 innings, rain delay 1:46 bottom 11th
6:24	Dunn Field, Elmira, NY	5/8/1965	Eastern League	Elmira Pioneers 2 Springfield Giants 1 in 27 innings
6:23	Judy Johnson Field, Wilmington, DE	7/5/1998	Carolina League	Wilmington Blue Rocks 3 Danville 97's 2 in 21 innings
6:22	Estadio Angel Flores, Culiacan, Mexico	10/22/1967	Mexican Pacific League	Obregon Yaquis 3 Culiacan Tomateros (Tomato Growers) 1 in 21 innings
6:22	Estadio Isidoro "Cholo" Garcia, Mayaguez, PR	12/22 & 12/23/1995 & 1/19/1996	Puerto Rican Winter League	Mayaguez Indios (Indians) 2 San Juan Senadores (Senators) 1 in 21 innings
6:20	Billy Hebert Field, Stockton, CA	9/5 & 9/6/1990	California League	Bakersfield Dodgers 5 Stockton Ports 4 in 22 innings
6:20	Evans High School Field, Augusta, GA	5/21/1993	High School League	Augusta Evans Knights 3 Marietta Sprayberry Yellow Jackets 2 in 17 innings
6:20	Dodd Stadium, Norwich, CT	7/13/2000	Eastern League	Altoona Curve 6 Norwich Navigators 5 in 19 innings
6:20	Shizuoka Kyujyo, Shizuoka, Japan	4/14/2002	Japanese Industrial League	Osaka Gas 6 Nissan Motors 5 in 17 innings
6:20	Knights Castle, Fort Mill, SC	8/15/2003	International League	Charlotte Knights 4 Indianapolis Indians 3 in 18 innings in first game, 250 Girl Scouts who were to have camped out in the outfield after the games slept all night in the Ball Park Café restaurant
6:19	Riverside Sports Complex, Riverside, CA	5/22/1988	California League	San Jose Giants 8 Riverside Red Wave 5 in 21 innings
6:19	Shimonoseki Kyujyo, Shimonoseki, Japan	9/8/1996	Japanese Central League	Yakult Swallows 6 Yokohama BayStars 5 in 14 innings
6:17	San Diego Stadium, San Diego, CA	8/15/1980	National League	Astros 3 Padres 1 in 20 innings

6:17	Humphrey Metrodome, Minneapolis, MN	8/31/1993	American League	Twins 5 Indians 4 in 22 innings
6:17	Oaks Oval, Lismore, Australia	12/31/1994	AAA Asian Under 19 Series	Australia 9 Chinese Taipei 8 in 20 innings, 2nd game postponed
6:15	Delano High School Diamond #4 & Varsity Field, Delano, CA	3/23/1967	High School League	Fresno McLane Highlanders 3 Fresno Warriors 2 in 21 innings, diamond switch delay from Diamond #4 to Varsity Field 0:15 top 8th
6:15	Cleveland Stadium, Cleveland, OH & R.F.K. Stadium, Washington, D.C.	9/14 & 9/20/1971	American League	Senators 8 Indians 6 in 20 innings in 2nd game
6:15	Citizens Bank Park, Philadelphia, PA	7/2/2004	American League at National League	Orioles 7 Phillies 6 in 16 innings
6:15	Wilson Field, Georgetown, KY	4/29/2005	NAIA	Lambuth Eagles 8 Pikeville Bears 5 in 22 innings
6:14	Nishi-Kyogoku Kyujyo, Kyoto, Japan	5/2/1959	Japanese Industrial League	Nippon Shinyaku 2 Kurashiki Reiyon 1 in 29 innings
6:14	Grayson Stadium, Savannah, GA	4/14/1973	Southern League	Columbus Astros 10 Savannah Braves 4 in 23 innings, 2nd game postponed
6:14	Stade Olympique, Montreal, Canada	8/23/1989	National League	Dodgers 1 Expos 0 in 22 innings
6:14	Commerce Bank Park, Bridgewater, NJ	8/16/2000	Atlantic League	Somerset Patriots 8 Newark Bears 7 in 17 innings
6:13	Managua, Nicaragua	late 1940s	Second Division Amateur League	Manta Nica defeated Schumann in 27 innings
6:13	College Stadium, Jamestown, NY	8/14/1965	New York-Penn League	Binghamton Triplets 4 Jamestown Tigers 4, 2nd game postponed
6:13	Fukuyama Kyujyo, Fukuyama, Japan	8/9/1998	Japanese Central League	Yokohama BayStars 14 Hiroshima Carp 6 in 15 innings
6:12	San Diego Stadium, San Diego, CA	8/25/1979	National League	Pirates 4 Padres 3 in 19 innings
6:10	Wrigley Field, Chicago, IL	8/17 & 8/18/1982	National League	Dodgers 2 Cubs 1 in 21 innings
6:10	Atlanta Stadium, Atlanta, GA	7/4/1985	National League	rain delay 1:24 at start, Mets 16 Braves 13 in 19 innings, 2nd rain delay 0:41 bottom 3rd
6:10	Veterans Stadium, Philadelphia, PA	7/7/1993	National League	Phillies 7 Dodgers 6 in 20 innings
6:09	Yankee Stadium (I), New York, NY	8/29/1967	American League	Yankees 4 Red Sox 3 in 20 innings in 2nd game
6:09	Wrigley Field, Chicago, IL	4/20 & 8/11/1986	National League	Pirates 10 Cubs 8 in 17 innings
6:09	Whataburger Field, Corpus Christi, TX	6/1/2005	Texas League	Wichita Wranglers 7 Corpus Christi Hooks 2 in 20 innings
6:07	Disch-Falk Field, Austin, TX	5/15 & 5/16/1981	NCAA	Texas Longhorns 7 Rice Owls 6 in 20 innings, rain delay 2:00 top 13th
6:07	Howser Field, Tallahassee, FL	4/7/2000	NCAA	Florida State Seminoles 14 Miami Hurricanes 13 in 17 innings
6:07	Pro Player Stadium, Miami, FL	4/27/2003	National League	Cardinals 7 Marlins 6 in 20 innings

6:06	Astrodome, Houston, TX	4/15/1968	National League	Astros 1 Mets 0 in 24 innings
6:06	Regional Park, Midwest City, OK	7/??/1973	American Legion	Post 170 (Midwest City) 2 Post 170 (Choctaw) 1 in 24 innings
6:06	Municipal Stadium, Taipei, Taiwan	9/15/1979	Taiwan University League	Weichuan Foods/Chinese Culture 1 Putaowang Biotechnology/ Fu Jen Catholic 0 in 21 innings
6:06	Anaheim Stadium, Anaheim, CA	4/13 & 4/14/1982	American League	Angels 4 Mariners 3 in 20 innings
6:05	County Stadium, Milwaukee, WI	5/1/1991	American League	Brewers 10 White Sox 9 in 19 innings
6:04	Keefe Stadium, San Antonio, TX	5/21/1987	Texas League	Shreveport Captains 4 San Antonio Dodgers 3 in 21 innings
6:03	Shively Field, Lexington, KY	6/3/1970	High School League	Madisonville Maroons 12 Lexington Lafayette Generals 11 in 22 innings
6:03	Comiskey Park (I), Chicago, IL	5/26 & 5/27 & 5/28/1973	American League	White Sox 6 Indians 3 in 21 innings, rain delay 0:17 top 14th
6:02	Webb Field, Modesto, CA	6/19/1970	California League	Modesto Reds 9 Reno Silver Sox 8 in 19 innings
6:02	Municipal Stadium, Greenville, SC	7/13 & 7/14/1984	Southern League	Memphis Chicks 3 Greenville Braves 2 in 19 innings in first game
6:02	Koshien Kyujyo, Osaka, Japan	5/24/2000	Japanese Central League	Chunichi Dragons 3 Hanshin Tigers 2 in 15 innings
6:01	Fairground Park, Fond du Lac, WI	7/31/1963	Amateur	Little Chute-Kimberly Papermakers 11 Fond du Lac 5 in 21 innings
6:01	Fenway Park, Boston, MA	9/3 & 9/4/1981	American League	Mariners 8 Red Sox 7 in 20 innings
6:01	Yankee Stadium (II), New York, NY	9/11/1988	American League	Yankees 5 Tigers 4 in 18 innings
6:01	Hiroshima Kyujyo, Hiroshima, Japan	10/1/1992	Japanese Central League	Hiroshima Carp 8 Yakult Swallows 7 in 13 innings
6:01	Estadio Angel Flores, Culiacan, Mexico	10/27/1995	Mexican Pacific League	Culiacan Tomateros (Tomato Growers) 3 Mazatlan Venados (Deer) 2 in 20 innings
6:00	Lawrence Hardball Park, Lodi, CA	8/31/1966	California League	Reno Silver Sox 6 Lodi Crushers 5 in 23 innings
6:00	Heart of Florida Medical Regional Center Field, Babson Park, FL	2/19 & 2/20/1999	NAIA	Nova Southeastern Knights 9 Webber Warriors 5 in 21 innings
6:00	Yankee Stadium (II), New York, NY	8/9/2002	American League	Athletics 3 Yankees 2 in 16 innings
6:00	Fukuoka Dome, Fukuoka, Japan	10/26/2002	Japanese University League	Nihon Bunri 2 Kyushu Kyoritsu 1 in 23 innings

Why is the Shortstop "6"?

As a baseball artifact, it's pretty special as it is.

It's a scorecard from August 5, 1891—a day when Buck Ewing drove in four runs off Cy Young and the New York Giants managed to hold off the Cleveland Spiders, 8–7, at the Polo Grounds. The book still shows the partial vertical fold its original owner might have created while stuffing it into a pocket as he raced to catch the steam-powered elevated train that would take him back downtown. And the scorecard pages themselves tell of a Cleveland rally thwarted only in the last of the ninth, when Spiders player-manager Patsy Tebeau, rounding third base, passed his teammate Spud Johnson going in the opposite direction—running his team into a game-ending double play.

The program is actually an embryonic yearbook. There are 14 photos and biographies of Giants players, and a wonderful series of anonymous notes under the heading "Base Hits" ("Anson next week. If we win three straights [sic] from him, we will be in first place"). But amid all the joyous nostalgia of a time impossibly distant—stuffed between the evidence that the owner saw Cy Young pitch in his first full major league season—hidden among the ads that beckon us to visit the Atalanta Casino or try Frink's Eczema Ointment or buy what was doubtlessly an enormous leftover supply of Tim Keefe's Official Players League Base Balls—we can throw everything out, except the top of page 10.

There, in six simple paragraphs, the scorecard's buyer is advised how to use it. "Hints On Scoring" tells us, simply, "On the margin of the score blanks will be seen certain numerals opposite the players' name. . . . The pitcher is numbered 1 in all cases, catcher 2, first base 3, second base 4, short stop 5, third base 6."

This is no mistake caused by somebody's over-indulgence at the Atalanta Casino.

The unknown editor offers a few sample plays, including: "If a ball is hit to third base, and the runner is thrown out to first base, without looking at the score card, it is known that the numbers to be recorded are 6-3, the former getting the assist and the latter the put-out. If from short stop, it is 5-3. . . ."

If we need any further confirmation that more has changed since 1891 than just the availability of Frink's Eczema Ointment,

the scorecard pages themselves provide it. In the preprinted lineups, third basemen Tebeau of Cleveland and Charlie Bassett of New York each have the number "6" printed just below their names. And the two shortstops, Ed McKean of the Spiders and Lew Whistler of the Giants, each have a "5."

We may view the system of numbers assigned to the fielding positions as eternal and immutable. But this 1891 Giants scorecard suggests otherwise, and is the tip of an iceberg we still don't fully see or understand—a story that anecdotally suggests a great collision of style and influence in the press box, no less intriguing than the war between that followed the creation of the American League.

The shortstop used to be "5," and the third baseman used to be "6."

We do not know precisely how and when it changed—there is a pretty good theory—but we do know that by 1909, the issue had been decided. In the World Series program for that year, Jacob Morse, the editor of the prominent *Base Ball Magazine,* gets seven paragraphs—the longest article in the book—to offer not "Hints On Scoring" but the much more definitive "How To Keep Score." And he leaves no doubt about it. "Number the players," Morse almost yells at us. "Catcher 2, pitcher 1; basemen 3, 4, 5; shortstop 6. . . ." The New York Giants themselves had reintroduced scorekeeping suggestions by 1915, and conformed to the method demanded by Morse, as if it had always been that way.

We can actually narrow the time frame of the change to a window beginning not in 1891, but closer to 1896. In the same pile of amazingly simple artifacts as that Giants scorecard is the actual softcover scorebook used by Charles H. Zuber, the Reds' beat reporter for the *Cincinnati Times-Star* five years later. Zuber employed a "Spalding's New Official Pocket Score Book" as he and the Reds trudged around the National League in the months before the election of President McKinley. Inside its front cover, one of the Great Spalding's many minions has provided intricately detailed scoring instructions. "The general run of spectators who do not care to record the game as fully as here provided," he writes with just a touch of condescension, "can easily simplify it by adopting only the symbols they need."

That this generous license was already being taken for granted is underscored by the fact that the Spalding editor suggests "S" for a strikeout, but writer Zuber ignores him completely and employs the comfortingly familiar "K." But the book's instructions are not entirely passé. They include the suggestion that the scorer use

KEITH OLBERMANN anchors MSNBC's nightly newscast, *Countdown,* and co-hosts a daily hour with Dan Patrick on ESPN Radio. A SABR member since 1984, he still regrets not acting on his intention to sign up during a visit to Cooperstown in 1983.

one horizontal line for a single, two for a double, etc.—which is exactly the way I was taught to do it, in the cavernous emptiness of Yankee Stadium in 1967.

The Spalding instructions go on for 11 paragraphs, and the official *rules* for scoring fill another 20. But remarkably, there is no guidance about how to numerically abbreviate the shortstop, third baseman, or anybody else who happened to be on the field. There isn't even the suggestion that a scorer must number the players, or abbreviate the players, according to their *defensive* positions: "Number each player either according to his fielding position or his batting order, as suits, and remember that these numbers stand for the players right through in the abbreviations."

In other words—use any system you damn well please. Number the shortstop "5" if you want, or "6." Or, if he's batting leadoff, use "1." Or if he's exactly six feet tall, try "72."

If by now you have wondered if the father of scorekeeping and statistics, Henry Chadwick, was not sitting there with smoke pouring from his ears over all this imprecision and laissez-faire, don't worry—he was. As early as his 1867 opus *The Game Of Base Ball* he was an advocate of one system and one system only—numbering the players based on where they hit in the order.

I realize that some of the most ardent of you, who have little shrines to Chadwick (in your minds, at least) as the ancient inspiration for SABR itself, must be reeling at the thought. Even if you think using "6" for the third baseman instead of the shortstop is a bit silly, it's a lot better than Chadwick's idea, surely the worst imaginable system of keeping score, based on the *batting lineup* ("groundout to short, 1 to 7 if you're scoring at home—no, check that, I forgot, the relief pitcher Schmoll took Robles' spot in the batting order in the double switch, so score it *9 to 7*").

Before we knock down the Chadwick statue outside SABR headquarters, this caveat is offered in his defense. In 1867, random substitutions were not permitted at all, and not until 1889 did they become even partially legal. Within a game, the batting order changed about as frequently as the designated hitter today assumes a defensive position. Chadwick's insistence on defensive numbering based on offensive positioning still doesn't make sense on a game-to-game basis, but at least he wasn't completely nuts.

But, as Peter Morris points out, Chadwick wanted to keep his system even as the substitution rule was changing. That same series of "Hints On Scoring" from the 1891 Giants scorecard first appeared, word for word, in a column in the *New York Mail and Express* in early 1889.

Weeks later, Chadwick is railing against it in the columns of *Sporting Life.* This new defensive-based scoring system is, he writes, "in no respect an improvement on the plan which has been in vogue since the National League was organized. If you name the players by their positions, and these happen to be changed in a game, then you are all in a fog on how to change them."

Chadwick was wrong about the ramifications but right about the coming fog.

Certainly, as the Giants scorecard and Charles Zuber's Spalding scorebook suggest, confusion would reign through the 1890s and into the new century. The New York scorecards soon reverted to "3B" and "SS" and dropped all hinting on what the bearer was supposed to do. Zuber's scoring system starts with the first baseman at "1," has the shortstop as "4," and the pitcher and catcher as "5" and "6." Only the Hall of Fame manager Harry Wright seems to have nailed it. In the voluminous scorebooks he kept through to his death in 1893, he has penciled in, in perfect, tiny lettering, the third baseman as "5" and the shortstop as "6."

So how was this chaos resolved?

This proves to have been the unexpected topic of conversation in the late 1950s between a budding New York sportswriter and one of the veterans of the business. Bill Shannon, now one of the three regular official scorers at Yankee and Shea Stadiums, was talking scorekeeping with Hugh Bradley. Bradley had been covering baseball in New York since the first World War, had been sports editor of the *New York Post* in the '30s, and was at the time of his conversation with Shannon a columnist with the *New York Journal-American.*

Shannon recalls that, out of nowhere, Bradley began talking about a great ancient conflict between rival camps of scorers, one of which favored the shortstop as "5" and the other as "6." The inevitable clash occurred, Bradley told him, at the first game of the first modern World's Series.

The World's Series, of course, had gone out with a whimper and not a bang in 1890. Though the Brooklyn Bridegrooms and Louisville Cyclones had been tied at three wins apiece, disinterest in that war-ravaged season was so profound that attendance at the last three games had been 1,000, 600, and 300, respectively. They didn't even bother to play the decisive game.

Thus when the series was restored 13 years later, every attempt was made to keep haphazardness and informality out of the proceedings. Not just *one* official scorer was required, but two—and the two foremost baseball media stars of the time: Francis C. Richter of Philadelphia, the publisher and editor of *Sporting Life,* and Joseph Flanner of St. Louis, editor of *The Sporting News.*

Hugh Bradley could not have witnessed it, but he could have heard it second- or thirdhand. As the rivals from the two publications filled out their scorecards, somewhere in the teeming confusion of the Huntington Avenue Grounds in Boston, somebody—probably the more volatile Flanner—peeked.

And he didn't like what he saw.

Richter was numbering Pittsburgh shortstop Honus Wagner as "5" and third baseman Tommy Leach as "6."

Questioned by Flanner, Richter supposedly responded that that was the way they kept score where *he* came from, and why would anybody do it any differently?

The basis of their argument was supposed to have been regional. The shortstop, Bradley told Shannon, was still a comparatively new innovation in the game, and it really defined two different positions. In Flanner's Midwest, he was positioned much like the softball short-fielders, not truly an infielder and thus not meriting an interruption of the natural numbering of the base-men. In Richter's East, the shortstop had developed into what he is today—the second baseman's twin. So what if he didn't anchor a bag? It was second baseman "4," shortstop "5," third baseman "6" and don't they have any good eye doctors out there in St. Louis, friend Flanner?

Bradley's recounting of the conflict had voices being raised and dark oaths being sworn before the more malleable Richter gave way, little knowing that he was ceding the issue forever on behalf of generations to come who saw the same logical flaw he had seen.

Bill Shannon's authority on such matters is near absolute. He can not only recount virtually every game he's ever seen, but can also run down the personnel histories of the sports departments at the dearly departed of New York's newspapers. He believes in the long-gone Bradley's saga of near-fisticuffs between Richter and Flanner—while 'Nuf Sed McGreevey and his Royal Rooters worked themselves into a frenzy before the first pitch of the 1903 Series—because of its likely provenance.

One of Bradley's writers when he was sports editor of the *Post* in the '30s was Fred Lieb, himself almost antediluvian enough to have witnessed the Flanner-Richter showdown. Shannon suspects Bradley got the story from Lieb, and that Lieb had gotten it from his fellow Philadelphian Francis Richter.

For now, that's all we've got—a pretty good-sounding anec-dote. There is nothing yet found in the files of *The Sporting News, New York Times, Washington Post,* or even in any of the con-temporary Spalding or Reach annual guides. No Flanner-Richter screaming match, no ruling on whether the shortstop or the third baseman was "5," no verified explanation as to how we got from the *hints* in the 1891 Giants scorecard to the *instructions* of the 1909 World Series program, no smoking gun proving when it became this way, as if there had never been any *other* way.

Needless to say, further research is encouraged and its results solicited.

In the meantime, dare I even mention that the 1891 Giants book also identifies the right fielder as "7" and the left fielder as "9"?

FRANK CERESI & CAROL McMAINS

Early Baseball in Washington, D.C.
How the Washington Nationals Helped Develop America's Game

Washington, D.C., is primarily known today as the home of our nation's central government and for its wealth of great museums. Very few people are aware that the city helped give the game of baseball its rich national identity over 150 years ago. A thorough review of the recent "find" of baseball materials, known simply as the "French Collection," which is in the archives of the Washington Historical Society, gives us a perfect opportunity to analyze Washington, D.C.'s significant role in the development of early baseball.[1]

Baseball's Birth

By 1840 changes were occurring swiftly as the country's new industrialism began to take hold and country life, so dependent on large areas of land, began to give way to crowded city life. New forms of leisure and recreation were needed as field sports and informal schoolyard games were becoming less available to workers in towns and cities. It was within this context that baseball, as we know it today, began as a game to be reckoned with.

The first real turning point in the development of baseball occurred in 1842 in the biggest, most bustling city of them all, New York City. A group of middle- and upper-class gentlemen in Manhattan met to play regularly scheduled games of baseball against each other "for health and recreation."[1] They formed a club and called themselves the Knickerbocker Base Ball Club of New York. Today, the Knickerbockers are universally regarded as the nation's first organized baseball club. They regularly met after work, generally around mid afternoon, to enjoy each other's company and the game that they found exhilarating.

Three years later, after losing their practice field in Manhattan, the club journeyed by ferry to Hoboken, New Jersey, to seek new grounds. There they played and practiced base ball on the Elysian Fields overlooking the Hudson River.[2] It was during this time that a serious young Knickerbocker, Alexander Cartwright, suggested to the others that the team become more organized. On September 23, 1845, approximately 30 members of the club convened at McCarthy's Hotel in Hoboken. At this meeting the idea of

FRANK CERESI and CAROL McMAINS, formerly of the National Sports Gallery in Washington, D.C., run FC Associates, a business that specializes in museum consulting and exhibit planning, the development and creation of spectacular exhibits, and professional and objective appraisals of sports artifacts and memorabilia.

formalizing new rules was put forth. The rules, forever known as the "New York" rules, were drawn up and codified, and the seeds of something big were sown.

Although other areas of the Northeast sprouted ball clubs of one form or another, organized competitive baseball was pretty much confined to New York City and its immediate suburbs. Even though "baseball momentum" clearly emerged from the valiant efforts of the Knickerbockers and their crosstown rivals, the Gothams, history tells us that in New York City the most popular outdoor team bat and ball sport of the late 1850s was not baseball but cricket. After all, it was little more than 75 years before that this young country had split from England, and old habits died hard. Even in Hoboken, right on Elysian Fields, the "home" grounds of the Knickerbockers, a crowd of 24,000 men and women gathered in 1859 to watch their favorite players in a cricket match.[3] That kind of crowd dwarfed the number of spectators attending baseball matches in the 1850s. That, however, was about to change. Within the next decade baseball would become far more popular than Alexander Cartwright, his Knickerbocker teammates, or anyone else could have possibly imagined.

The Baseball Explosion Begins: Here Come the Nationals

During this time interest in baseball began to stir in Washington, D.C., the nation's capital, a city on the verge of being swept into the great Civil War. It began innocently enough when a group of mostly federal government employees took a cue from their counterparts up north and formed an organized baseball team. It would be known as the Washington Nationals, a team that would be significant to the development of the national pastime.

That the men were civil servants gave the group an air of respectability, for government workers of that era were a considerable force in the social and economic life of the city. The group, though certainly not wealthy, was comprised of upper-middle-class workers who were envied for their guaranteed wage and job security. Accounts of the day report that many were "thrilled" by the prospect of deserting taverns and the Willard and Ebbitt Hotel bars for the "wholesome, invigorating outdoors."[4] Quickly, and with a determination that would make any governmental bureaucrat proud, the officers undertook the task of writing rules for their club,[5] the Washington Nationals Base Ball Club. They elected James Morrow, a clerk from the Pension Office, as president, and Joseph L. Wright, the Official Doorkeeper of the United States House of Representatives, as vice president. Arthur Pue

Gorman, the 22-year-old chosen as secretary, also worked on Capitol Hill. He later made his mark, becoming a reliable player for the Nationals, an organizer who helped hatch the team's "grand tour of the west" directly after the Civil War, and a longtime United States senator from Maryland.

Because of the recent find of baseball documents in the French Collection, we are able to peek inside the team's rule book and get a flavor of the game as it existed at the time of the Civil War.[6] The book tells us that baseball, when the Nationals first formed, was clearly an amateur sport. Not only were there no salaried players, but membership on the Nationals required dues to be paid *by* the players to the club, initially of 50 cents and 25 cents each month thereafter. Second, the membership was exclusive. Article I of the Constitution declared that the club would have no more than 40 members, and "gentlemen wishing to become members may be proposed" and thereafter would be "balloted for." Article II set up a "committee of inquiry" and membership would be denied by "three black balls."

The rules within the Constitution's Bylaws set forth a stringent code of conduct for the ballplayers. The club wanted the men on the field of play to be exemplary and polite. This was clearly thought to be a way to weed out riffraff and gamblers who frequented horse races and boxing matches.[7] Article II of the Bylaws admonished that a fine of 10 cents would be levied at any member who used "improper or profane language." It didn't stop there! If you, as a member of the Nationals, "disputed an umpire's call" you "shall" be fined a quarter. Worse yet, if you "audibly expressed [your] opinion on a doubtful play before the decision of an umpire," you would be a dime poorer. Anyone "refusing obedience to a team captain" would be fined 10 cents.

Other rules are not quite as quaint when viewed through the lens of contemporary life, but they certainly illustrate the game as it was played. Though baseballs were specific as to size and weight, they were harder and smaller than what is used today. Also, wood bats were limited in dimension, but they were larger and longer than those commonly used in the modern game. Baseball in 1860 was definitely a hitter's (called the "striker") game. Article III, Rule 6 of the Bylaws nails that point. It specifies that the ball must be "pitched," not "jerked or thrown" to the striker. The rule directed the pitcher to heave the ball, in a discus-like motion, toward the striker. As was the baseball custom of the day, the striker could tell the pitcher exactly where to place the ball. If the pitcher didn't "pitch" the ball to the striker's liking, but instead "threw or jerked" it in a confusing manner, the umpire could call out a warning, "Ball to the bat!" and walk the striker after only three called balls.[8]

On July 2, 1860, the *Washington Star* recorded the first box score for teams representing the District of Columbia.[9] Art Gorman scored six runs and Mr. French added five of his own, as the Nationals beat the Washington Potomacs Ball Club. The Potomacs, likely filled with other men with government-related jobs, did not have the staying power of the Nationals, and any reference to "the Potomacs" shortly disappeared from local papers.

They apparently were not that great, either, as the Potomacs got trounced, 46–14, by the stronger Nationals club in Washington's historic first recorded game.[10]

The Civil War Years

Washington, D.C., was, of course, in the "eye of the hurricane" during the Civil War years. For citizens of the District of Columbia, those were tense and trying times because not only was the city the focal point and symbol for a unified nation, but it was very precariously situated. After all, Richmond, the capital of the Confederacy, was less than a 100 miles south of the District line. Yet, through it all, baseball in Washington, as in many parts of the Northeast, did not halt. The game actually flourished.

One of the reasons that baseball prospered during the war was, unlike many other sporting and recreational games, it was portable: it could be played in any relatively open field. All you needed was a bat or large stick, a ball, at least some knowledge of the rules of the game, and willing participants. Unlike cricket, you did not need nicely manicured grass. For the soldier on the field whose days were spent either drilling or being terrified that they might soon be engaged in combat, the game was a welcome relief. In short, not only did it lend itself to the feeling of being part of a team, a nice feature in a military setting, but also it was fun. One soldier from Virginia in 1862 said it best when he wrote:

> It is astonishing how indifferent a person can become to danger.... The report of musketry is heard a little distance from us ... yet over there on the other side of the road is most of our company playing Bat Ball and perhaps in less than a half an hour they may be called to play a ball game of a more serious nature.[11]

In the meantime, the Washington Nationals were doing their part to keep the game going during the Civil War. Although the Potomacs disbanded, the Nationals kept playing whenever and wherever possible. One of the Nationals' biggest games of 1861 was played on July 2 against the 71st New York Regiment. The team of New Yorkers was well schooled in the intricacies of the game, and their superiority on the field showed as they won 41–13.[12] That game would be, however, the New Yorkers' last bit of frivolity, for that regiment was on its way to Manassas, Virginia. Within a few short days the 71st would be surprised by the strength of the Confederate Army, and the regiment sustained heavy losses in the Battle of Bull Run.[13]

For the next two years, most of the Nationals' games were played locally. All of the ball clubs in the Washington area that sprouted up during this time sported names that perfectly captured the tenor of the times and Washington's prominence as the capital city—the Nationals, Unions, and Jeffersons. After all, this was a period of intense patriotism in the city that housed the federal government during the time when the outcome of the Civil War was far from certain. The Nationals played both of the other District teams, winning every time.[14] For the first game of the 1862 season, on May 20, the Nationals welcomed the newly formed "Jeffersons" into the baseball community by tattooing them, 62–22. Ned Hibbs of the Nationals socked five home runs in that game, future senator Gorman hit three, and Mr. French tallied nine runs. The game was covered in a local newspaper, and the following telling line was recorded : "The spectators of the game were numerous and cheered bravely whenever a home run or fine catch was made."

In August 1862 the Nationals again played against New York's 71st Regiment in Tenleytown, Maryland (now part of the District of Columbia). This time, however, the result of the rematch game would be different, as the Nationals were victorious 28–13. At first glance the final score indicates that the Nationals were becoming more talented on the field, although the New York 71st manpower was, by then, depleted due to the war. The box score and roster of the game, the only one known to exist, is neatly handwritten in the French Collection materials, presumably by French himself.[15] By midseason the following year, the Nationals kept playing despite the increased volatility of life in the nation's capital. In July 1863, as the Battle of Gettysburg raged north of the city in Pennsylvania, the Nationals played ball and were drawing crowds wherever they went. They won all games they played against the Jeffersons, the Unions, and a new Baltimore club, the Pastimes.

Members of the Nationals team were gaining stature outside of the baseball diamond as well. Crafty second baseman Arthur Gorman, newly elected as the team president, was named the Postmaster of the Senate.[16] His climb up the political ladder would in time benefit the team greatly. Others who played, or who would play, for the Nationals saw significant combat action during the war. One such ballplayer, Seymour Studley, was not only wounded but almost died of heat stroke while fighting for the Union.

The Nationals continued to test their skills against Union soldiers until the very end of the war. For example, on May 17, 1865, the team battled the 133rd Regiment of New York in a game played at Fort Meigs in Maryland as the Union troops were mustering out of the military. What is most interesting about that particular game is the almost genteel tone of the game summary that appeared in the unidentified newspaper clipping found in the French Collection. Its substance is very revealing especially when the reader considers the light mood that must have pervaded the soldiers as well as the civilians on the Nationals ball club, for this game took place barely six weeks after General Lee surrendered to General Grant at Appomattox. It was reported, "Each and all of the nines [the starting lineup] played in first class style endeavoring to make it an interesting and agreeable match." Further, the men apparently worked up a nice appetite, as the paper reported, matter-of-factly, "During the progress of the game a handsome collation [light meal] was spread and the urbanity of the officers and members of the 133rd added much to the entertainment!"[17]

Hungry or not, 1865 was quite a year, as the Nationals ballplayers kept winning. The Civil War had ended and Washingtonians were ready to celebrate. Baseball helped fill that void and the game's popularity was cemented in the capital city forever. Nice-sized crowds, from several hundred into the thousands, saw the team take on and beat all comers, from the Baltimore Pastimes and that city's newly formed Enterprise Club to the Nationals' old rivals, the Washington Unions. On August 22, 1865, the Nationals beat the Jeffersons in what the newspapers dubbed the "Great Baseball Match for the Championship of the South." This might have been a bit of local hyperbole, probably induced by their newly elected president, the clever and politically connected Postmaster Gorman. However, the Nationals did win the "championship" game, 34–14, and within a couple of days two of the "better" Northern teams accepted an invitation from Mr. Gorman himself to play the "champs" in a "baseball tournament" in the capital city.[18]

Baseball and High Society in the Nation's Capital

The teams that Mr. Gorman invited to the tournament were the two most powerful baseball clubs in the country during the 1865 season. The Atlantics from Brooklyn, New York, were undefeated, winning all 18 of their games.[19] That team featured the very popular Dickey Pearce, a great shortstop who some credit with having invented the bunt.[20] The Philadelphia Athletics were no slouches, either. They won all except three of their games for the year and showcased the talented and influential Albert Reach,[21] who later made a fortune manufacturing baseball equipment.[22]

With this impressive talent on its way down from the north, the wily Mr. Gorman knew what to do to put the Nationals on the front pages. A newspaper story dated August 28 tells the tale.[23] Arthur Gorman met the ball clubs at the train station in Washington in what turned out to be a very significant three-day stay. Gorman rolled out the red carpet in a serious way. He led the visiting ball clubs by four horse coaches draped with American flags for a special tour of the United States Capitol and followed by taking his visitors to the White House. Though the players missed President Andrew Johnson, they met him the following day at the presidential home. This was the very first time a sports team would be received by the President of the United States.

After the White House visit, the guests went to their rooms at the Willard Hotel, and then joined the Nationals at the "Presidential Grounds" to play baseball.[24] The game might have been interesting, but the show was really in the stands. What stands, say you? It seems that Mr. Gorman was able to not only arrange the team's presidential visit, but he made sure that spectator seats were erected on the Presidential Grounds where the gentlemen of the government, including Cabinet-level appointees, escorted their "belles of the capital" in their finery to watch the contest.[25] Not only that, but the fans had the privilege of actually *paying* a hefty one dollar charge to enter the grounds to watch the affair. Even though the Philadelphians, and next day the New Yorkers, won both games, 5,000 of Washington's elite witnessed more than a pair of baseball games—they witnessed a tournament turned into a social event at a most opportune time. The gala atmosphere was just what the war-weary city, indeed the nation, really needed. The game of baseball, almost as a backdrop, had now really come into its own. Also, the "battle" for sports supremacy was now over and baseball was the victor. As the *American Chronicle of Sports and Pastimes* stated in 1868, baseball had changed more in 10 years than cricket had in 400—because it adapted to the American circumstances.[26]

For the next year and a half, the Nationals capitalized on their popularity in the Washington region and continued to battle clubs from other areas of the country as well. The Nationals again played a New York team on October 9, 1865, the excellent Excelsiors Club from Brooklyn, beating them in a "close" game, 36–30. This entitled the club the prestigious "trophy ball."[27] They also continued a tradition that was becoming standard for major ball clubs of the day. Since the game was played on their "home field," the boys hosted a magnificent feast for their guests after the game, with rounds of toasts, speeches, and general all-around merriment.[28]

During 1866 the club was sharpening their collective skills in preparation for what would be their grand "tour of the west" a year later, a tour that would forever confirm the influence of the Washington Nationals over the game of baseball. During the summer they won every game they played against the other local baseball clubs, the Jeffersons and the Unions.[29] After they dispensed with the local talent, the team traveled south into the former Confederacy to play and beat the Monticellos from Charlottesville, 37–7. They topped off the mini tour and traveled east to crush the Unions of Richmond, 143–11. They were now ready to head north to make good on their promise the previous year to visit the clubs from New York that had come to Washington in 1865.

Reality set in during that trip. The Nationals' only defeats in 1866 came in New York City, still the hotbed of organized baseball, where the most talented players in the country resided. As much of a mark as the Nationals had made in the capital region, New York was still the baseball capital. In fact, the New York–based National Association of Base Ball Players (NABBP) was at its height as an organization. The Association saw its membership numbers rise dramatically during the first full year after the Civil War ended. Arthur Pue Gorman officially left the Washington Nationals as a player and officer to become president of that Association. Gorman was, after all, an ambitious man, and the presidency of the only organized baseball association was prestigious. However, Gorman would be perfectly positioned to shortly help guide his old team, but from behind the scenes, in what would become the team's finest moment.

The Nationals took on baseball's "best of the best" during the 1866 trip, including the nation's strongest club during that season, the Unions from Morrisania, New York. But they simply could not get over the top. They lost to the Unions twice as well as to New York City's excellent Excelsior and Gotham ball clubs.[30] By the end of the year, the Nationals would claim dominance in the Washington area, as they were even dubbed "champions of the south," and they clearly were considered peerless and polite hosts when the New York boys visited town for a friendly game on the Nationals' home turf.[31] However, the 1866 trip "up north"

revealed that the Washington team needed to strengthen itself if they were to make their mark on the national stage.

The Nationals' Great 1867 Tour of the West

Certainly 1867 was *the* banner year for the Washington Nationals. The need for shaking things up fell into the capable hands of the club's new president, the former Union officer Colonel Frank Jones. The Colonel had found employment at the Treasury Department after the war. That department, Washington's largest, was an easy walk to many a baseball game in and around the National Mall, as baseball contests dotted the landscape by the war's end. Although Art Gorman's time was cramped due to his political and NABBP responsibilities, he was still able to offer Jones advice and political goodwill. The men struck upon an idea that they felt certain had merit.

Why not take the Nationals on the road into America's heartland to showcase the game they loved? Although baseball clubs had previously traveled up and down the Northeast for years, said "tours" were really very limited and confined to the Northeast and the capital city's immediate south. The Washington pair correctly thought that a "grand tour of the west," a first for any baseball club, would *really* put their team on the map, help spread the baseball gospel, and ultimately cement the Washington Nationals' rightful place in history.[32] They would be right.

From the Nationals' New York travels in 1866, they were well aware of the fine play demonstrated by a 20-year-old, George Wright, who played for the nation's top team, the Unions from Morrisania. Young Mr. Wright not only played for the team that thrashed the Nationals, 22–8, but he also came from impressive baseball stock. He was the son of a renowned cricketer and younger brother of Harry, whose baseball roots went back all the way to the great Knickerbocker teams of the late 1850s. Perhaps it was a promised job as a clerk at the Treasury Department that did the trick—after all, a steady paycheck was a nice thing to have—or it could have been Colonel Jones's evocative talk of taking his team "on a grand tour of the west," a first for any organized club. Either way, Wright was approached and agreed in April to play with the Nationals for the 1867 season.[33]

The Nationals followed their Wright score by quickly landing two other New Yorkers, catcher Frank Norton, a whiz with his bare-handed grabs, and the impressive first baseman George Fletcher from the same Brooklyn Excelsior club that edged Washington, 32–28, the previous year. Norton had led the Excelsiors with 70 runs in 20 recorded games during the 1866 season, and Fletcher came in second for the club with 62 runs.[34] Shortstop Ed Smith, formerly of the Brooklyn Stars, Harry McLean, who at one time played with the Harlem Club, and from the Brooklyn Eckfords, the talented George H. Fox rounded out the New York contingent. The boys from the north were joined by the veteran Washington Nationals players; Will Williams, an excellent pitcher who was also a law student at Georgetown University; Henry Parker of the Internal Revenue Service, fleet outfielder; and Civil War veterans Harry Berthrong and Seymour Studley. Both Berthrong and Studley worked at the Treasury, Henry at the Office of the Comptroller and Seymour as a clerk.[35]

Excitement was in the air as the fully assembled team began the 20-day, 10-stop western tour by railway on July 11, 1867. It would be covered not only by the *Washington Star*, but also by the influential and important weekly journal known as *The Ball Players Chronicle*. The man credited with being the nation's first daily baseball journalist, Henry Chadwick, also traveled with the team to cover the games. Not only did "Father Henry," as he was affectionately known, write the content and edit *The Ball Players Chronicle* and contribute columns to assure *Star* coverage, but he also provided up-to-the-minute details of the tour to other traveling journalists from the *New York Times*, *New York Mercury*, and *New York Clipper*.[36] The result would be that the Nationals' tour received press coverage that far exceeded anything ever done in sports before. Colonel Jones and Art Gorman, who would join the team in Chicago, were ecstatic!

The first game of the tour was played against the Capitals of Columbus, Ohio. Let's let Mr. Chadwick set the stage:

The arrangements for the match were excellent, a roped boundary enclosing the field, and all the base lines laid down properly. Tables were provided for the scorers and members of the press, seats for the players, with a retiring tent, and also seats for ladies. A cordon of carriages, mostly filled with the fair belles of Columbus, occupied two-thirds of the outer portion of the field, and the surroundings of the grounds with the white uniform of the Columbus players—the flags and the assemblage, altogether made up a very picturesque scene indeed. Though it was but ten o'clock in the morning, an hour when hundreds who desired to witness the game could not well get away, quite a numerous assemblage of spectators were present, the delegation of ladies being very numerous, something we are glad to record.[37]

The game showed the team, and the throngs of spectators who watched, just how powerful the Nationals were. The Capitals scored the first two runs of the game, but things quickly got out of hand for the host team. Each of the Nationals scored at least seven runs, as they walloped the Columbus Capitals, 90–10. At that point the game was called after an abbreviated seven innings, the dinner bell rang, and the teams went on to enjoy the post-game feast, a routine that would occur in virtually each city on the 10-stop tour. It was, as Chadwick duly noted, a "pleasant and rational opening" for the Nationals' tour.[38]

It was thought that things would be a bit tougher for Washington the next day in Cincinnati for their game against the Red Stockings. After all, this team featured Harry Wright, George's older brother and an old hand from the Knickerbocker days of yore. The locals were impressed with the Nationals' blue pants, white woolen shirts, and blue caps and cheered the team's arrival. But the home team had little to cheer about as Washington, led by the younger of the Wright brothers, thrashed the Red Stockings,

53–10.[39] The Nationals played again in Cincinnati the next day and spanked the Red Stockings' crosstown rivals, the Buckeyes, 88–12.

Things continued in favor of the touring Nationals for the next several stops. George Wright and George Fletcher each hit three homers on their way to an 82–12 victory over Louisville. The next day, George Wright bashed *five* homers to lead the team over Indianapolis. Fletcher hit only three homers, but the others began to flex their collective muscle. The final score? 106–21! After two days during which the team crossed the Mississippi by steamboat, the Nationals downed the Unions from St. Louis, in scorching heat of up to 104 degrees, 113–26. That very afternoon, in the same sweltering heat, they played in the same city again. This time it was closer, but the Empires could barely hang on as the Washington club bested them, 53–26.

This was to be the beginning of the final leg on the tour, as the train took the players to Chicago for the last three games. The boys were tired from the trip and those hot days in St. Louis but soon, it was thought, they would be heading back in triumph to the nation's capital. By any measure, the tour was far more successful than even Colonel Jones or Art Gorman could have possibly imagined. Crowds from all over the Midwest met the players at every stop. They were wined and dined in each city, even those where they annihilated the hometown ball club. Handsome George Wright, slugger George Fletcher, pitcher Will Williams, and the others had their own flock of fans to contend with, both male and female.[40] Thanks to the omnipresent pen of Henry Chadwick, and other journalists who were now reporting in their own newspapers as each game unfolded, each Nationals game, and the exploits of the individual players, were followed in every major city. The baseball gospel *was* indeed spreading!

When the team arrived in Chicago, they were met by hundreds of fans as well as the ballplayers of all three of the Chicago-area teams they were to play, the rival Atlantic and Excelsior squads and the much less experienced Forest City Club from Rockford, Illinois. The latter club had traveled 100 miles from their home to "host" the Nationals for the first game. It was to be a tune-up for the stronger Excelsior and Atlantic clubs that hailed from Chicago proper.[41] However, things did not go as everyone predicted. The long tour, the July heat, and the hoopla finally caught up with the Nationals. The Forest City Club, led by 16-year-old pitching sensation Albert Spalding, jumped to an early lead in a game that was marred by two rain delays.[42] The "corn crackers" from Rockford never relinquished their lead.[43] The final score was 29–23. That was the only loss the Nationals sustained during the entire tour.

The Nationals' defeat, however, only heightened an already enthusiastic fan base for the remaining two games. After all, the home team newspapers blared, if the less experienced Forest City Club could win, think of what the two major big city clubs could do! Not much, it seems, for the Nationals, having been able to rest for a day, came roaring back. In front of a crowd that was estimated to be 8,000 strong, they first annihilated the Excelsiors, 49–4, and finished their tour taking apart the Chicago Atlantics, 78–17.[44]

The boys really ended on a high note. The team had traveled to parts of the country that had never really seen the evolving game played so "splendidly," they had won nine of ten games, and they outscored their opponents 735 to 146 (see Appendix)![45]

The Nationals' Legacy

By the end of the decade that defined baseball's explosion, the Washington Nationals' fingerprints were everywhere. Their influence would be felt locally and nationally. For a baseball club that began less than a year before 1860, it is amazing what the team accomplished in such a short period of time. Not only did the Nationals help keep the game alive during the Civil War by hosting ball games with visiting Union soldiers, but by 1865, as the war ended, at a critical time when the weary country needed a shot in the arm, the team for the first time was able to meld the excitement of the national pastime into an exuberant patriotic celebration that involved even the President of the United States.[46] Additionally, their baseball dominance locally sowed seeds of the game within the *entire* city, and those seeds helped sprout not only significant white teams but African American teams as well.[47]

Last, the Nationals will forever be known for their groundbreaking "grand tour of the west," where they introduced to scores of people the game that would quickly be recognized as our country's national game. Forty years after the tour, the then "grand old man" of baseball, Henry Chadwick, made that point many times, and even the influential *Spalding's Baseball Guide* credits the Nationals for "opening the eyes of the people" to the beauty of the game and the tour for serving "to intensify the passion for the game by stimulating the formation of clubs that wanted to achieve similar renown."[48]

Appendix

Results from the Nationals of Washington Tour of 1867

Date	Opponent	Location	Score
7/13	Capitals	Columbus, OH	90-10
7/15	Cincinnati	Cincinnati	53-10
7/16	Buckeyes	Cincinnati	88-12
7/17	Louisville	Louisville	82-21
7/20	Indianapolis	Indianapolis	106-21
7/22	Unions	St. Louis	113-26
7/23	Empires	St. Louis	53-26
7/25	Rockford Forest Citys	Chicago	23-29
7/27	Excelsiors	Chicago	49-4
7/29	Chicago Atlantics	Chicago	78-17

Notes

1. Geoffrey C. Ward and Ken Burns, *Baseball: An Illustrated History* (New York: Knopf, , 1994), 4.
2. What we now call baseball was originally referred to as two words, base ball. By the end of the Civil War most references are to the word "baseball" as we know it today.
3. Seymour, *Baseball: The Early Years*, 14. FULL CITATION NEEDED Au: Please supply.
4. Shirley Povich, *The Washington Senators* (New York: G.P. Putnam's Sons, 1954), 1.
5. That the men would form a "gentleman's society" to play baseball in 1859 was hardly surprising. During the 1840s and '50s, a whole host of societies and associations sprang forth. Political groups and trade unions were formed. Likeminded folks banded together to form everything from anti-slavery societies to the Ancient Order of Hibernians and B'nai B'rith. Things went so far that one poor soul lamented, "A peaceful man can hardly venture to eat or drink, or go to bed or get up, to correct his children or kiss his wife without obtaining the permission or direction of some . . . society." Seymour, *Baseball: The Early Years*, 13.
6. The materials in the French Collection were donated to the Historical Society of Washington, D.C., by Miller Young in 1999. The documents and memorabilia were part of the estate of Nicholas Young, a founder of the Olympic Base Ball Club in Washington, D.C., in 1866.
7. In fact, Rule 30 of the Bylaws forbade betting. French Collection, HSWDC, 17.
8. Stephen D. Guschov, *The Red Stockings of Cincinnati: Base Ball's First All-Professional Team and Its Historic 1869 and 1870 Seasons* (Jefferson, NC, and London: McFarland, 1998), 39. The appearance of the curveball in 1867, years after the Nationals first wrote their rules, obviously caused quite a stir. When the "secret pitch" was unleashed by one William "Candy" Cummings as his New York club played Harvard University's top team, Charles W. Eliot, President of Harvard, said with disdain, "I am instructed that the purpose of the curve ball is to deliberately deceive the batter. Harvard is not in the business of teaching deception." Ward and Burns, *Baseball: An Illustrated History*, 20.
9. Morris A. Bealle, *The Washington Senators: The Story of an Incurable Fandom* (Washington: Columbia, 1947), 8.
10. Exaggerated scores were not uncommon during the early years of baseball. Some teams were simply more skilled than others.
11. Ward and Burns, *Baseball: An Illustrated History*, 32.
12. Confirmed by handwritten notes likely by Mr. French himself. French Collection, HSWDC, 43.
13. Seymour, *Baseball: The Early Years*, 41.
14. Bealle, *The Washington Senators*, 9.
15. French Collection, HSWDC, 48.
16. Bealle, *The Washington Senators*, 9.
17. French Collection, HSWDC, 52.
18. French Collection, HSWDC, 54.
19. Marshall D. Wright, *The National Association of Base Ball Players, 1857–1870* (Jefferson, NC and London: McFarland., 2000), 98.
20. The Society for American Baseball Research, *Nineteenth Century Stars* (Kansas City, MO: SABR), 101. Au: Need date of publication.
21. Wright, *The National Association*, 15.
22. SABR, *Nineteenth Century*, 106.
23. French Collection, HSWDC, 55.
24. The "Presidential Grounds," later called the "White Lot," is now commonly known as the Ellipse.
25. French Collection, HSWDC, 55.
26. John P. Rossi, *The National Game: Baseball and American Culture* (Chicago: Ivan R. Dee, 2000), 5.
27. The "trophy ball" was, in reality, the game ball that contained the clubs' names and the score printed neatly on it. It was customarily lacquered for protection and preservation and given to the captain of the winning club with great pomp and circumstance.
28. French Collection, HSWDC, 65. Mr. French himself "presided" over the gala affair.
29. Wright, *The National Association*, 117.
30. Bealle, *The Washington Senators*, 11.
31. William J. Ryczek, *When Johnny Came Sliding Home: The Post-Civil War Baseball Boom, 1865–1870* (Jefferson, NC and London: McFarland, 1992), 116. Curiously, the team did not play the newly formed Washington Olympics in 1866. That team, initially organized by Washington resident and former Civil War soldier Nicholas Young, would, in the early 1870s, overtake the Nationals as the area's top team. Young himself was also to become an extraordinarily important figure in the development of the game during the next several decades. He was not only a founding member of the National League in 1876, the same major league that exists to this day, but he also ran a school for umpires in Washington, D.C. In his later years he became one of the 19th century's elder spokesmen for the game of baseball. PROBABLY BETTER PLACED BEFORE THE YOUNG ENTRY IN THE FOOTNOTES Au: See note for yourself. Frank Ceresi, Mark Rucker, and Carol McMains, *Baseball in Washington, D.C.* (Charleston, SC: Arcadia, 2002), 11.
32. The goal of Jones and Gorman's to make the western tour one of historic proportions is clearly reflected in the ball club's Constitution, which was revised on April 1, 1867, less than four months before the tour. The Constitution states that the club's "object shall be to improve, foster and perpetuate the American game of baseball and advance socially and physically the interests of its members." French Collection, HSWDC, 25.

33. Ryczek, *When Johnny*, 116. Wright's occupation would be listed as that of Treasury Department clerk, although apparently young George earned a few extra dollars as "clerk of Cronin's cigar store and baseball headquarters," according to historian and author Morris Bealle. See Bealle, *The Washington Senators*, 6.

34. Wright, *The National Association*, 116.

35. Ryczek, *When Johnny*, 118, and Bealle, *The Washington Senators*, 6.

36. French Collection, HSWDC, 210, and *The Ball Players Chronicle*, July 18, 1867. In the revised Constitution for the Nationals, dated April 1, 1867, Chadwick became an "honorary member" of the ball club. French Collection, HSWDC, 23.

37. Henry Chadwick, *The Ball Players Chronicle*, Vol. 1, No. 7, July 18, 1867.

38. Henry Chadwick, *The Ball Players Chronicle*, Vol. 1, No. 7, July 18, 1867.

39. Ironically, the whipping at the hands of the Nationals ignited the Red Stockings into immediate action. Within two years they would field the first professional team, do a tour of their own, and win every game they played in 1869. Au: Repetition not needed? They would travel to Washington, D.C., and beat both the Nationals and the Olympics during their famous 1869 tour.

40. The team's celebrity with the ladies apparently continued when they returned to Washington. A yellowed column in the French materials, written more in the style of a fashion guide than a sports section, reports that amongst the fans watching the Nationals in August 1867 were "several hundred ladies, who watched with glistening eyes peering from beneath charming little jockey hats, saucily perched forward, and dainty bugle trimmed parasols elevated more from force of habit than from necessity." French Collection, HSWDC, 210.

41. Ryczek, *When Johnny*, 122, citing the *Henry Chadwick Scrapbooks*.

42. Albert Spalding would become one of the most influential figures in the history of the game. The teenager became an excellent pitcher, winning over 250 games during his playing career. He then extended his influence as the longtime owner of the Chicago White Stockings and eventually opened a sporting goods company, Spalding and Brothers, that would make him a millionaire by the end of the century. Spalding is a member of the National Baseball Hall of Fame.

43. Ryczek, *When Johnny*, 124, citing the *Spirit of the Times*, August 3, 1867.

44. French Collection, HSWDC, 193. At one point the Nationals were winning, 33 to 0.

45. Ryczek, *When Johnny*, 126, citing the *Spirit of the Times*, July 20, 1867.

46. In a sense the hoopla surrounding the presidential meeting and visit arranged by the Nationals in 1865 predated the famous "Presidential First Pitch" tradition that was to begin 60 years later when President Taft threw out the first pitch to inaugurate the 1910 Major League Baseball season.

47. In 1867, the very year of the Nationals' grand tour, the Washington Alerts and Mutuals, two of the earliest African American ball clubs, formed in the District. Charles Douglass, the son of Frederick Douglass, during the 1867 to 1870 time period played for both teams. In fact, as secretary of the Mutuals in 1870, Charles contacted the Nationals and successfully arranged access for his club to use the Nationals' ball field for the Mutuals' series with the visiting powerhouse Philadelphia Pythians black ball club. Charles Douglass to J.C. White, September 10, 1869, Leon Gardiner Collection, Historical Society of Pennsylvania.

48. See for example, Ryczek, *When Johnny*, 126, citing the *Henry Chadwick Scrapbooks*. The annual Spalding Guides were published in the late 19th century by the sporting company owned by the very same Albert Spalding who led the Forest City Club to the victory over the Nationals . . . their only defeat! Bealle, *The Washington Senators*, 7–8.

From the *Washington Post* of February 6, 1900, "Base Ball Notes" column

One of the best second basemen the game has ever seen was the colored diamond athlete, Hughey Grant, who was at his best when he played on the Buffalo team," says Tom Brown. "Grant's great forte as a fielder was his sure-fire hands. He was as near to perfection in gauging swift grounders as Heine Reitz, than whom no finer hand-worker ever lived. Grant, however, had Reitz distinctly beaten as an all-around fielder, as he was faster of foot, covered larger area of ground, and was surer and quicker on double plays. He was a natural batsman, as many a twirler found to his sorrow. Grant played no favorites at the bat. High incurves, low outshoots, or slow teasers served at a shot-putting gait all looked the same to Grant. The pitchers seemed to take a fiendish delight in deliberately firing the ball at his head with the intention of driving him from the plate, but they never succeeded in taking his nerve. In the annals of the game and in the achievements of such second basemen as Burdock, Ross Barnes, Fred Pfeffer, and Yank Robinson the name of Hugh Grant has been overlooked, though if he were a white man he would stand abreast of the others in the red-letter chapters of baseball."

Contributed by Bob Schaefer

PHIL BIRNBAUM

Are Traded Players "Lemons"?

In 2001, economist George Akerlof won a Nobel Prize for Economics for his work on the theory of the "market for lemons." The idea is this: suppose in the population of otherwise identical used Chevrolets, some will be defective "lemons," while some will be very reliable "cherries." The owner of the car knows, from his repair bills, whether his car is a lemon or a cherry. But the prospective buyer does not.

The theory of the "market for lemons" shows that in this situation, where buyer and seller have asymmetric information, there will be a much larger proportion of lemons for sale. The reason: anyone with a lemon will have incentive to sell it, since the buyer won't know it's a lemon and may pay more than what it's worth. Similarly, the owner of a cherry has no way of proving to the buyer that it is indeed worth more than average, and is therefore more likely to hang on to it.

The result is that when sellers have more information than buyers, the overall quality of goods for sale is lowered, since there is no possibility of getting full value for high-quality goods.

Which leads to the question: if this is true for Chevrolets, is it also true for baseball players? A team that trades a player can be assumed, perhaps, to have more information about the player than the team trading for him. While both have access to the player's season and career statistics, the trading team might know his arm has been hurting lately, or his attitude isn't what it should be, or that he's not keeping himself in shape the way he used to. According to the lemon theory, we should find that, on average, traded players won't turn out to be as good as their statistics suggest. This study attempts to see if that's really the case.

The Study

How can we tell, in retrospect, if a traded player wasn't as good as we thought he was? I tried to measure this by using Bill James's "Favorite Toy." The Favorite Toy (TFT) is a method for estimating the probability of a player achieving a certain future goal (for instance, 3,000 hits). If the lemon theory applies to ballplayers, then traded players as a group should be less likely to reach a TFT goal than players who were not traded.

So what I did was this: for all players from 1901 to 1975, I found qualifying players who changed teams during or after one of those years; 1975 was chosen because prior to 1975, it can safely be assumed that players would change teams only as a result of being traded or sold.

For each player I calculated TFT's "projected remaining runs created" for his career as of the end of that season. I then checked how many players achieved their projections plus 50%. The TFT formula predicts that the chance of a player achieving his projection plus 50% is 1 in 6, or 17%.

I added the 50% because Bill James stressed that TFT is valid only for exceptional players attempting to achieve a difficult goal. I assume that a goal with a 17% chance of success counts as difficult.

And also, because the players must be "exceptional," I limited the study to players who had accumulated 1,000 runs created by the end of the qualifying season. I also eliminated players who did not play at all after their qualifying season, for whatever reason (injury, retirement, etc.).

Example: Hank Aaron

Take Hank Aaron. After the 1969 season, TFT projected Hammerin' Hank to create an additional 369 more runs by the end of his career. Our test sees if he will create 150% of that, or 552 runs. In fact, Aaron outdid even the 150% goal, creating 577 more runs before retiring in 1976.

Aaron was not traded after the '69 season, but he *was* traded after the 1974 season. At that time he was expected to create 116 more runs. He failed to achieve 150% of that (and he even failed to achieve 100% of that), creating only 87 runs over the next two seasons before retiring.

I repeated this calculation for every player from 1901 to 1975 who had 1,000 runs created under his belt at the time. I then separated those players into those who were traded (like Aaron in 1974) and players who weren't (like Aaron in 1969).

Results

Including both traded and non-traded cases, there were 678 qualifying player-seasons in the study.

Of these 678 seasons, 148 had the player began the next season with another team (by changing teams during or after the previous season). Of those 148, 10 of them reached the goal.

In the other 530 seasons, the player was not traded. Of those 530, 109 of them, or 21%, achieved the goal.

It certainly looks like there's a large lemon effect here: players not traded were three times more likely to achieve the goal as traded players.

Table 1. Players with at least 1000 career RC who played again after the current season

	Total	Achieving 150% of projection	%
Only non-traded players	530	109	21%
Only traded players	148	10	7%
All qualifying players	678	119	18%

Test 2

Now, as mentioned, TFT is supposed to work only on "exceptional" players. Perhaps we got the results we did because the traded players weren't "exceptional." Perhaps they accumulated their 1,000 runs created, but then were in the twilights of their careers, playing part-time, or pinch-hitting. That might make them different from the non-traded players, which might skew the results.

To test this, I tightened the criteria for inclusion. In addition to having 1,000 runs created, I limited the sample to players who:

1. Had at least 90 runs created in the previous year; and
2. Had a TFT "established level" (weighted average of the past three years) of at least 80 RC.

I ran the study again. The results (see Table 2) were even more dramatic. None of the traded players—zero—achieved the goal.

Table 2. Players with at least 1,000 career RC who played again after the current season, with at least 90 RC that season and an established level of 80 RC, achieving 150% of their Favorite Toy projection

	Total	Achieving 150% of projection	%
Only non-traded players	170	42	25%
Only traded players	19	0	0%
All qualifying players	189	42	22%

Test 3

Now, 22% is already a small proportion of successful seasons. Also, those 42 successful seasons aren't by 42 different players—some players have multiple successes, often in consecutive seasons. For example, Hank Aaron accounted for 13 of the 42, from 1962 to 1973, plus 1975. (He was recorded as successful in the first 9 of those 13 seasons.) Perhaps, then, it's just by chance that the lemon effect seems so large, due to the list's domination by the most successful players.

To check that, I changed the study so that instead of requiring 150% of the expected RC to count as successful, only 100% would be required. This should bring the success rate, in theory, to 50%.

Here are the results:

Table 3. Players with at least 1,000 career RC who played again after the current season, with at least 90 RC that season and an established level of 80 RC, achieving their Favorite Toy projection

	Total	Achieving 100% of projection	%
Only non-traded players	170	86	51%
Only traded players	19	3	16%
All qualifying players	189	89	47%

Again, there's a strong effect here: players whose teams kept them were more than three times as likely to achieve expectations than traded players. Looked at another, equally shocking way — only one out of six traded players achieved the expectations you'd expect from a player of that age and performance. You'd expect 50% of those players to be below what was expected, but a full 84% had careers that fizzled out early.

Test 4

Perhaps, I thought, it's an age thing: maybe the traded players were old, and TFT just doesn't work as well for old players. But the results turned out to be similar. Here are the results for players younger than 35:

Table 4. Players with at least 1,000 career RC who played again after the current season, with at least 90 RC that season and an established level of 80 RC, who were 34 or younger in the current season

	Total	Achieving 100% of projection	%
Only non-traded players	105	53	50%
Only traded players	13	1	8%
All qualifying players	127	52	41%

And here are the players 35 or older:

Table 5. Players with at least 1,000 career RC who played again after the current season, with at least 90 RC that season and an established level of 80 RC, who were 35 or older in the current season

	Total	Achieving 100% of projection	%
Only non-traded players	65	33	51%
Only traded players	6	2	33%
All qualifying players	71	35	49%

Conclusions

It does seem that there's a lemon effect for baseball players—traded players do seem to be damaged goods, at least compared to what you'd expect (or what TFT would expect) from their statistics.

However, TFT is a blunt tool, and using TFT limited the sample to certain types of players. A more comprehensive study would use a different projection method, one that applies to all traded players, not just outstanding ones.

One possibility is to use Bill James's Brock2 method. Fed a career so far, Brock2 projects the player's career totals, and can be used for all players (although I think the player must have at least three years' worth of major league statistics). The disadvantage is that the algorithm is difficult to implement without a spreadsheet (although if anyone has a VB implementation they are willing to share, please drop me a line).

Alternatively, the editors of *Baseball Prospectus* talk about their "Pecota" method, which projects a player's career by finding retired players most similar at the same age, and averaging their stats. However, the *BP* editors do not explain their proprietary method in full.

If the difficulties of either of these methods can be resolved, it would be fairly easy to do a full test of all players and see to what extent, if any, the lemon effect continues to appear.

Technical Notes

The basic version of the Runs Created formula was used throughout the study. The player's age was taken as of December 31 of the year before starting the next season with the new team. The "16% chance of reaching 150%" does not consider the Favorite Toy's "97%" rule. Raw data for each test can be found online at www.philbirnbaum.com/lemondata.txt.

TOM RUANE

In Search of Clutch Hitting

Clutch hitting is back in fashion in the baseball research community. For years many of us looked in vain for the existence of some persistent clutch-hitting ability and, failing to find it, came to the conclusion that such an ability must not exist. The pioneer of this approach was Dick Cramer, who wrote an article on this subject in the 1977 *Baseball Research Journal*, but many of us have done similar studies. First, you determine who performs better than normally one year in "clutch situations" (and the definitions of these situations change from study to study) and then you see if these players have a tendency to repeat their performance the next season. They don't, which has led a generation of baseball researchers to roll their eyes whenever announcers start rhapsodizing about Joe Blow's ability to come through when it counts.

In "Underestimating the Fog," an article in the 2005 *Baseball Research Journal*, Bill James argues that we were wrong to think that such an approach "proved" anything. There is so much random noise inherent in this method, so much "fog," that we shouldn't expect to see anything when looking for clutch ability in this manner. I might get around to testing this hypothesis at some point, but for now I thought I'd take a different tack. I thought it might be interesting to compare a player's ability in both clutch and non-clutch situations over the course of his career. I'm not really looking for persistence in results from one year to the next, but rather I'll be looking for results that are not what we'd expect to see if there were only random forces at work. Hopefully, dealing with much larger groups of at-bats will help to thin out the fog somewhat.

Identifying "Clutch"

The first problem facing anyone undertaking a study like this is that we don't really know what "clutch" means. Or rather, it seems to mean something different whenever it's used, depending upon the point we are trying to make. Ted Williams was once accused of not being a clutch player based upon his performance in a handful of games, selected both because they had a significant impact on his team's chances to win a world championship and because he performed relatively poorly in them. Games in the middle of a

TOM RUANE is a computer programmer and Retrosheet volunteer living in Poughkeepsie, New York. This is his third appearance in *The Baseball Research Journal*.

tight pennant race weren't clutch, only a couple at the very end of a few seasons. Others have defined terms like "Late Inning Pressure Situations" to identify players who perform well or poorly in a handful of at-bats near the end of close games.

One lazy way out of this problem (hint: it's the one I'll be taking) is to define a clutch situation as an at-bat with runners in scoring position. In a sense, this is nonsense: a leadoff hitter in the late innings of a tie game is usually a much more clutch situation than a batter at the plate with a runner on second and a 15–2 lead. Still, it's often what we mean by "clutch." I don't know about you, but when someone talks about how well this or that player has hit in the clutch, I usually test the statement by checking to see how the man has hit with men in scoring position. These at-bats may not all be the most pressure-packed of the season, but they probably come close enough for our purposes.

Situational Biases

There is a problem with taking this approach, however: batters do not hit equally well in all situations. Table 1a contains a breakdown of batter stats for each of the 24 game situations from 1960 to 2004. Note: this data is not complete for these years, and for the purposes of this article we will be ignoring any games for which we are missing play-by-play information.

I thought it might be easier to see some trends if I compressed the data in a few ways. Aggregate performance by outs is listed in Table 1b, Aggregate performance with men on base is in Table 1c, and with runners in and out of scoring position in Table 1d.

With men in scoring position, batters have just about the same slugging percentage and a higher on-base percentage than they do in their other at-bats. So they hit somewhat better in these situations. Except, of course, that they don't.

There are two deceptive things about comparing situational statistics in this manner. First of all, sacrifice flies occur only with a lead runner on third or (very rarely) on second. These are about the same as run-scoring groundouts, and the decision not to count these as at-bats is a mistake first adopted in 1889 (when, who knows, perhaps it made sense), a mistake which has gone in and out of fashion over the years. I'm not sure how many of the sacrifice flies hit from 1960 to 2004 were actually struck with a sacrificial intent, but I'd be surprised if all but a handful of these were merely failed attempts at getting a hit. So the first thing we're going to do in our study is to treat sacrifice flies as at-bats.

The second thing that's misleading is walks. Walk rates vary

Table 1a.

FST	Out	AB	H	2B	3B	HR	BB	IBB	HBP	SF	OBP	SLG	OPS
---	0	1532622	397872	70352	10052	41281	124600	6	9597	0	.319	.399	.719
---	1	1089667	272485	47627	6764	26633	93420	24	6859	0	.313	.380	.693
---	2	855785	211439	37083	4936	21779	82275	91	5645	0	.317	.378	.696
x--	0	321722	91402	14907	1921	8458	21371	3	2354	0	.333	.421	.755
x--	1	396177	111618	18431	2313	10860	27732	36	2658	0	.333	.422	.755
x--	2	400916	103338	17374	2518	10836	32030	131	2531	0	.317	.395	.711
-x-	0	98402	24968	4104	654	1967	10171	621	862	6	.329	.369	.698
-x-	1	184504	45058	8137	1278	4269	30453	8618	1494	35	.356	.372	.727
-x-	2	218447	52285	9214	1509	5045	45860	17097	1757	0	.375	.365	.740
xx-	0	75884	20950	3420	411	2045	5327	16	660	7	.329	.413	.742
xx-	1	154245	40316	7178	961	4073	11667	52	1175	26	.318	.400	.718
xx-	2	199902	47270	8384	1422	4753	17909	168	1540	0	.304	.364	.668
--x	0	17713	5348	953	195	388	2276	181	178	2835	.339	.443	.783
--x	1	53374	17321	3045	514	1356	9344	2363	663	9639	.374	.477	.851
--x	2	90284	21777	3907	628	2075	16646	3975	799	0	.364	.367	.731
x-x	0	29489	9865	1653	192	865	2459	340	309	5351	.336	.492	.828
x-x	1	60054	19653	3278	460	1728	5483	786	598	11295	.332	.483	.816
x-x	2	91638	23143	4109	667	2179	8579	472	773	0	.322	.383	.705
-xx	0	16965	5153	920	165	437	3173	1304	203	2882	.367	.455	.822
-xx	1	36700	10873	1957	319	809	16311	11963	452	6302	.462	.433	.896
-xx	2	49866	11563	2089	347	1062	14106	7438	476	0	.406	.352	.757
xxx	0	19001	6248	1064	128	599	1367	0	216	3466	.326	.493	.818
xxx	1	48260	14911	2646	384	1406	3396	0	503	8762	.309	.467	.776
xxx	2	68338	16292	2938	553	1710	5491	1	529	0	.300	.373	.673

Table 1b. . . .

Out	AB	H	2B	3B	HR	BB	IBB	HBP	SF	OBP	SLG	OPS
0	2111798	561806	97373	13718	56040	170744	2471	14379	14547	.323	.405	.728
1	2022981	532235	92299	12993	51134	197806	23843	14402	36059	.328	.397	.725
2	1975176	487107	85098	12580	49439	222896	29373	14050	0	.327	.378	.705

Table 1c. . . . by men on

FST	AB	H	2B	3B	HR	BB	IBB	HBP	SF	OBP	SLG	OPS
---	3478074	881796	155062	21752	89693	300295	121	22101	0	.317	.388	.705
x--	1118815	306358	50712	6752	30154	81133	170	7543	0	.327	.412	.739
-x-	501353	122311	21455	3441	11281	86484	26336	4113	41	.360	.368	.728
xx-	430031	108536	18982	2794	10871	34903	236	3375	33	.313	.385	.699
--x	161371	44446	7905	1337	3819	28266	6519	1640	12474	.365	.412	.777
x-x	181181	52661	9040	1319	4772	16521	1598	1680	16646	.328	.434	.762
-xx	103531	27589	4966	831	2308	33590	20705	1131	9184	.423	.397	.820
xxx	135599	37451	6648	1065	3715	10254	1	1248	12228	.307	.423	.730

Table 1d. . . . with runners in and out of scoring position

	AB	H	2B	3B	HR	BB	IBB	HBP	SF	OBP	SLG	OPS
Not RISP	4596889	1188154	205774	28504	119847	381428	291	29644	0	.319	.394	.713
RISP	1513066	392994	68996	10787	36766	210018	55396	13187	50606	.345	.392	.737

quite a bit from situation to situation. With men on second and third and one out, a batter is nearly five times more likely to get a walk than he is with the bases loaded and one out. Most of this difference is due to intentional walks, which are easy to remove (and we will), but large differences in walk rates still remain even without them. Not only are these differences significant, but they vary quite a bit from batter to batter. The reason for this, of course, is that in some situations (most frequently with first base open)

some batters are "pitched around" and sent to first via a non-intentional intentional walk. The decision to pitch to a batter in this manner is largely made based upon his reputation, the relative handedness of the pitcher and batter, and often simply because of a manager's hunch.

As a result, in addition to treating sacrifice flies as outs in this study, I'm also going to ignore walks. This is not to say that walks aren't important, or are not in many instances the outcome

Table 2a.

FST	Out	AB	H	2B	3B	HR	AVG	SLG	BPS
---	0	1532622	397872	70352	10052	41281	.260	.399	.659
---	1	1089667	272485	47627	6764	26633	.250	.380	.630
---	2	855785	211439	37083	4936	21779	.247	.378	.625
x--	0	321722	91402	14907	1921	8458	.284	.421	.705
x--	1	396177	111618	18431	2313	10860	.282	.422	.704
x--	2	400916	103338	17374	2518	10836	.258	.395	.652
-x-	0	98408	24968	4104	654	1967	.254	.369	.622
-x-	1	184539	45058	8137	1278	4269	.244	.372	.616
-x-	2	218447	52285	9214	1509	5045	.239	.365	.604
xx-	0	75891	20950	3420	411	2045	.276	.413	.689
xx-	1	154271	40316	7178	961	4073	.261	.400	.661
xx-	2	199902	47270	8384	1422	4753	.236	.364	.600
--x	0	20548	5348	953	195	388	.260	.382	.643
--x	1	63013	17321	3045	514	1356	.275	.404	.679
--x	2	90284	21777	3907	628	2075	.241	.367	.609
x-x	0	34840	9865	1653	192	865	.283	.416	.699
x-x	1	71349	19653	3278	460	1728	.275	.407	.682
x-x	2	91638	23143	4109	667	2179	.253	.383	.636
-xx	0	19847	5153	920	165	437	.260	.389	.648
-xx	1	43002	10873	1957	319	809	.253	.370	.622
-xx	2	49866	11563	2089	347	1062	.232	.352	.583
xxx	0	22467	6248	1064	128	599	.278	.417	.695
xxx	1	57022	14911	2646	384	1406	.261	.395	.657
xxx	2	68338	16292	2938	553	1710	.238	.373	.611

Table 2b. Performance by outs

Out	AB	H	2B	3B	HR	AVG	SLG	BPS
0	2126345	561806	97373	13718	56040	.264	.402	.666
1	2059040	532235	92299	12993	51134	.258	.390	.649
2	1975176	487107	85098	12580	49439	.247	.378	.624

Table 2c. ... by men on

FST	AB	H	2B	3B	HR	AVG	SLG	BPS
---	3478074	881796	155062	21752	89693	.254	.388	.642
x--	1118815	306358	50712	6752	30154	.274	.412	.686
-x-	501394	122311	21455	3441	11281	.244	.368	.612
xx-	430064	108536	18982	2794	10871	.252	.385	.638
--x	173845	44446	7905	1337	3819	.256	.382	.638
x-x	197827	52661	9040	1319	4772	.266	.398	.664
-xx	112715	27589	4966	831	2308	.245	.365	.610
xxx	147827	37451	6648	1065	3715	.253	.388	.641

Table 2d. ... with runners in and out of scoring position

	AB	H	2B	3B	HR	AVG	SLG	BPS
Not RISP	4596889	1188154	205774	28504	119847	.258	.394	.652
RISP	1563672	392994	68996	10787	36766	.251	.380	.631

of "clutch" at-bats, only that it is difficult to level the playing field with respect to walks and I don't want a batter's reputation inflating (or deflating) his apparent performance in clutch situations.

Finally, I'm also going to remove hit by pitches. Not that it can't be clutch (and painful) to take one for the team, but I'd like to concentrate on the hitting aspect of batting rather than getting hit. With these changes made, here are the new situational breakdowns (see Tables 2a through 2d).

So with these adjustments, it's clear that batters actually hit worse with runners in scoring position than they do otherwise.

Since batters hit best with a man on first, I thought it might be interesting to see how right-handed and left-handed hitters do in these situations (See Table 3a and Table 3b).

Table 3a. Righties

FST	AB	H	2B	3B	HR	AVG	SLG	BPS
- - -	2090674	523625	92577	11626	54934	.250	.385	.635
x - -	677801	181155	30450	3739	18246	.267	.404	.671
- x -	300296	72633	12563	1876	6802	.242	.364	.606
xx -	263504	65779	11630	1539	6715	.250	.382	.632
- - x	105321	26474	4667	733	2358	.251	.377	.628
x - x	120675	31523	5479	714	2932	.261	.391	.653
- xx	70013	17130	3107	482	1490	.245	.367	.611
xxx	92149	22948	4151	579	2244	.249	.380	.629

Table 3b. Lefties

FST	AB	H	2B	3B	HR	AVG	SLG	BPS
- - -	1387400	358171	62485	10126	34759	.258	.393	.651
x - -	441014	125203	20262	3013	11908	.284	.425	.708
- x -	201098	49678	8892	1565	4479	.247	.374	.621
xx -	166560	42757	7352	1255	4156	.257	.391	.647
- - x	68524	17972	3238	604	1461	.262	.391	.653
x - x	77152	21138	3561	605	1840	.274	.407	.681
- xx	42702	10459	1859	349	818	.245	.362	.607
xxx	55678	14503	2497	486	1471	.260	.402	.663

As expected, left-handed hitters are able to take more advantage of the man on first situation, since holding the runner on opens up a hole on the right side.

Since I want to do away with as much of the fog as possible in this study, I'm going to consider only those players with at least 3,000 at-bats (including sacrifice flies). This group of players should be significantly better hitters than the ones with less than 3,000 at-bats for two reasons. First of all, requiring a significant number of at-bats will eliminate all pitchers from the mix. And second, I'm assuming that batters with longer careers are better than those with shorter careers.

Before going much further, then, I wanted to see if my target group showed a similar decline with runners in scoring position. Table 4 displays the statistics for the two groups of batters.

The percentage declines were about the same for the two groups. This isn't what I would have expected if clutch hitting is a talent that some players have and others don't. I would have assumed that the more talented group of hitters would have done better. Of course, there's no reason why talent and clutch ability have to go hand in hand.

Still, I was surprised that batters, both good and bad, hit worse with men in scoring position. Much of this is due to the big spike in performance that occurs when there's a man on first. Another reason is the presence of force-outs and fielder choices that aren't available with no one on.

Still, the single worst hitting situation is second and third with two outs. One reason for this could be a selection bias: good hitters are often walked in these situations. As a result, the quality of hitters batting at these times is lower than at others. I thought this might be something we could look at. Here are the average BPSs of the hitters up in each of the 24 game situations:

FST	0 Out	1 Out	2 Out
- - -	.646	.640	.647
x - -	.655	.659	.647
- x -	.656	.651	.648
xx -	.664	.652	.634
- - x	.648	.662	.651
x - x	.664	.658	.642
- xx	.656	.643	.636
xxx	.651	.641	.630

Table 4.

1–2999	AB	H	2B	3B	HR	AVG	SLG	BPS
Not RISP	1748765	414965	70688	9459	35513	.237	.349	.587
RISP	588724	135614	23479	3614	10466	.230	.336	.566

3000+	AB	H	2B	3B	HR	BAVG	SLG	BPS
Not RISP	2848124	773189	135086	19045	84334	.271	.421	.693
RISP	974948	257380	45517	7173	26300	.264	.406	.670

There's something to this theory, as the quality of hitters at the plate with men on second and third and two out is among the worst.

Later on, we will explore some other possible explanations for the drop-off in performance with runners in scoring position.

The Players

Enough talk. So who were the greatest clutch hitters from 1960 to 2004, the players who were able to raise the level of their game when it mattered most (or at least when runners were on second or third)? Here they are:

Name	B	AB	NO-RISP AB	NO-RISP BPS	RISP AB	RISP BPS	Diff
Bill Spiers	L	3430	2548	.607	882	.722	.115
Mike Sweeney	R	3760	2673	.764	1087	.867	.103
Pat Tabler	R	3948	2815	.626	1133	.725	.099
Jose Valentin	B	4882	3678	.666	1204	.765	.099
Wayne Garrett	L	3308	2557	.557	751	.643	.087
Sandy Alomar	B	4748	3831	.519	917	.592	.073
Tony Fernandez	B	7972	6100	.665	1872	.736	.071
Rennie Stennett	R	4554	3520	.612	1034	.682	.070
Joe Girardi	R	4150	3117	.596	1033	.666	.070
Rick Miller	L	3910	2991	.599	919	.668	.069
Larry Parrish	R	6848	5075	.679	1773	.747	.068
Carlos Beltran	B	3508	2587	.748	921	.815	.068
Tony Taylor	R	6587	5304	.597	1283	.663	.067
Scott Fletcher	R	5294	4014	.583	1280	.649	.066
Johnny Edwards	L	4585	3471	.575	1114	.638	.063
Brent Mayne	L	3652	2701	.590	951	.649	.059
Troy O'Leary	L	4043	2917	.700	1126	.758	.058
Miguel Tejada	R	4277	3115	.726	1162	.782	.057
Orlando Merced	B	4028	2883	.682	1145	.738	.056
Henry Rodriguez	L	3054	2243	.719	811	.776	.056
Edgardo Alfonzo	R	4981	3700	.702	1281	.758	.056

Diff: BPS with runners in scoring position minus BPS without

Just who I expected to see: Bill Spiers, Wayne Garrett, Rennie Stennett, Rick Miller ... and the other side of the coin:

Name	B	AB	NO-RISP AB	NO-RISP BPS	RISP AB	RISP BPS	Diff
Richard Hidalgo	R	3193	2252	.821	941	.614	-.207
Jermaine Dye	R	3863	2750	.772	1113	.611	-.161
Al Martin	L	4269	3233	.753	1036	.598	-.155
Larry Brown	R	3472	2729	.574	743	.423	-.151
Earl Williams	R	3058	2186	.701	872	.554	-.147
Hal Morris	L	4037	2952	.769	1085	.624	-.145
Jim Edmonds	L	5139	3739	.868	1400	.727	-.141
Jim Morrison	R	3414	2494	.708	920	.570	-.139
Dean Palmer	R	4953	3586	.753	1367	.617	-.137
Pete Ward	L	3088	2253	.690	835	.553	-.136
Lee Maye	L	3849	2978	.708	871	.577	-.130
Mark Kotsay	L	3756	2898	.734	858	.611	-.123
Don Slaught	R	4101	3020	.721	1081	.599	-.122
Pat Borders	R	3183	2364	.662	819	.541	-.121
Todd Walker	L	3704	2772	.749	932	.630	-.119
Reggie Smith	B	7119	5306	.797	1813	.680	-.117
Shawn Green	L	5566	4102	.814	1464	.700	-.114
Tony Bernazard	B	3735	2808	.671	927	.558	-.114
Kevin Young	R	3944	2814	.721	1130	.608	-.113
Phil Bradley	R	3716	2836	.730	880	.618	-.112
Warren Cromartie	L	3958	3022	.705	936	.593	-.112
Lee Lacy	R	4582	3502	.718	1080	.606	-.112

For lack of a better term (and so I don't have to keep writing "the difference between a batter's BPS with and without runners in scoring position"), I'm going to call this difference ("DIFF" in the charts above) Clutch Percentage. I know it's not really "Clutch" and not really a "Percentage," but it's the best I could come up with.

The poor Clutch Percentages are more extreme than the positive ones, partly because the median of the group is not zero but rather -.027.

I'm not sure what I expected to see here. I doubt that if I had presented these two lists of players to you and told you that one was a list of the best clutch hitters and the other the worst, you could have figured out which was which.

One of the things that bothers me about the last list is that 12 of the 20 players on it have less than 1,000 at-bats with runners in scoring position. Of the 727 players in the study, only a little more than 30% (222) fell into that category. If the differences we're looking at were caused more by chance than talent, you'd expect to see players with small sample sizes at the two extremes.

Is the Data Random?

Could these results have been random? The way I usually approach this kind of question is with brute force. Rather than attempting to finesse the issue with mathematics, I run over it with simulation. My approach this time is perhaps best shown by example.

In the games we have, Vada Pinson had a runner on second or third in 2,114 of his 8,954 at-bats, or 23.6096%. So to simulate his random career, I generated 8,954 random numbers (one for each at-bat) between 0 and 1. If the number was less than .236096, I counted it as an at-bat with runners in scoring position. When I was done, I had randomly selected around 2,114 at-bats that I'm considering to be clutch. Using these two pools of at-bats (the ones selected by this process and the ones not selected), I computed his simulated Clutch Percentage.

One problem with this approach is that we already know that the data is not random. Players on average hit worse (in terms of BPS, 27 points worse)[1] with men in scoring position. Our random tests will not reflect this. Since we're doing these simulations to see how much random variation there will be in the data, this problem might not be fatal, but it does complicate things. For example, we will want to compare the amount of spread in both the real and simulated data. This spread will be centered around -.027 in the real run and .000 in the simulated runs.

I did 1,000 of these simulations. What did I find out? Well, there was nothing terribly unusual in the spread of the real data. In the random run the average distance from each player's Clutch

Table 5

	-J	-I	-H	-G	-F	-E	-D	-C	-B	-A	A	B	C	D	E	F	G	H	I	J
Real	1	3	6	5	15	21	46	76	77	115	105	88	69	41	31	13	10	1	3	1
Fake	1	2	3	7	14	26	45	70	94	109	109	92	68	45	26	14	7	3	2	1

Percentage and the expected value varied from a low of .2872 to a high of .3512. The actual values differed by .3314, which was a little high but nothing out of the ordinary (117th place out of 1,001). In addition to looking at the spread, I also broke the range of values into 20 groups (each .015 wide except for the first and last) and saw if the distribution of the players were similar in both the real and the simulated worlds. Note that the midpoint in the two worlds is different, since the expected Clutch Percentage is -.027 for the actual values and .000 for the simulated ones. In Table 5, as a result, group A contains the count of players from .000 to .015 over the expected value, B contains the count of players from .015 to .030, and so on. Not too surprisingly, -A contains the count of players from .000 to .015 below the expected value, -B contains the count of players from .015 to .030 below, and so on (see Table 5).

Our real distribution is very similar to the average of the fake ones. But it is important to note that this doesn't prove anything. While a very different spread and distribution could be used to demonstrate that Clutch Percentage is not random, the fact that these results are similar is not evidence that only random forces are at work here.

Potential Problems

This section explores factors that may complicate things, causing batters to hit worse (or better) with runners in scoring position.

The first thing that occurred to me is that batters might be facing a platoon disadvantage more often with runners in scoring position than they might otherwise. To test this, I looked at batters who hit right, left, and from both sides of the plate, and determined how well they did against right and left pitchers. I next computed what types of pitchers they faced both with and without runners in scoring position and used that information to generate an expected BPS (batting average plus slugging percentage) given the mix of pitchers they saw in both situations. Here's the data:

	Count	AB	BPS	BPSvR	BPSvL	No RISP PLAT%	No RISP ExBPS	RISP PLAT%	RISP ExBPS
Right	402	5247	.679	.662	.714	36.8	.679	34.1	.677
Left	219	5298	.693	.718	.612	75.9	.694	71.8	.689
Both	106	5220	.652	.651	.647	50.9	.652	50.0	.651
Total	727	5259	.679	.677	.673	50.6	.679	47.8	.677

```
Count:  Number of batter included in sample
AB:     Average number of at-bats in group
BPS:    Average overall BPS
BPSvR:  Average BPS against right-handed pitchers[2]
BPSvL:  Average BPS against left-handed pitchers
PLAT%:  Percentage of times having the platoon advantage
ExBPS:  Expected BPS given the mix of pitchers faced
```

This table presents a lot of unfamiliar information, so it might be a good idea to go over a sample line. There are 402 right-handed hitters in our study. The average righty in the study had 5,247 at-bats and an overall BPS of .679. As expected, he hit lefties better than the righties (.714 to .662), but had a platoon advantage only 36.8% of the time with no runners in scoring position. Now, I didn't assume that all right-handed hitters had a platoon advantage against left-handed pitchers. Instead, I determined which type of pitcher each batter performed better against over the course of his career. Most of the time, hitters did better against pitchers who threw from the other side, but not always. Given the percentage of pitchers of each type our hitters faced with no one in scoring position, and how they hit against these pitchers, righty hitters had an expected BPS of .679 in these situations. When runners were on second or third, the platoon advantage and BPS drop slightly to 34.1% and .677 respectively.

You should not assume from the chart above that switch-hitters had no platoon advantage or disadvantage. The reason why they hit almost the same against both righties (.651) and lefties (.647) is that the platoon differentials of switch-hitters tended to cancel each other out. To illustrate this, here are the players with 3,000 or more at-bats with the greatest platoon differentials:

Name	B vs. P	BPSvR	BPSvL	Diff
Rob Deer	R vs. L	.599	.801	.202
Adrian Beltre	R vs. R	.750	.667	.083
Tom Goodwin	L vs. L	.599	.621	.021
Randy Bush	L vs. R	.666	.369	.298
Dave Hollins	B vs. L	.608	.806	.198
Wally Backman	B vs. R	.652	.365	.287

```
B: Handedness of the batter (Right, Left, Both)
P: Handedness of the pitcher (Right, Left)
BPSvR: BA + SLG against right-handed pitchers
BPSvL: BA + SLG against left-handed pitchers
Diff: Difference
```

The average platoon differential is greatest for the lefties in our study (.107), and just about the same for right-handed hitters (.058) and switch-hitters (.057). People often assume that just because a batter hits from both sides of the plate that he hits equally well from each side. This is not the case, although it isn't always obvious which side is their weakest (unless it's someone like Wally Backman).

Platoon advantages by themselves are not sufficient to explain the fact that hitters tend to perform worse with runners in scoring position. The average dropoff is about 23 points of BPS (.693 to .670), and the expected dropoff due to platoon disadvantages is only two points for right-handed hitters, five points for lefties, and one point for switch-hitters. Of course, this effect is different for each player. Frank Howard, for example, punished lefties so much that he seldom faced them with men in scoring position, causing him to have a platoon disadvantage of 17 points. Tony Batista, on the other hand, is a right-handed hitter who has hit righties better than lefties over the course of his career. As a result, he has a platoon advantage of three points with runners in scoring position.

Another factor we might want to take into account is that the quality of pitchers is often worse in these situations. This makes sense. After all, when you're up with men in scoring position, you are usually facing the pitcher who permitted those runners to reach base, something that happens a lot more frequently with a Jaime Navarro on the mound than a Roger Clemens. To determine how much worse they are, for each at-bat by one of the batters in

Table 6.

Name	B	AB	NO-RISP		RISP		Diff	PlatF	OppF	PRat
			AB	BPS	AB	BPS				
Bill Spiers	L	3430	2548	.607	882	.722	.115	-.006	.003	.999
Mike Sweeney	R	3760	2673	.764	1087	.867	.103	.003	.013	.998
Pat Tabler	R	3948	2815	.626	1133	.725	.099	-.001	.008	1.005
Jose Valentin	B	4882	3678	.666	1204	.765	.099	-.001	.013	1.007
Wayne Garrett	L	3308	2557	.557	751	.643	.087	-.004	.008	.994
Sandy Alomar	B	4748	3831	.519	917	.592	.073	-.000	.005	1.008
Tony Fernandez	B	7972	6100	.665	1872	.736	.071	.000	.008	1.003
Rennie Stennett	R	4554	3520	.612	1034	.682	.070	-.004	.011	1.004
Joe Girardi	R	4150	3117	.596	1033	.666	.070	.001	.005	1.011
Rick Miller	L	3910	2991	.599	919	.668	.069	-.010	.012	1.002
Larry Parrish	R	6848	5075	.679	1773	.747	.068	-.001	.003	1.001
Carlos Beltran	B	3508	2587	.748	921	.815	.068	-.001	.006	1.008
Tony Taylor	R	6587	5304	.597	1283	.663	.067	-.001	.007	1.007
Scott Fletcher	R	5294	4014	.583	1280	.649	.066	-.003	-.005	1.001
Johnny Edwards	L	4585	3471	.575	1114	.638	.063	-.003	.010	1.004
Brent Mayne	L	3652	2701	.590	951	.649	.059	-.002	.012	1.024
Troy O'Leary	L	4043	2917	.700	1126	.758	.058	-.005	-.001	1.003
Miguel Tejada	R	4277	3115	.726	1162	.782	.057	-.000	.008	1.002
Orlando Merced	B	4028	2883	.682	1145	.738	.056	-.001	.009	1.006
Henry Rodriguez	L	3054	2243	.719	811	.776	.056	-.004	.003	1.007
Edgardo Alfonzo	R	4981	3700	.702	1281	.758	.056	-.000	.008	1.010

Name	B	AB	NO-RISP		RISP		Diff	PlatF	OppF	PRat
			AB	BPS	AB	BPS				
Richard Hidalgo	R	3193	2252	.821	941	.614	-.207	.000	.006	.996
Jermaine Dye	R	3863	2750	.772	1113	.611	-.161	-.001	.005	1.003
Al Martin	L	4269	3233	.753	1036	.598	-.155	-.017	.002	1.011
Larry Brown	R	3472	2729	.574	743	.423	-.151	-.004	.005	1.001
Earl Williams	R	3058	2186	.701	872	.554	-.147	.000	.002	1.000
Hal Morris	L	4037	2952	.769	1085	.624	-.145	-.002	.017	1.006
Jim Edmonds	L	5139	3739	.868	1400	.727	-.141	-.008	.005	1.001
Jim Morrison	R	3414	2494	.708	920	.570	-.139	-.001	.004	1.000
Dean Palmer	R	4953	3586	.753	1367	.617	-.137	-.006	-.001	1.003
Pete Ward	L	3088	2253	.690	835	.553	-.136	-.002	.013	1.005
Lee Maye	L	3849	2978	.708	871	.577	-.130	-.006	-.005	.990
Mark Kotsay	L	3756	2898	.734	858	.611	-.123	-.001	.006	1.006
Don Slaught	R	4101	3020	.721	1081	.599	-.122	-.003	-.004	.995
Pat Borders	R	3183	2364	.662	819	.541	-.121	-.001	.005	.999
Todd Walker	L	3704	2772	.749	932	.630	-.119	-.007	.007	1.011
Reggie Smith	B	7119	5306	.797	1813	.680	-.117	.001	.001	1.006
Shawn Green	L	5566	4102	.814	1464	.700	-.114	-.006	-.001	1.006
Tony Bernazard	B	3735	2808	.671	927	.558	-.114	.000	.005	1.006
Kevin Young	R	3944	2814	.721	1130	.608	-.113	-.002	.008	1.000
Phil Bradley	R	3716	2836	.730	880	.618	-.112	-.003	.000	1.005
Warren Cromartie	L	3958	3022	.705	936	.593	-.112	-.004	.001	1.001
Lee Lacy	R	4582	3502	.718	1080	.606	-.112	-.003	-.001	1.001

PlatF: Platoon advantage or disadvantage with runners in scoring position
OppF: Expected BPS increase or decrease based upon the quality of pitchers

our study, I calculated the pitcher's opponents' BPS, taking into account the handedness of the batter. I found that the average pitcher when runners are in scoring position is about three to four points worse (in BPS) than those on the mound when there aren't. Not a big deal and a result that seems to balance out the platoon disadvantage, except, as with the platoon disadvantage, there are differences from player to player. The most extreme cases among the players in our study are Hal Morris, who has faced pitchers 17 points worse with runners in scoring position, and Larry Walker, who has faced pitchers 11 points better. All in all, I think it's a good thing to check before anointing someone either a great or a poor clutch hitter.

The last thing we want to look at is any possible park effects. After all, there are more runners in scoring position in good-hitting parks. So I calculated the average park factor for the two situations and, to make a long story even longer, here's what I found:

	AB	PFact
No RISP	2848124	1.0048
RISP	974948	1.0084

PFact: Average park factor

Since there are more at-bats in a typical game in a hitter's park than there are in a pitcher's park, it's not too surprising that the average park factor in both groups would be greater than one. Note that the advantage with runners in scoring position is slight. Still, this is not insignificant for all players. The two extremes:

Name	No RISP PFact	RISP PFact	PRat
Lee Maye	.980	.970	.990
Todd Helton	1.214	1.259	1.037

PRat: RISP park factor divided by the NO-RISP park factor.

It is perhaps not too surprising that a member of the Colorado Rockies got the biggest park factor boost with runners in scoring position.

A Last Look at the Players

I wanted to take one last look at the players at the top and bottom of our lists, this time with their platoon, strength of opposition, and park factors included.

Some of these hitters (Mike Sweeney, Jose Valentin, Rennie Stennett, and Johnny Edwards) got a bigger than average boost by facing weaker pitchers with runners in scoring position, and Brent Mayne had the advantage of both facing weaker than normal pitching and hitting in these situations in friendlier parks. My feeling is that Mayne would not have been on the list without this help; see Table 6.

It looks like only Al Martin (with a bad platoon factor) and Lee Maye (who seemed to have everything go against him in these situations) could claim to owe their spots on this list to forces

beyond their control. Hal Morris, on the other hand, had reasonably good factors and still hit poorly with runners in scoring position.

Conclusion

So did I find evidence of clutch hitting? Not really. I did come up with lists of players who performed well and poorly in this area. Along the way I presented quite a bit of data on situational hitting, platoon advantages, opposition pitching strength, and park effects, and I attempted to both understand and explain what I found. At the end of all this, however, I guess I'm still not convinced that the players owe their inclusion on these lists of mine to talent rather than luck. Even when dealing with sample sizes of several thousand at-bats, the amount of random variation that I found in my simulations was very close to what I found in the real data. As I mentioned before, this doesn't necessarily mean that there aren't some real differences buried in all that noise, only that I'm not sure I found them. One could argue that the forces at work here, if they exist, must be awfully weak to so closely mimic random noise, and if they are really that inconsequential, perhaps we could assume they don't exist without much loss of accuracy.

Notes

1. Earlier I had mentioned the players as a whole hit an average of 23 points worse with men in scoring position. But the average Clutch Percentage is -27 points. This might seem confusing but hopefully won't after an example. Let's say there are three players: Moe, Larry, and Curly. Here are the performances both with and without men in scoring position:

Name	No RISP AB	No RISP BPS	RISP AB	RISP BPS	CLP
Moe	50	.600	20	.200	-.400
Larry	150	.600	30	.500	-.100
Curly	200	.700	50	.800	.100
Total	400	.650	100	.590	-.060

So as a group, they hit 60 points worse with men in scoring position, but this counts Curly's contribution much more heavily than Moe's. If we average their respective Clutch Percentages (and so count each player equally), we get .633 in the "NO RISP" group ([.600+.600+.700] / 3), .500 in the "RISP" group ([.200+.500+.800] / 3), and an average difference of 133 points.

2. Some of these averages look weird. For example, the overall BPS for switch-hitters (.652) is greater than the players' averages against *both* righties (.651) and lefties (.647). This would seem, on the face of it, to be a mathematical impossibility. It is caused by the manner in which I determined the averages, and is best shown by example. Let's say we have two players, Moe and Larry, who have the following right-left splits:

	vs. R AB	vs. R BPS	vs. L AB	vs. L BPS	Total AB	Total BPS
Moe	10	.200	90	.600	100	.560
Larry	90	.600	10	.200	100	.560
Total		.400		.400		.560

So when I average these, I do not weight them by at-bats, which would cause the players with more at-bats to influence the results more than someone just over the 3,000 at-bat minimum, but just take an average of the averages. And since players tend to have fewer plate appearances when they do not have the platoon advantage (as I showed in an extreme example above), the results can look a little strange at times.

GABRIEL COSTA, MICHAEL HUBER, & JOHN SACCOMAN

Cumulative Home Run Frequency and the Recent Home Run Explosion

British Prime Minister Benjamin Disraeli once remarked that there are three kinds of falsehoods: lies, damned lies, and statistics. While this may be debated on political and philosophical levels, there *are* circumstances where statistics (and graphs and charts) can shed some truth and light. Perhaps this is one of those times.

In this paper we define a measure which we call the *cumulative home run ratio* (CHR). We consider every player in history who has slugged 500 home runs, and compute their year-to-year total of home runs (HR) divided by their at-bats (AB). After which, we compare this accumulated HR/AB ratio to the slugger's corresponding age.

For example, from Table 1 below, in 1914 Babe Ruth hit 0 HR in 10 AB. This gives the 19-year-old Ruth a proportion of HR to AB equal to 0.000000. The next year (1915), Ruth hit 4 HR in 92 AB; Ruth's cumulative home run ratio over his two years as a pro becomes 0.039216 (4 HR in 102 AB) at age 20. Since he hit 3 HR in 136 AB in 1916, his CHR at the age of 21 is computed to be 0.029412 (7 HR in 238 AB). The data in Table 1 continues Ruth's major league career and provides his CHR for each season.

Table 1. Babe Ruth

Year	AB	HR	Age	CHR
1914	10	0	19	0.000000
1915	92	4	20	0.039216
1916	136	3	21	0.029412
1917	123	2	22	0.024931
1918	317	11	23	0.029499
1919	432	29	24	0.044144
1920	458	54	25	0.065689
1921	540	59	26	0.076850
1922	406	35	27	0.078361
1923	522	41	28	0.078393
1924	529	46	29	0.079663
1925	359	25	30	0.078746
1926	495	47	31	0.080561
1927	540	60	32	0.083888
1928	536	54	33	0.085532
1929	499	46	34	0.086086
1930	518	49	35	0.086763
1931	534	46	36	0.086716
1932	457	41	37	0.086899
1933	459	34	38	0.086159
1934	365	22	39	0.085025
1935	72	6	40	0.085010

Figure 1. Babe Ruth's Cumulative Home Run Ratio

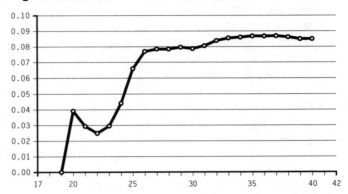

Figure 1 shows the plot of Ruth's age (horizontal axis) versus his CHR (vertical axis) over his career. Ruth's CHR seems to level off in his mid-to-late 20s, and remains fairly constant for the next 10 years or so. Graphically, we can see that Ruth's CHR levels off toward a limiting value of roughly .085 or 8.5 HR per 100 AB for his career. In fact, this limiting value seems to "converge" to a "natural" or a "predictable" number, since from 1928 through the end of his career in 1935, his CHR hovered near this value.

One particular question which arises is the following: "Did most, if not all, 500+ home run hitters level off with respect to CHR around the same age as Ruth?"

In Figure 2, we present the CHR for Hank Aaron, the all-time home run leader. We see here that Aaron's CHR, like that of Babe Ruth's, has relatively little variation from his mid-20's onward. We note that his final CHR value converges nicely to approximately .061, very near his CHR from the age of 28 onward.

Figure 2. Hank Aaron's Cumulative Home Run Ratio

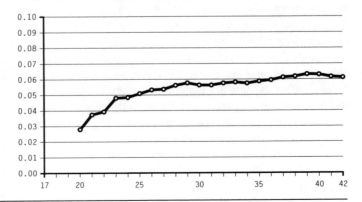

At the end of this article, we have provided the cumulative home run ratio charts—in roughly chronological order, dating from their first home run—for all 20 members of the 500 Home Run Club (see Appendix).

Some interesting observations about CHR can be made:

- Sluggers like Mel Ott and Frank Robinson have CHRs which are nearly constant, as reflected in their charts by virtually flat lines.
- Most 500+ home run hitters attain a final CHR which could have been accurately estimated by the time they reached their mid-to-late 20s.
- Multi-seasonal 50+ home run hitters like Ruth, Foxx, Mantle, and Mays all level off by their mid-20s.
- Third baseman Eddie Mathews is the only member of the 500 Home Run Club to have peaked in his early 20s and then have his CHR actually decline over his career.
- For the most part, consistency in CHR is independent of lifetime batting average: Ted Williams at .344, Mel Ott at .304, or Reggie Jackson at .262.
- For the most part, consistency in CHR is independent of players with frequent injuries (e.g., Mickey Mantle), interrupted careers (e.g., Ted Williams and Willie Mays), or longevity of careers (e.g., Willie McCovey).

We have seen that as the sluggers' careers progressed, their CHR reached a particular value and remained there. This was true of Aaron, who had a slight increase in CHR in his early 30's, but very little "variability" thereafter; it was true of Willie Mays; ditto for Mike Schmidt. In fact, the CHR for Hall of Famers such as Jimmie Foxx, Mel Ott, Frank Robinson, and Reggie Jackson have virtually the same graphical trends as the sluggers who played before them. The bottom line appears to be that the great sluggers have CHRs which level off (or reach a limit) as they enter their late 20's.

While the observations above are generally true, we find exceptions, particularly with players who starred over the past decade or so. The home run explosion over the past 10 years has generated many questions spanning quite a few areas. For many, the names of Mark McGwire, Sammy Sosa, and Barry Bonds bring these questions and a host of emotions to the foreground. How can such players hit home runs with an increasing frequency so relatively late in their careers? Is the pitching that much worse? Are other factors involved?

Figures 3, 4, and 5 represent the CHRs of the aforementioned McGwire, Sosa, and Bonds. The trends of these graphs appear to be significantly different than the CHRs of the others. In fact, the following three graphs reflect unparalleled performances, because of the increasing—rather than the leveling-off—CHRs.

Figure 3. Mark McGwire's Cumulative Home Run Ratio

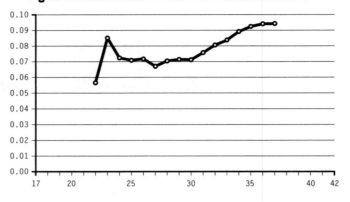

Figure 4. Sammy Sosa's Cumulative Home Run Ratio

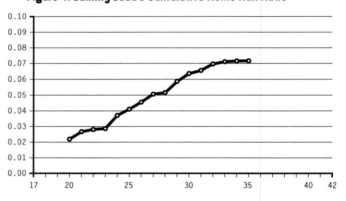

Figure 5. Barry Bonds' Cumulative Home Run Ratio*

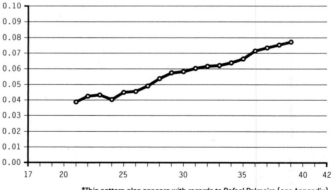

*This pattern also appears with regards to Rafael Palmeiro (see Appendix).

FATHER GABRIEL B. COSTA and **LIEUTENANT COLONEL MICHAEL R. HUBER** teach mathematics at the United States Military Academy; **PROFESSOR JOHN T. SACCOMAN** teaches mathematics and computer science at Seton Hall University. They also teach courses on sabermetrics. Their all-time favorite players are Babe Ruth, Paul Blair and Willie Mays, respectively. All three authors hold doctorates in mathematics, are members of SABR and have previously published in the BRJ.

Appendix

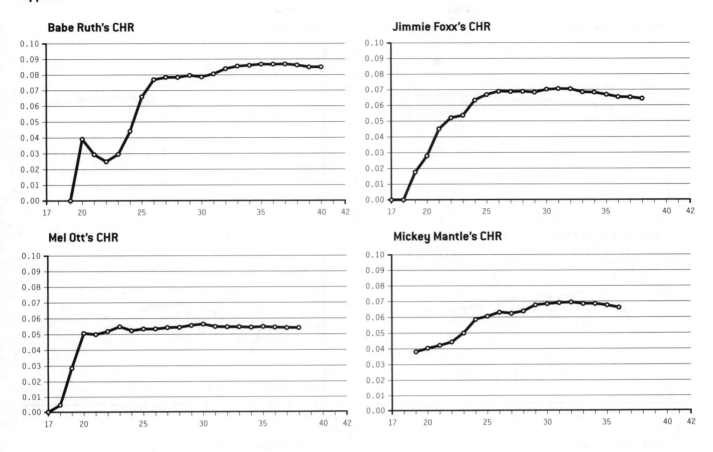

Mickey Mantle

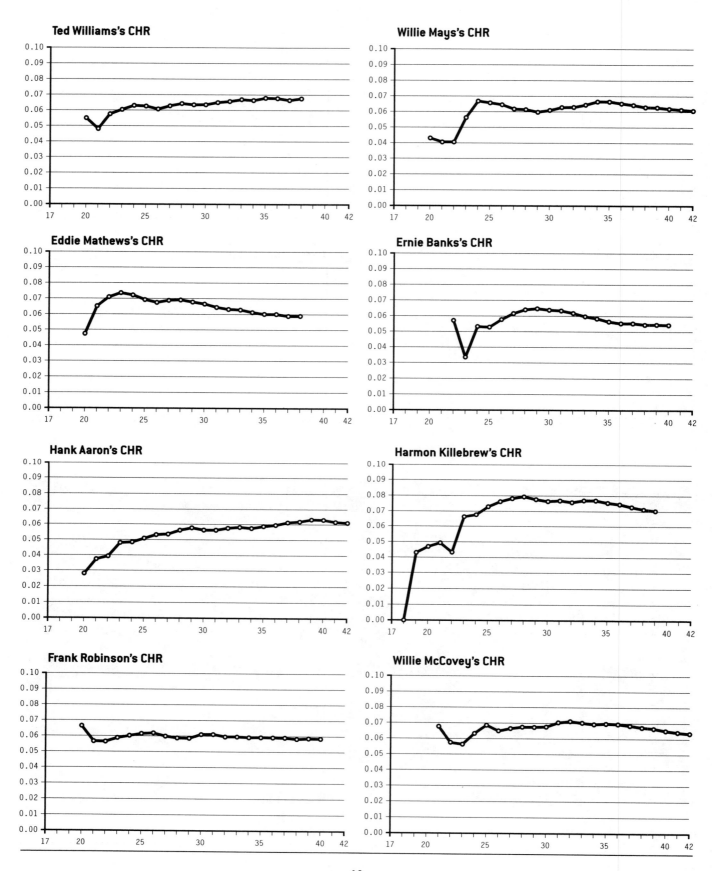

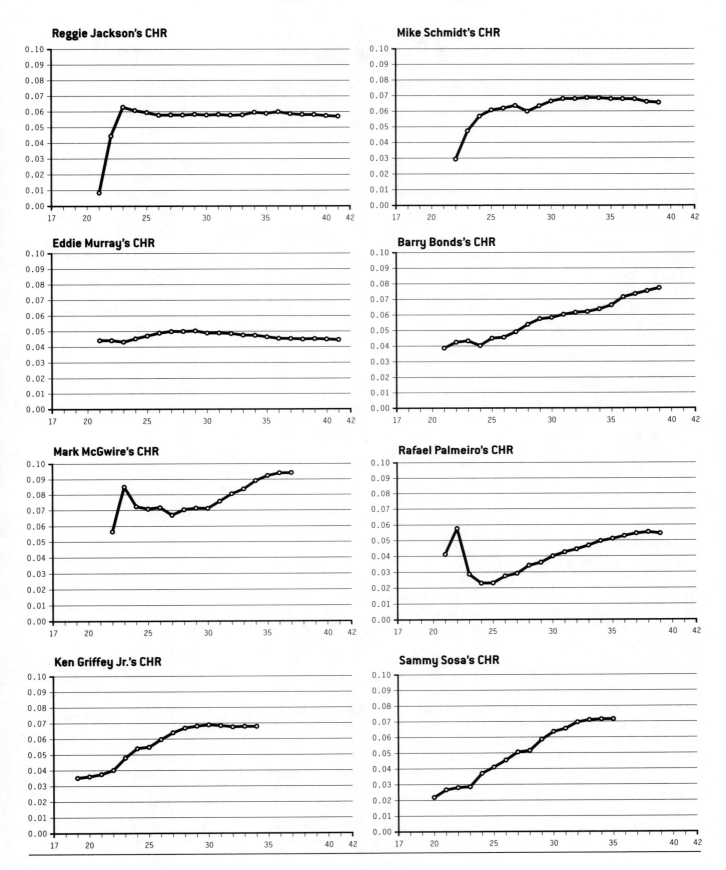

BRUCE COWGILL

Should a 22-Game Season Sweep Have Occurred?
An Examination of Season Sweeps and Near-Sweeps

After the Dodgers' win over the Pirates on August 5, 2004, the game's broadcasters announced that the Dodgers had just achieved a season sweep of the Pirates. The announcers added that it was the Dodgers' first season sweep since moving to the West Coast in 1958. First, I found it surprising that this was their first sweep, given the short season series on today's schedule. Second, a six-game season sweep did not sound like that great a feat.

It turns out that the Dodgers have swept several three-game season series over the last few years, including the Orioles just two months prior to the Pirates sweep. However, if we exclude these small series, the announcers were correct that the Dodgers' sweep of the Pirates was their first since 1958. Actually, the "Dodgers" franchise (including the Brooklyn Superbas) had *never* swept a season series in the 20th century. One has to go all the way back to 1899, when the Brooklyn Superbas swept a 14-game season series against the Cleveland Spiders.

To my second point, a six-game season sweep is no great feat. In 2004, four other teams achieved such a mark, and two teams had seven-game sweeps. In 2005, three teams swept: Twins vs. Devil Rays, Phillies vs. Padres, and Astros vs. Phillies (note, this is the Astros' second in a row season sweep of the Phillies, making it 12 straight).

Sweep History

If six-game sweeps are somewhat common, what is the record? The most games won in a sweep since 1900 was 13 by the 1993 Atlanta Braves over the expansion Colorado Rockies. There have also been several instances of 12–0 sweeps, most recently the 1999 Texas Rangers over the Minnesota Twins. In baseball history, the record holder is the 1885 Chicago White Stockings' 16-game sweep of the Buffalo Bisons. In 1899, the Cleveland Spiders were on the losing end of two 14-game sweeps by the Brooklyn Superbas and the Cincinnati Reds. This is not too surprising considering that the Spiders managed to win only 20 games out of 154 that season, and the most games they won against any of the 11 other teams was four.

Since 1871, only 21 season sweeps of 10 games or more have

BRUCE COWGILL is Vice President, Quantitative Research for Paragon Research & Consulting, a marketing research firm, specializing in the pharmaceutical industry.

occurred, with only nine of these happening since 1900. Only nine? The first season sweep of significance did not take place until the Baltimore Orioles' 12-game sweep of the Kansas City Royals in 1970. Table 1 lists all sweeps in baseball history of 10 games or more.

Table 1. Season Sweeps (min 10 games)

Year	Winner	Loser	Win	Loss
1885	CHN	BFN	16	0
1883	BSN	PHI	14	0
1899	BRO	CL4	14	0
1899	CIN	CL4	14	0
1892	BSN	BLN	13	0
1993	ATL	COL	13	0
1896	BLN	PHI	12	0
1896	CIN	SLN	12	0
1897	NY1	SLN	12	0
1970	BAL	KCA	12	0
1988	KCA	BAL	12	0
1990	OAK	NYA	12	0
1994	MON	SDN	12	0
1996	CLE	DET	12	0
1999	TEX	MIN	12	0
1978	BAL	OAK	11	0
1875	BS1	NY2	10	0
1875	HR1	BR2	10	0
1876	BSN	CN1	10	0
1876	CHN	CN1	10	0
1998	NYA	KCA	10	0

Prior to 1961, and the arrival of increasingly shortened season meetings, season sweeps would have been quite an accomplishment. From 1904 to 1961, each league had eight teams who played each other 22 times (excluding the 1918–19 WWI-shortened seasons). During that time period, no team ever swept a 22-game season series! However, four teams came close with 21–1 records and another with a 20–1 record:

1909 Chicago Cubs vs. Boston Braves (Doves)
1909 Pittsburgh Pirates vs. Boston Braves (Doves) (20–1)

The Cubs won 104 games that season, surprisingly only good for second place behind the 110-win Pirates. The Cubs lost 4–2 to Braves rookie pitcher "Red" White at home in their third meeting of the season.

The Braves almost achieved the dubious honor of going 1–21 against two teams in one season but remained 1–20 against the Pirates, picking up their lone victory in game one of a September 2 doubleheader. Cliff Curtis, pitching in his second major league start, defeated rookie Babe Adams and the Pirates, 1–0.

1927 New York Yankees vs. St. Louis Browns

The "Murderers Row" Yankees won 110 games that season, while the Browns would manage only 59 wins. The game on September 11 marked the last meeting of the two clubs that year. To that point, the Yankees had won 21 straight against the Browns—one more win for a 22-game season sweep. The Yankees were playing at home. Future Hall of Famer Herb Pennock was on the mound. Babe Ruth would hit home run number 50. But pitcher Milt Gaston gave up only five hits and the Browns beat the Yankees, 6–2.

1937 Pittsburgh Pirates vs. Cincinnati Reds

The Reds won their lone game against the Pirates, 8–3, in the first game of a May 31 doubleheader (their fifth meeting of the season), then lost a NL post-1900 record 20 straight to the Pirates. Seventeen of the losses came in 1937.

1945 Chicago Cubs vs. Cincinnati Reds

The Cubs were 21–1 vs. the Reds (losing their 16th meeting) and won the pennant by just three games over the Cardinals. Interestingly, the Reds managed a 9–13 record against the Cardinals. This was much better than the Cubs' 6–16 mark against second-place St. Louis, which was the Cubs' only losing record to a team that season. (Note: Table 9 shows all near-sweeps of at least 10 games played.)

Research Questions

While certainly better than 6–0, how does the Braves' 13–0 mark compare with the Dodgers' feat? How does the Braves' sweep compare to the 21–1 near-sweeps? My question was from a statistical viewpoint, not one based on differences in era that might make it more or less possible (e.g., travel comforts, personal assistants, day vs. night games, etc.). I realize in the "interesting statistical feats" category, a 13-game sweep does not deserve even a footnote in comparison to feats such as Dimaggio's hitting streak. But regardless, 13–0 is a decent record, especially if one considers that only six teams have gone 12–0 since 1970. If that is the case, then 21–1 seems that much more remarkable despite missing the sweep (let's face it, there is not much difference in the court of humiliation between 22–0 and 21–1).

My questions are:

- How likely were the Dodgers to sweep the Pirates?
- How likely were the Braves to win 13 games against the Rockies?
- How does the Braves' 13–0 compare to the teams who achieved 21–1 records?
- How likely is a 22-game season sweep?
- Should a 22-game season sweep have occurred in history?

Calculating Team vs. Team Sweep Probabilities

Rather than taking a slightly easier road using each team's overall win-loss record, I decided to examine the impact of each team's record at home and away as the basis for my analysis. Table 2 shows each team's overall record, place finished in league (division rank in 2004 and 1993), and home-and-away splits.

There are some interesting findings in Table 2. First, only the 1909 Pirates' near-sweep of the Braves was achieved by a first-vs. last-place team. However, in the other cases, either a first-place team or a last-place team was involved. Second, although somewhat obvious, if the head-to-head record is removed for these teams, their overall records suffer (or improve) quite a bit. That is, removing 21 wins (or 21 losses) has a substantial impact on a team's record. This is most evident in the case of the 1937 Pirates. If the Pirates had not nearly swept the Reds, their record would have been below .500 (65–67, .492)! Conversely, the Reds' record would be 55–77, .417. Third, three of the 12 teams had a

Table 2. Records for Teams in Sweeps or Near-sweeps

	Team	Overall	%	Finish	Home	%	Away	%
6-0	2004 Dodgers	93-69	.574	1	49-32	.605	44-37	.543
	2004 Pirates[1]	72-89	.447	5	39-41	.488	33-48	.407
13-0	1993 Braves	104-58	.642	1	51-30	.630	53-28	.654
	1993 Rockies[2]	67-95	.414	6	39-42	.481	28-53	.346
21-1	1909 Cubs	104-49	.680	2	47-29	.618	57-20	.740
	1909 Braves	45-108	.294	8	27-47	.365	18-61	.228
21-1	1927 Yankees	110-44	.714	1	57-19	.750	53-25	.679
	1927 Browns[3]	59-94	.386	7	38-38	.500	21-56	.273
21-1	1937 Pirates[4]	86-68	.558	3	46-32	.590	40-36	.526
	1937 Reds	56-98	.364	8	28-51	.354	28-47	.373
21-1	1945 Cubs	98-56	.636	1	49-26	.653	49-30	.620
	1945 Reds[5]	61-93	.396	7	36-41	.468	25-52	.325
20-1	1909 Pirates	110-42	.723	1	56-21	.727	54-21	.720
	1909 Braves	45-108	.294	8	27-47	.365	18-61	.228

better record on the road than at home: 1993 Braves, 1909 Cubs, and the 1937 Reds (see Table 2).

Using the home-and-away winning percentages, I calculated each team's probability of winning at home and away using a variation of the log5 method.[6] Table 3 shows the single-game probabilities of each "sweep" team (the first team listed) winning based on their home-and-away records from Table 2.

Table 3. Single Game Win Probability

	Pr (HomeWin)	Pr (AwayWin)
2004 Dodgers vs. Pirates	.713	.547
1993 Braves vs. Rockies	.763	.671
1909 Cubs vs. Braves	.846	.832
1927 Yankees vs. Browns	.889	.679
1937 Pirates vs. Reds	.708	.669
1945 Cubs vs. Reds	.796	.650
1909 Pirates vs. Braves	.900	.817

Intuitively, the probabilities are what one would expect from teams that have a high winning percentage when playing teams with very low winning percentages. Noteworthy is the 1909 Cubs' and Pirates' expected dominance over the Braves at home <u>and</u> away. Also, the 1909 Pirates' home probability is astounding (with today's schedule, if the Pirates played only the Braves, they would be 73–8 at home).

Since these are single-game probabilities, the next step is to calculate the probability of winning a series of games. For the 1993 Braves, who won all 13 games, the calculation is fairly easy. The probability of winning 13 games in a row is the product of each game's probability. In 1993, the Braves played six home games and seven away games against the Rockies (note that the order of the games does not matter in this calculation):

```
Pr(Braves winning 13 in a row vs. Rockies) =
    .763 x .763 x .763 x .763 x .763 x .763 x
  .671 x .671 x .671 x .671 x .671 x .671 x .671
         = 0.0121 or about 1 in 83
```

Table 4. Sweep and Near-Sweep Probability

	Pr (6-0)	
2004 Dodgers vs. Pirates	.0564	1 in 18

	Pr (13-0)	
1993 Braves vs. Rockies	.0121	1 in 83

	Pr (22-0)		Pr (21-1)	
1909 Cubs vs. Braves	.0210	1 in 48	.0887	1 in 11
1927 Yankees vs. Browns	.0039	1 in 258	.0255	1 in 39
1937 Pirates vs. Reds	.0003	1 in 3,715	.0027	1 in 372
1945 Cubs vs. Reds	.0007	1 in 1,406	.0062	1 in 161
1909 Pirates vs. Braves[8]	.0340	1 in 29	.1252	1 in 8
Parity series[9]	.00000024	1 in 4,194,304	.0000052	1 in 190,650

The formula for 22–0 follows the same logic, with an even split of 11 home games and 11 away games. The probability that the 1927 Yankees would sweep the Browns is 0.0039 or about 1 in 258.

The calculation for 21–1 is slightly more complicated, due to the fact there are 22 different ways for a team to have a record of 21–1 (as opposed to only one way for a team to have a record of 22–0). That is, a team could lose game 1 and win games 2 through 22, or win games 1 through 9, lose game 10, win games 11 through 22, or win games 1 through 21 and lose game 22 (as the 1927 Yankees did). Table 4 summarizes these calculations.[7]

As I suspected, the 2004 Dodgers' six-game sweep is not that impressive. However, although relatively high, the probability is lower than I expected for a six-game sweep. This is more a function of the relatively small winning-percentage differential between these two particular teams.

Because of the large winning-percentage differential of the 1909 Cubs and Braves, it was actually more likely for the 1909 Cubs or Pirates to have a 22–0 record than the 1993 Braves to have a 13–0 record. And, 21–1 was almost expected of the Cubs or Pirates. With a 1 in 39 chance in 1927 and many other dominant years, one should not be surprised that there would be a Yankee season with a 21–1 record at some point. With each team playing seven 22-game series each year, 1 in 39 amounts to less than 1 in 6 team seasons (assuming the same dominance over those seasons).

The 1937 Pirates were the most unlikely of these teams to go 21–1. This is because they were not that strong a team, finishing third that year with a .558 record, resulting in the smallest winning-percentage differential. The 1 in 372 translates to 1 in 53 team seasons.

Should a 22-Game Sweep Have Occurred?

Upon further examination of the above figures, I became less impressed. In fact, I am somewhat surprised that a 22–0 record never happened.

From 1904 to expansion in 1961, there have been 111 league seasons that included 22-game series (excluding 1918–19). With eight teams in a league, there are 28 22-game series that occur each season. Twenty-eight series over 111 seasons equals 3,108 total 22-game series. Accounting for the fact that both teams in a series have a chance for a sweep, there have been 6,216 opportunities for a sweep. None have happened. Zero. Baseball is 0 for 6,216 in 22-game sweeps! Given that the 1937 Pirates had a 1 in 3,715 chance as a third-place team with a relatively poor record at sub-.600, it presented me with the initial justification to examine my "less than impressed" intuition.

While the 1909 Cubs at 1 in 48 chance and the 1927 Yankees at 1 in 258 chance are probably not common, I suspect that there have to be numerous combinations of similar winning-percentage differentials between two teams. In fact, in both of these cases, there were other combinations of teams in those very years who were *more* likely to be involved in a season sweep: the 1909 Pirates vs. Braves and the 1927 Yankees vs. Red Sox (five times as likely as the Yankees vs. Browns). These other combinations result in higher winning-percentage differentials (which leads to a higher sweep probability), and I doubt that these are the largest differentials over 111 seasons.

Should a 22–0 sweep have occurred? Over 3,000 series, many teams with 90 or more wins, many teams with less than 60 wins, dynasties, eternal cellar dwellers?

Calculating Season Sweep Probabilities Among Multiple Teams: 1909 NL

Of the teams examined, I decided to start with the 1909 NL season because it included *two* near-sweeps of relatively high probability (yes, 3% is relatively high).

For this phase, I chose to use each team's overall record and ignored home-and-away splits. The sole reason for this decision is to reduce the number and complexity of the calculations required. The first analysis focused on Team A vs. Team B. To determine the probability of a 22-game sweep in one season requires a more formidable task of examining all 28 season series: Team A vs. B, A vs. C, A vs. D, E, B vs. C, B vs. D, etc., thus a simplified approach seemed reasonable.

Using the 1909 NL final results, the next step is to calculate the probability of Team A winning over Team B for all 28 combinations: Pr(a,b). We also need the probability of Team B winning over

Team A, Pr(b,a); fortunately, that is just 1-Pr(a,b). This produces a grid of 56 probabilities for all possible head-to-head matchups. As noted earlier, the probability of a team winning 22 games out of 22 is Pr(a,b) raised to the 22nd power. In the initial calculations, I cared only about the Cubs sweeping the Braves, but now I have to factor in the probability of the Braves sweeping the Cubs (however remote), so all 56 combinations need to be calculated.

Log5 Issue

The problem when calculating all combinations of head-to-head probabilities in a league is that a team's average log5 Win% across all the teams does not equal its actual Win%. This is because teams do not play identical schedules. For instance, the .724 Pirates did not have to play themselves, while the hapless .294 Braves did not benefit from playing the hapless .294 Braves. Therefore, the Pirates log5 probability will be overstated and the Braves will be understated. To account for this, a technical adjustment needs to be made to each team's actual winning percentages before applying log5. Interested readers can see Table 5 for the adjustment, and a full explanation can be found in SABR's *By the Numbers*.[10] Table 5 shows that, after adjustment, the resulting probabilities are nearly identical to the actual Win%.

Back to 1909

Once adjusted, I recalculated all 56 sweep probabilities. Most matchups have very small sweep probabilities, but a few stand out. The near-sweep Cubs over the Braves' probability is 0.0128. The Pirates over the Braves is 0.0258, double that of the Cubs' chances. The only other probabilities close to 0.01 are the Pirates over the Cardinals (0.0098) and the Pirates over the Dodgers (0.0092).

A few more calculations: the probability of *neither* team winning 22 out of 22 games and the probability of *no* 22-game sweep occurring in *any* series in that season. For the 1909 NL, the probability of *no* sweep is equal to 0.9298. So, the probability of *at least one* sweep occurring in 1909 NL equals 0.0702 or a 1 in 14 chance.

In the 1909 NL, there was a 1 in 14 chance of a 22-game sweep! That seemed fairly significant to me. Assuming that chance over 111 league seasons results in a probability of 0.9997! This is

Table 5. 1909 NL Differences in actual Win%, Log5 Win%, and Adjusted Log5 Win%

Team	Actual Win %	Log5 Average %	Δ Actual Win %	Adjusted Win%[11]	Log5 Average % using AdjWin %	Δ Actual Win%[12]
Pirates	.724	.737	.013	.710	.724	.000
Cubs	.680	.689	.009	.669	.679	-.001
Giants	.601	.606	.005	.595	.600	-.001
Reds	.503	.503	.000	.503	.503	.000
Phillies	.484	.483	-.001	.485	.484	-.000
Dodgers	.359	.352	-.007	.368	.360	.001
Cardinals	.355	.348	-.007	.364	.356	.001
Braves	.294	.282	-.012	.307	.294	.000

about as near to a statistical guarantee as one can get.

So far my thinking was correct: a 22-game sweep should have occurred. Correct? Not exactly.

Calculating More Probabilities: Beyond 1909 NL

If the 1909 NL season is representative of the other 110 seasons, then one would expect a sweep to have occurred. However, I suspect that the 1909 NL is *not* like other seasons. In that season the top team's Win% was 0.724 and the last-place team's was 0.294, a difference of over 0.400. That seems quite large to me. For perspective, the 1998 114-win Yankees' 51-game lead over the expansion Devil Rays amounted to a differential of "only" .315.

To further place the 1909 season in context, I examined a league of total parity. That is, all the teams finished with a 0.500 record. In this scenario, the chances of at least one 22-game sweep occurring over 111 parity league seasons is only 0.0015 or 1 in 675. So, this suggests that in seasons where there is competitive balance, the chance of a sweep occurring is low.

Conversely, less competitive balance results in higher probabilities of a sweep. In fact, even small deviations from parity result in significantly higher probabilities. For example, consider a league with a 0.600 team, a 0.400 team, and six 0.500 teams every season. This would result in about a 1 in 20 chance over 111 seasons. This is 34 times the likelihood of a total parity league.

The difference between the top and bottom team is not the only difference that matters. Since each team plays each other, the deviation across all eight teams contributes to increasing the likelihood of a sweep occurring. The standard deviation of Win% from the 1909 NL season is 0.159.[13] I calculated the other near-sweep years' standard deviation along with their sweep probabilities. Table 6 compares these seasons.

Table 6. Probability comparison of a season sweep occurring

Year	Win% Std Dev	Pr (≥1 sweep)	Pr (≥1 over 111 seasons)
Parity	0.000	0.000013 (1 in 74,899)	0.0015
1909 NL	0.159	0.0702 (1 in 14)	0.9997
1927 AL	0.123	0.0192 (1 in 52)	0.8838
1937 NL	0.099	0.0027 (1 in 365)	0.2623
1945 NL	0.115	0.0099 (1 in 101)	0.6676

Table 6 illustrates how changes in the Win% standard deviation impact the probability of a season sweep occurring. The 1927 AL deviation may appear only slightly smaller than the 1909 NL, but statistically the difference is substantial. In the 1927 AL, the Yankees did dominate but the other teams in the mix did not, at least not to the same extent as the 1909 NL teams. In the 1909

NL, there were three teams over .600 and three teams below .400. In the 1927 AL, only the Yankees were above .600 and only two teams were below .400. So, in this comparison, the 1927 AL was more competitively balanced (I am sure we have never heard that before) and results in a lower standard deviation. This lower deviation subsequently results in a season-sweep probability of 0.0192, considerably less than 1909's. However, like the 1909 NL, 111 seasons of 1927 AL would result in a very high probability of a 22-game sweep. This is not quite the case for the 1937 NL. While the 1937 NL had two teams above .600 and two teams below 0.400, the spread was tighter. In fact, the top team was only 0.625 and the last-place team was 0.364. With 111 seasons like the 1937 NL, the probability of a sweep is much less than 50%.

So where are we? Some seasons produce a high likelihood of sweeps while others produce hardly any chance. Using these near-sweep seasons as our test sample is probably not reasonable, simply for the fact that they produced matchups resulting in 21−1 records. Yet it is important to point out that collectively these four league seasons alone had a 1 in 10 chance (0.0996) of producing at least one season sweep. And, we still have to account for another 107 league seasons. One can reasonably assume that at least some of those other seasons will have high standard deviations. Any additional poor competitive balance seasons would contribute heavily to the chances of a sweep occurring, thus supporting my initial hypothesis that a 22-game sweep should have occurred.

With four seasons already accounted for, the next step was to examine the remaining 107 seasons of data. Examining each season's records proved informative. The standard deviations of unadjusted Win% for all 111 league seasons ranged from 0.049 to 0.159 with an average of 0.101. As it turns out, the highest standard-deviation season was the 1909 NL! (With my sample of four containing an outlier, my hypothesis was in jeopardy.) In that season, the difference between the first- and last-place team's Win% was .430 or 65.5 games back. This was not the largest differential. That occurred in the 1906 NL, with the Cubs having a .439 differential over the Beaneaters (Braves), who were 66.5 games back. The smallest deviation (.049) occurred in the 1915 NL, where the Phillies' differential over the Giants was only .138, a mere 21 games back.

These extreme seasons produced a season-sweep probability of 0.0757 for the 1906 NL and 0.00013 for the 1915 NL, a difference by a factor of 582. Unfortunately, I was disappointed to learn that the average single-season sweep probability was under 1% at 0.0088. With a low average single-season sweep probability coupled with an outlier as part of my test sample, I knew that the likelihood of at least one 22-game sweep occurring over 111 seasons was no longer a statistical guarantee.

Over the 111 league seasons, the probability of *at least one* 22-game season sweep occurring turned out to be 0.6288, nearly a two in three chance.[14] Although a far cry from a statistical sure thing, a 22-game sweep was more likely to occur than not.

Therefore, I can still conclude that I am "somewhat" surprised that a 22-game sweep did not occur.

Revisiting Sweep Probabilities

Since my initial team vs. team sweep probabilities were based on the log5 method using actual Win% as shown in Tables 2, 3, and 4, I recalculated these probabilities using adjusted Win% and maintained the home-and-away ratio of wins in order to make an "apples to apples" comparison. The results are shown below in Tables 7 and 8. In Table 7, the win probability for each series decreases only about one or two percentage points. However, this relatively small decrease dramatically impacts each team's sweep probability, as seen in Table 8.

Summary

Between 1904 and 1961, despite a roughly two in three chance, no team ever swept a 22-game season series. Only five teams came close to accomplishing such a feat. Even after expansion, when season series were reduced to 18 games, no team achieved an 18–0 sweep. It was not until 1970, one year after schedules included 12-game series, that a sweep occurred. Amazingly, only nine teams since 1900 have swept a season series of 10 games or more. While today's schedule, with several smaller-length series, has produced numerous season sweeps, very few are noteworthy. Yet today's schedule does include 19 games against division rivals, so maybe, just maybe, we might witness a season sweep of significance in our lifetime.

Caveats

It is important to note that when performing these types of calculations, several assumptions have to be made. Some more implicit than others. For example, we do not really know the probability of team A winning vs. team B. We use each team's record to estimate such a probability, but it is still just an estimate. In this research, this estimate is taken a step further as each team's record is adjusted or "normalized" to account for scheduling discrepancies between teams. The approach I took is a reasonable one, but others also may be just as reasonable.

Some teams match up better or worse against certain teams. That fact is evident in this research by examining the 1937 Pirates, who were a sub-.500 ball club that happened to win 21 out of 22 games against one of their opponents. The 1927 Yankees beat up on the Browns, losing only once, but managed to lose four games (I almost said "four times as many") against a Red Sox team that was 8½ games *behind* the Browns. There are examples like this every season, but we assume each team's record is reasonable to

Table 7. Comparison of unadjusted and adjusted single-game probabilities

	Method	Pr (winning at home)	Pr (winning away)
1909 Cubs vs. Braves	UnAdj	.846	.832
	Adj	.832	.813
1927 Yankees vs. Browns	UnAdj	.889	.679
	Adj	.875	.650
1937 Pirates vs. Reds	UnAdj	.708	.669
	Adj	.690	.650
1945 Cubs vs. Reds	UnAdj	.796	.650
	Adj	.780	.625
1909 Pirates vs. Braves	UnAdj	.900	.817
	Adj	.889	.797

Table 8. Comparison of unadjusted and adjusted sweep and near-sweep probabilities

	Method	Pr (22–0)	Pr (21–1)
1909 Cubs vs. Braves	UnAdj	.0210 (1 in 48)	.0887 (1 in 11)
	Adj	.0136 (1 in 74)	.0644 (1 in 15)
1927 Yankees vs. Browns	UnAdj	.0039 (1 in 258)	.0255 (1 in 39)
	Adj	.0020 (1 in 496)	.0151 (1 in 66)
1937 Pirates vs. Reds	UnAdj	.0003 (1 in 3,715)	.0027 (1 in 372)
	Adj	.0002 (1 in 6,770)	.0016 (1 in 623)
1945 Cubs vs. Reds	UnAdj	.0007 (1 in 1,406)	.0062 (1 in 161)
	Adj	.0004 (1 in 2,706)	.0036 (1 in 279)
1909 Pirates vs. Braves[15]	UnAdj	.0340 (1 in 29)	.1252 (1 in 8)
	Adj	.0226 (1 in 44)	.0943 (1 in 11)

estimate head-to-head probabilities.

Another "leap" is that we assume the head-to-head probability is constant. That is, we assume the 1927 Yankees' probability of winning at home vs. the Browns is 0.875 (from Table 9) for all 11 home games. In reality, there may be several factors that cause this figure to deviate: travel schedule preceding a series (especially pre-airlines), injuries, illness, etc. Would the Yankees' probability of winning be affected if Ruth sat out a game in 1927 against the Browns (he played in only 151 of 154 games that season)? Finally, the starting pitchers may have the largest impact on game-to-game probability deviation. Maybe the Yankees' Win% against the Browns would be 0.892 over 11 games, but depending on the pitching matchup, it might be .900 one day, .700 the next, .500 the next, and so on.

Even if we could agree on all the factors to include, I doubt we could agree on the proper adjustments for each factor affecting a

Table 9. Near-season sweeps (min 10 games played)

Year	Winner	Loser	W	L	T	Win%	Year	Winner	Loser	W	L	T	Win%	Year	Winner	Loser	W	L	T	Win%
1909	CHN	BSN	21	1	0	0.955	1991	TOR	CLE	12	1	0	0.923	1999	TOR	BAL	11	1	0	0.917
1927	NYA	SLA	21	1	0	0.955	1992	OAK	SEA	12	1	0	0.923	1897	CL4	SLN	11	1	1	0.846
1937	PIT	CIN	21	1	0	0.955	1995	CIN	HOU	12	1	0	0.923	1894	NY1	CHN	11	1	2	0.786
1945	CHN	CIN	21	1	0	0.955	1995	NYA	TOR	12	1	0	0.923	1895	CL4	SLN	11	1	2	0.786
1909	PIT	BSN	20	1	0	0.952	1996	BOS	DET	12	1	0	0.923	1880	TRN	CN1	10	1	0	0.909
1904	BOS	WS1	20	2	0	0.909	1877	BSN	CN1	11	1	0	0.917	1895	BLN	LS3	10	1	0	0.909
1904	NY1	BSN	20	2	0	0.909	1878	BSN	ML2	11	1	0	0.917	1897	BLN	LS3	10	1	0	0.909
1907	PIT	SLN	20	2	0	0.909	1879	BFN	TRN	11	1	0	0.917	1977	BOS	SEA	10	1	0	0.909
1908	PIT	SLN	20	2	0	0.909	1879	BSN	TRN	11	1	0	0.917	1988	NYN	LAN	10	1	0	0.909
1911	PHA	SLA	20	2	0	0.909	1880	CHN	BFN	11	1	0	0.917	1997	BAL	MIN	10	1	0	0.909
1928	SLN	PHI	20	2	0	0.909	1880	TRN	BFN	11	1	0	0.917	1997	BAL	TEX	10	1	0	0.909
1931	SLN	CIN	20	2	0	0.909	1882	BFN	WOR	11	1	0	0.917	1997	LAN	PHI	10	1	0	0.909
1935	PIT	BSN	20	2	0	0.909	1882	CL2	WOR	11	1	0	0.917	1998	BAL	DET	10	1	0	0.909
1953	BRO	PIT	20	2	0	0.909	1884	SLU	KCU	11	0	1	0.917	1874	BS1	BL1	9	1	0	0.900
1954	CLE	BOS	20	2	2	0.833	1893	CL4	WSN	11	1	0	0.917	1874	BS1	HR1	9	1	0	0.900
1889	BR3	LS2	19	1	0	0.950	1893	PIT	BLN	11	1	0	0.917	1874	CH2	BL1	9	1	0	0.900
1912	BOS	NYA	19	2	0	0.905	1894	BLN	WSN	11	1	0	0.917	1874	NY2	CH2	9	1	0	0.900
1887	SL4	CL3	18	1	0	0.947	1895	BRO	LS3	11	1	0	0.917	1874	PH1	PH2	9	1	0	0.900
1889	CN2	LS2	18	2	0	0.900	1895	NY1	SLN	11	1	0	0.917	1875	BS1	HR1	9	1	0	0.900
1890	BRO	PIT	18	2	0	0.900	1896	CHN	PIT	11	1	0	0.917	1876	BSN	PHN	9	1	0	0.900
1891	BS2	WS9	18	2	0	0.900	1897	CIN	SLN	11	1	0	0.917	1876	CHN	BSN	9	1	0	0.900
1902	PIT	PHI	18	2	0	0.900	1969	BAL	KCA	11	1	0	0.917	1876	CHN	LS1	9	1	0	0.900
1919	NYA	PHA	18	2	0	0.900	1969	CHN	SDN	11	1	0	0.917	1876	HAR	CN1	9	1	0	0.900
1889	SL4	LS2	18	2	1	0.857	1969	HOU	MON	11	1	0	0.917	1876	HAR	PHN	9	1	0	0.900
1902	SLA	BLA	18	2	1	0.857	1969	NYN	SDN	11	1	0	0.917	1884	BL2	IN2	9	1	0	0.900
1886	CHN	KCN	17	1	0	0.944	1969	SFN	MON	11	1	0	0.917	1884	CL5	PT1	9	1	0	0.900
1886	CHN	WS8	17	1	0	0.944	1970	NYA	KCA	11	1	0	0.917	1884	CNU	KCU	9	1	0	0.900
1887	PHI	IN3	17	1	0	0.944	1971	KCA	BOS	11	1	0	0.917	1884	LS2	IN2	9	1	0	0.900
1962	PHI	HOU	17	1	0	0.944	1974	KCA	MIL	11	1	0	0.917	1884	LS2	TL1	9	1	0	0.900
1965	MIN	BOS	17	1	0	0.944	1975	CIN	CHN	11	1	0	0.917	1884	NY4	PT1	9	1	0	0.900
1974	ATL	SDN	17	1	0	0.944	1975	TEX	DET	11	1	0	0.917	1884	SL4	PT1	9	1	0	0.900
1986	NYN	PIT	17	1	0	0.944	1976	NYA	CHA	11	1	0	0.917	1977	MIN	TOR	9	1	0	0.900
1886	DTN	WS8	17	1	1	0.895	1977	SLN	ATL	11	1	0	0.917	1978	BAL	SEA	9	1	0	0.900
1891	SL4	WS9	17	2	1	0.850	1979	MIN	TOR	11	1	0	0.917	1978	MIL	OAK	9	1	0	0.900
1884	PRO	DTN	15	1	0	0.938	1980	ATL	PIT	11	1	0	0.917	1978	NYA	CHA	9	1	0	0.900
1885	CHN	DTN	15	1	0	0.938	1980	HOU	CHN	11	1	0	0.917	1978	TEX	CLE	9	1	0	0.900
1885	NY1	BFN	15	1	0	0.938	1980	LAN	MON	11	1	0	0.917	1979	MON	ATL	9	1	0	0.900
1918	NY1	BSN	15	1	0	0.938	1980	SDN	NYN	11	1	0	0.917	1994	CHA	SEA	9	1	0	0.900
1884	SLU	BLU	14	1	0	0.933	1983	LAN	PHI	11	1	0	0.917	1994	SEA	TEX	9	1	0	0.900
1883	PH4	CL5	13	1	0	0.929	1984	TOR	MIN	11	1	0	0.917	1999	BOS	ANA	9	1	0	0.900
1892	CL4	LS3	13	1	0	0.929	1988	LAN	PHI	11	1	0	0.917	1999	CLE	ANA	9	1	0	0.900
1899	CHN	CL4	13	1	0	0.929	1988	MIN	DET	11	1	0	0.917	1999	CLE	BAL	9	1	0	0.900
1899	NY1	CL4	13	1	0	0.929	1989	CAL	DET	11	1	0	0.917	1999	NYA	SEA	9	1	0	0.900
1899	SLN	CL4	13	1	0	0.929	1989	TOR	CHA	11	1	0	0.917	1999	OAK	TBA	9	1	0	0.900
1894	NY1	LS3	12	0	1	0.923	1993	HOU	NYN	11	1	0	0.917	1876	HAR	LS1	9	1	1	0.818
1983	CHA	SEA	12	1	0	0.923	1995	CLE	KCA	11	1	0	0.917	1884	CN2	IN2	9	1	1	0.818
1985	NYA	BAL	12	1	0	0.923	1996	CLE	BOS	11	1	0	0.917	1884	NY4	BR3	9	1	1	0.818
1986	DET	BAL	12	1	0	0.923	1997	ANA	OAK	11	1	0	0.917	1893	PHI	CIN	9	1	1	0.818
1987	BOS	BAL	12	1	0	0.923	1997	CHA	KCA	11	1	0	0.917							
1987	TOR	BAL	12	1	0	0.923	1998	NYA	TBA	11	1	0	0.917							
1991	OAK	CAL	12	1	0	0.923	1998	SDN	CIN	11	1	0	0.917							

Source: Retrosheet

The 1945 Chicago Cubs

team's chances. SABR research on Dimaggio's hitting streak sheds further light on many of the factors involved and the subsequent difficulty of such estimates. In reality, the true probability of such events will never be known. Yet we should be able to accept such estimates knowing that their precision is based on a reasonable set of assumptions.

That said, I thought it might be worthwhile to point out how these estimates are affected by even small changes in the assumptions. Consider the following:

- Team A has a 0.600 probability of winning vs. Team X every game (constant probability).
- Team B's overall probability of winning vs. Team X is also 0.600, but each game alternates between 0.700 and 0.500.

The probability of winning back-to-back games is 0.360 for Team A and 0.350 for Team B—not much difference between the two. However, consider a 22-game sweep: Team A's chances are 1 in 76,000 and Team B's are 1 in 104,000. That is much more significant. The point is that each change, while relatively small as an individual change, becomes amplified over repeated calculations.

Special thanks to David Smith, Phil Birnbaum, Ray Ciccolella, Abba Krieger, Alice Muehlhof, David Paulson, and Marc Alan Jones

Notes

1. Unlike the other series listed, the Dodgers (West) and the Pirates (Central) are in separate divisions.
2. The San Diego Padres record was actually worse at 61–101.
3. The Boston Red Sox record was worse at 51–103, but they managed a few additional wins to finish with a 4–18 record vs. their former pitcher's new team
4. Finished third, 10 games back of the Giants
5. The Philadelphia Phillies finished 15 games below the Reds in last place at 46–108.
6. Pr(A wins at home vs. B) = [(A HomeWin%) x (B AwayLoss%)] / [(A HomeWin%) x (B AwayLoss%)] + [(A HomeLoss%) x (B AwayWin%)]
7. Although the above long-hand probability calculations are not difficult, the binomial distribution function, found in any introductory statistics textbook, simplifies the process further and is available in standard spreadsheet programs. However, the home and away split does add a few extra steps to the normally straight-forward formula.
8. The probability of a 20–1 record equals .1440 or about 1 in 7.
9. As a point of reference, I included probabilities for a .500 team vs. another .500 team.
10. Ciccolella, Ray, "Log5: Derivations and Tests", *By the Numbers*, August 2004.
11. Adjusted Win% = Win% + [(0.500 – Win%) / N] where N is set to minimize the error. Rather than use a fixed N for all seasons, I calculated the N that minimized each season's sum of squares error. For most of the seasons, I found N=10 minimized the error, but N ranged from 8 to 16.
12. Ciccolella's procedure reduces the log5 probability error by a factor of nearly 200.
13. Standard deviation is a statistical calculation used to measure the amount of spread within a set of data relative to the average. The higher the deviation, the larger the spread. In this case, higher standard deviations indicate large differences between teams' winning percentages, i.e., poor competitive balance.
14. Incidentally, prior to using Adjusted Win%, the probability of a sweep occurring exceeded 0.800.
15. The probability of 20–1 after adjustment is now .1111 or about 1 in 9.

Sources
Retrosheet
Sinins' Sabermetric Encyclopedia
Total Baseball 8th edition
ProQuest

DAVID W. SMITH

Do Batters Learn During a Game?

It is common to hear batters and pitchers comment on the value of being able to "make adjustments" during a game. For example, pitchers speak of "setting a batter up" by a certain sequence of pitches, which may take several at-bats to accomplish. Similarly, batters often remark that they "look for" a certain type of pitch or in a certain location after considering what the pitcher has thrown before. Although it makes sense that a player might very well alter his mental approach as a result of earlier success or failure, I decided to go beyond the anecdotal interviews and ask if there was any tangible evidence indicating that these adjustments actually take place.

My approach was to examine matchups between starting batters and starting pitchers, giving the greatest opportunity to discover changes during the course of a game. Given the realities of modern pitcher usage, it is very uncommon for a batter to face the same relief pitcher more than once in a game, and therefore the relievers were excluded. The batting performance of pitchers was also removed. I analyzed every play of every game from 1960 through 2005, which covered 92,271 games and more than seven million plate appearances. The play-by-play information comes from Retrosheet (www.retrosheet.org).

There are a variety of performance measures used today within the baseball analysis community. I use the three standard aggregate measures: batting average, on-base average, and slugging average. These three quantities reflect different aspects of batter performance, and I therefore suspected that they might not all show the same patterns of change during a game. Table 1 presents the results for the first four matchups within a game for all games from 1960 through 2005. There were a few cases of a batter facing a starting pitcher five times in one game, but these are too rare to be useful in this analysis.

In addition to noting how uncommon it is for a starting batter to face a starting pitcher four times in a game, we see clear patterns of improvement, or batter learning, in all three values as the game progresses. However, the three averages do not increase at the same rate. On-base average rises slowly, only 2.1% from the first to fourth time at bat, while batting average and slugging average go up much more rapidly, 6.1% and 6.4% respectively. The most rapid change in the data is in slugging average from

DAVID W. SMITH received SABR's highest honor, the Bob Davids Award, in 2005. He is the founder and President of Retrosheet.

Table 1. Batting by number of appearances within a game, both leagues, 1960–2005

	PA	BA	OBA	SA
1	1,530,593	.259	.328	.393
2	1,456,880	.269	.331	.416
3	1,151,387	.274	.336	.427
4	394,251	.275	.335	.418

the first to second time up. In the 1950s Branch Rickey and Allan Roth developed a measurement called *isolated power* to examine extra-base hits separately from singles. Isolated power is simply the difference between slugging average and batting average. For all at-bats over the 46 years studied (not just for the starters), the isolated power is .135 (batting average of .259 and slugging average of .394, see Table 3). For the data in Figure 1, the isolated power values for the four times at bat are .134, .147, .153, and .143. My interpretation is:

1. The first time up, batters are more concerned with making contact than hitting with power.
2. The second and subsequent times up, they are adjusting with the result that they are able to swing more confidently and with greater power.
3. The isolated power of the non-starter appearances is lower than that of the starters.

This pattern was remarkably constant over the period studied (data not shown), even though the total level of baseball offense varied considerably over the years. There was also no discernible difference between the two leagues, either before or after the advent of the designated hitter in the American League in 1973. However, there was a definite in the pattern for home and road teams, as shown in Table 2 and Figures 1 and 2.

Table 2. Home and road batting by number of appearances, 1960–2005

	Home Teams		
	PA	BA	OBA	SA
---	---	---	---	---
1	764,687	.266	.337	.405
2	725,211	.272	.336	.424
3	559,561	.277	.341	.433
4	173,132	.278	.340	.425

	PA	BA	OBA	SA
		Road Teams		
1	765,906	.252	.318	.382
2	731,669	.265	.325	.408
3	591,826	.271	.331	.421
4	221,119	.272	.331	.412

Home & Road Combined for Starters vs. Starters			
	BA	OBA	SA
Home	.272	.338	.420
Road	.263	.325	.403
All	.267	.331	.411

There are rather large differences between the two, both in absolute value of the numbers and in the pattern of changes. The home team has an overall nine to 17 point superiority in these three measures, as shown in the bottom portion of Table 2. However, the greatest differences are in the pattern of the changes, as shown in Figure 1 and 2, which come from the data in the first two portions of Table 2. In all three parameters, the rates of increase are steeper for players on the visiting team than they are for those who are playing at home. Interestingly enough, slugging average for all players drops from the third to fourth times at bat. By the fourth time at bat, the performance differences for the home and road players are much more similar than they were earlier in the game.

This pattern is initially surprising, since it is not obvious why the road team batters should display so much more learning than the home team batters. However, we must remember that there are two sides to each matchup and consider the pitchers as well, since both are presumably capable of making adjustments. One of the great differences usually identified between different parks is the mound, and many visiting pitchers comment that it takes time to get used to a new mound on the road. Therefore, it is reasonable to consider that there are two kinds of learning going on. The first is the mental part of the pitcher-batter confrontation, which we have seen to favor the batter, and the second is the physical adjustment by the pitcher to the mound. Presumably the home team pitchers are more familiar with the mound than the road team pitchers are, and they should have less of this adjustment to do. Let us consider the home vs. road differences again, remembering that the difference between home and road batters narrows as the game proceeds. By this argument, the learning displayed by the road team batters would therefore result mostly from the mental aspects, since the home team pitchers are not affected as much by the mound. On the other hand, the road team pitchers are starting the game at a relative disadvantage as they deal with the idiosyncrasies of that particular mound. Therefore, the performance by home team batters starts off at a higher level, but does not increase as rapidly, because there is less room for improvement before they reach the maximum. However, it must be true that the road team pitchers have been successful in their adjustments, or else one would expect that the performance by home team batters would continue beyond what is observed.

Figure 1. Batting performance in different times at bat for home teams, 1960–2005

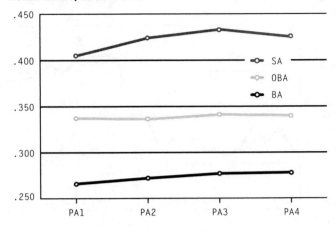

Figure 2. Batting performance in different times at bat for road teams, 1960–2005

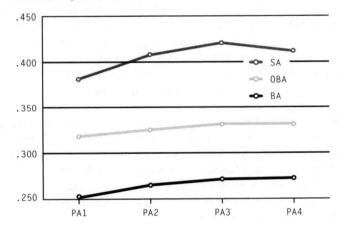

There is one additional factor that might affect the batters, and that is the nature of the hitting background. Although the center field background does vary among parks, there is much less variation here than there is in the mound. One way to examine the effect of the hitting background would be to compare the performance of road team batters in the first game of each series to the later games in the series. If the background was a significant factor, then one would expect the first game performance to be different. I did not subdivide the results in this way, so this possibility remains unexplored.

There are many aspects of batter performance which have changed since 1960, including strike zone rule changes, the rise and decline of artificial surface fields, the designated hitter (DH) rule, and profoundly new patterns of relief pitcher usage. It occurred to me that the percentage of plate appearances which were between starters might show variation as well. Figure 3 addresses the DH effect. From 1960 to 1972, the two leagues were very similar in the percentage of plate appearances that

Figure 3. Percentage of plate appearances by starters vs. starters, 1960-2005

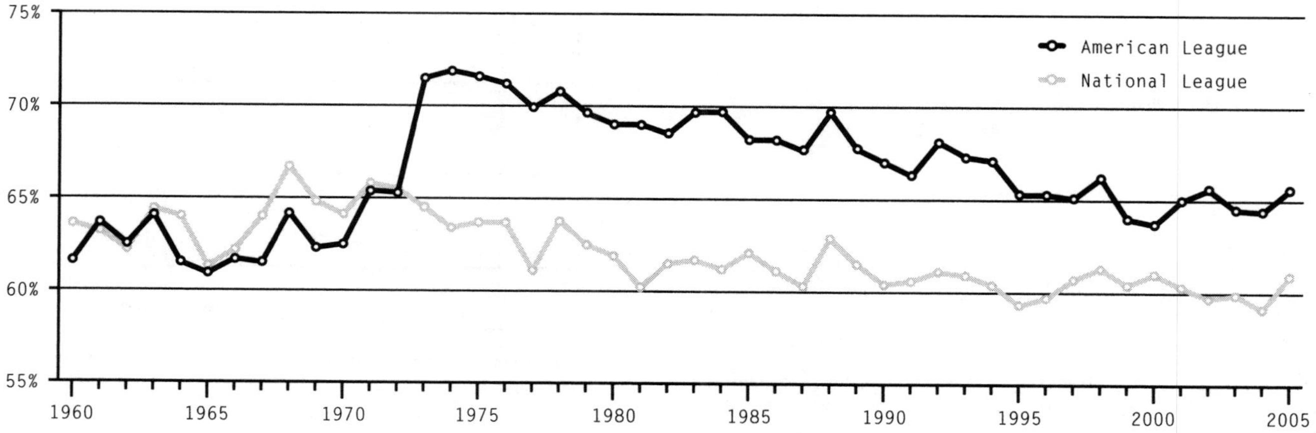

involved starting batters and starting pitchers, with variation from about 61% to 67%. In 1973 with the advent of the DH, the curves for the two leagues diverge sharply, as the American League percentage jumps to nearly 72% while the National League values show little change. Both leagues have seen a continual decline since then, as the difference between the two has narrowed from a maximum of about eight percentage points to the current difference of about four points. The relationship now is essentially what it was in the pre-expansion era. However, even with these striking changes over time, the results in terms of batter learning did not change in a corresponding way (data not shown).

One more interesting feature of this analysis is the different performance levels of the starters and non-starters. Table 3 shows that the starting batters are noticeably more effective than the overall average, as would be expected. However, it must be noted that the overall values include pitchers as batters as well as the effect of specialist relief pitchers.

Table 3. Batting performance of starters vs. all batters, 1960–2005

	BA	OBA	SA
Starter vs. Starter	.267	.331	.411
All Batters vs. All Pitchers	.259	.326	.394

I would like to emphasize that I presented no information for individual teams or players. It is always true in a study such as this that the results get less clear as the sample size gets smaller, with random statistical noise playing a larger part. I therefore studied aggregates, with home vs. road as the only subdivision. When the results are divided more finely, to single teams or single batters, there will inevitably be many exceptions that cloud the issue. I have chosen to avoid this confusion.

In conclusion I note that I began this study with the question: Do batters learn during a game? It is clear that the general answer is: yes, they do. However, it is also clear that the situation is a little more complicated than that and a better understanding can be obtained by considering other factors. The biggest one I could identify was the effect of playing at home vs. on the road. So the next time you hear a batter say that he improved his performance by making adjustments during a game, there is a good chance you should believe it. On the other hand, if you hear a pitcher say it, then you might be a little suspicious.

A preliminary version of this paper with a smaller data set was presented at the SABR national convention in June 1996.

DAVID L. FLEITZ

The Honor Rolls of Baseball

Who deserves to be inducted into the Baseball Hall of Fame, and who does not? The Hall of Fame electors wrestle with this question every year. The selection process for players causes controversy on an annual basis, but the institution, since its inception, has also grappled with the issue of recognition for non-playing contributors. Some believe that Hall membership should be reserved for players alone, while others contend that executives, umpires, managers, and sportswriters deserve equal acknowledgment. The Hall of Fame has modified its eligibility rules for both playing and non-playing personnel numerous times over the years, and many of those changes have drawn waves of criticism in the press. "It appears," stated an editorial in *The Sporting News* after one Hall election, "that the entire Hall of Fame scheme is in need of a complete overhauling."

The erstwhile "Bible of Baseball" was not referring to the electoral changes of the last few years. Rather, the above statement appeared in the weekly newspaper nearly 60 years ago, after the Hall of Fame made an ill-advised attempt to honor non-playing contributors to the national pastime. On April 23, 1946, the Hall of Fame's Permanent Committee (which evolved into the now familiar Veterans Committee) announced the selection of 11 old-time players to the Hall of Fame. The committee also revealed the names of 39 others—managers, executives, umpires, and sportswriters—to the new "Honor Rolls of Baseball."[1]

In creating the Honor Rolls, the Hall constructed a second level of induction. It allowed the Hall to recognize the accomplishments of a non-playing contributor without according him the same status (that is, a plaque on the wall) as a Babe Ruth or a Ty Cobb. The Honor Rolls also marked the first attempt by the Hall of Fame to create an appropriate recognition for the contributions of sportswriters, although the concept was roundly criticized and was ultimately judged a failure. Before long, the Honor Roll award died of neglect, and it is almost completely forgotten today.

Background

When the National Baseball Hall of Fame and Museum was created in the mid-1930s, Commissioner Kenesaw M. Landis gave the right to select honored players to the Baseball Writers Association of America. Two hundred and twenty-six sportswriters participated in the first election, held in January 1936, and named Ty Cobb, Babe Ruth, Honus Wagner, Christy Mathewson, and Walter Johnson to the Hall. In 1937 the writers elected Tris Speaker, Napoleon Lajoie, and Cy Young; in 1938 only Grover Cleveland

Alexander gained enough votes for enshrinement; and in 1939 George Sisler, Willie Keeler, and Eddie Collins joined the others.

At the same time, the Hall of Fame debated the issue of electing early players, executives, and other deserving contributors. A separate election for 19th-century players was held in 1936, but the voting process was not well planned. When no one gained the required number of votes for selection, sports columnists across the country criticized the Hall of Fame electors for ignoring the contributions of early players.

In response, Landis appointed a committee consisting of himself, the two league presidents, a retired league president, and the president and chairman of the minor leagues. This was called the Centennial Commission, and was given the responsibility of electing 19th-century players and builders of the game to the Hall. This committee elected seven men to the Hall in 1937 and 1938, including the first baseball writer, Henry Chadwick. In 1939 a smaller committee consisting of Landis and the two league presidents elected six more men, including old-time players Cap Anson and Buck Ewing, to the Hall of Fame.

Questions about the committee choices arose early in the selection process. In December 1937 the Centennial Commission selected managers Connie Mack and John McGraw, league presidents Ban Johnson and Morgan Bulkeley, and early shortstop George Wright to the Hall. Some sportswriters, led by Richards Vidmer of the *New York Herald Tribune*, suggested that the members of the committee might have confused George Wright with his brother Harry, the first professional baseball manager, whom they saw as a more deserving candidate.[2] In any event, George Wright had died only a few months before, and his selection marked the first instance of a Hall candidate being helped by the "death effect," a boost in a candidacy caused by a recent demise.

Some observers also criticized the enshrinement of Morgan Bulkeley, who served as National League president for only ten months. Bulkeley was nothing more than a figurehead, but was selected to the Hall of Fame because he was the first National League leader. William Hulbert, the true creator of the league, was

DAVID L. FLEITZ is a from Bowling Green, Ohio. He is the author of *Shoeless: The Life and Times of Joe Jackson, Louis Sockalexis: The First Cleveland Indian,* and *Ghosts in the Gallery at Cooperstown.* His latest book, *Cap Anson, the Grand Old Man of Baseball,* was published by McFarland in 2005.

not elected until 1995.

After the 1939 selections were made, Commissioner Landis appointed a new four-man board, the Old-Timers Committee, charged with electing players and contributors from the distant past. This board consisted of Philadelphia Athletics manager Connie Mack, executives Ed Barrow and Bob Quinn, and veteran writer Sid Mercer. However, from 1939 to 1944, this committee could never arrange a meeting to elect new members to the Hall of Fame. In the meantime, the BBWAA decided to vote every three years instead of every year. It elected Rogers Hornsby in 1942 and no one else from 1940 to 1947.

In 1944, after the Hall had inducted only one man in the previous five years, Landis made significant changes to the Old-Timers Committee. He added two more members, Boston writer Mel Webb and Hall of Fame president Stephen C. Clark. Landis also empowered the committee members to act as trustees of the institution, allowing them to set policy concerning the selection process for Hall of Fame honorees. The committee, renamed the Permanent Committee, met for the first time in December 1944 and named the recently deceased Landis to the Hall.

The Permanent Committee exercised its power for the first time in 1945. In January of that year, the BBWAA held its first vote since 1942. Because of the large number of qualified candidates, the voting was widely split among many deserving players, and no one managed to gain the required number of votes for election to the Hall. In response, the Permanent Committee met on April 25, 1945, and unilaterally elected what Bill James called "a bargeload of 19th-century guys" to the Hall of Fame.[3] At one stroke, 10 new Hall of Famers entered the doors of Cooperstown. The Committee, much to the dismay of the BBWAA, also gave itself the responsibility for electing players whose careers extended up to 1910.

The Permanent Committee hoped that this move would clear up the voting stalemate, but it did not. In January 1946, after the BBWAA decided to resume its annual voting, it once again failed to elect anyone to the Hall of Fame, even after a runoff vote. On April 23, 1946, the Permanent Committee struck again. In a meeting held on that date in the offices of the New York Yankees, the committee selected 11 more new Hall members. In the words of respected columnist Dan Daniel, the Permanent Committee "announced the baseball beatification of a vast number of worthies" and "decided to load up the Cooperstown pantheon by the wholesale."[4] The BBWAA was not happy that the committee selected Ed Walsh, Joe Tinker, Jack Chesbro, and other stars who played most or all of their careers after 1900.

The Honor Rolls of Baseball

The Permanent Committee made one other decision that has been almost forgotten by history. The committee, which had just elected 11 men to the Hall, also named another 39 individuals to the "Honor Rolls of Baseball."

The Honor Rolls consisted of four lists of five managers, 11 umpires, 11 executives, and 12 sportswriters. The Permanent Committee decided, completely on its own, to establish a second level of honor to the Hall of Fame, with the first level—plaques on the wall—being reserved for the outstanding players of the past, along with certain pioneers of the game.

No one had asked the committee to establish this new type of recognition, but since the commissioner had empowered the committee members to act as trustees of the institution, the board acted within the scope of its powers. No one knows who first proposed the idea, but the Honor Rolls of Baseball emerged from the meeting as a fait accompli.

Here is the list of the 39 members of the Honor Rolls:

Writers	Managers
Walter Barnes, BOS	Ned Hanlon*
Tim Murnane, BOS	Bill Carrigan
Harry Cross, NY	John M. Ward*
William Hanna, NY	Miller Huggins*
Sid Mercer, NY	Frank Selee*
Bill Slocum, NY	
George Tidden, NY	**Executives**
Joe Vila, NY	Ed Barrow*
Frank Hough, PHI	Bob Quinn
Francis Richter, PHI	Ernest S. Barnard
Irving E. Sanborn, CHI	John E. Bruce
John B. Sheridan, STL	John T. Brush
	Barney Dreyfuss
Umpires	Charles H. Ebbets
Bill Klem*	August Herrmann
Tommy Connolly*	John A. Heydler
Bill Dinneen	Arthur Soden
Billy Evans*	Nicholas Young
John Gaffney	
Thomas Lynch	
Tim Hurst	
John Kelly	
Silk O'Loughlin	
Jack Sheridan	
Bob Emslie	*now in Hall of Fame

The Honor Roll recognition was not meant to be a final destination for anyone in these four groups. The committee made it clear that any of the men named to the Honor Rolls would be eligible for full admission to the Hall in the future, "as the pillars of baseball take in their proper alignment in history through the years," in the words of historian and Hall of Fame director Ken Smith.[5]

Smith, in the 1974 edition of his book *Baseball's Hall of Fame*, offered a possible rationale behind the committee's selection of 60 men (21 Hall of Fame inductees and 39 Honor Roll members) in 1945 and 1946. The museum itself had recently undergone an expansion, and Smith wrote that the Hall directors "wanted faster action [in creating honorees] for the fine new hall where there was to be room for seventy plaques."[6] Perhaps the committee took it upon itself to create so many new honorees, implied Smith, because before 1945 there were only 27 plaques on the wall and the display room was two-thirds empty.

Reaction to the new designation was swift and almost uniformly negative. *The Sporting News* devoted an editorial to the Honor Rolls, stating, "Either a man is worthy of the Hall of Fame, or he isn't. Rigging what might be regarded as an out-and-out expedient to dispose of 39 cases whose claims may have harassed the committee cheapens the entire Cooperstown enterprise.

"There was no demand for a new list of sub-greats. There will never be any cogent reason for that phony type of baseball beatification. If a man was a great umpire or an outstanding writer, he should be elected to the diamond Pantheon, and not placed in an annex of that edifice, so to speak.

"While the failure of the writers to name anybody in their most recent two elections was deplorable," continued *The Sporting News*, "it is still more deplorable to load up the Hall of Fame, and to confuse the fan as to who is in the Pantheon and who is in the newly-created Array of Almosts."[7]

The Permanent Committee perhaps missed its best chance at gaining support when it failed to select J. G. Taylor Spink of *The Sporting News* to the Honor Rolls. Spink's father founded the magazine in 1886 and built it into the "Bible of Baseball," the most important and widely-read baseball weekly in the nation. Spink became editor and publisher in 1914 and played a major role in uncovering the Black Sox scandal and in popularizing the sport (by distributing the magazine to soldiers in both World Wars). The negative editorial concerning the Honor Rolls, which was published in the magazine on May 2, 1946, suggested that the election process "is in need of a complete overhauling."[8] The editorial did not carry a byline, but was likely written by Spink himself.

There was already a certain amount of tension between the Permanent Committee and the BBWAA, stemming from the fact that the committee had unilaterally elected 21 new Hall of Famers due to the failure of the BBWAA to do so in 1945–46. The creation of the Honor Rolls, and the inclusion of sportswriters, merely added to the friction. The committee, in making its selections to the Honor Rolls, did not solicit advice from the BBWAA, preferring instead to decide for itself which writers were most deserving of recognition. The introduction of the Honor Rolls made it appear that no other writers would be joining Henry Chadwick with full Hall membership in the future; instead, deserving writers would be shunted off to the Honor Rolls.

Most of the nation's sportswriters rejected the Honor Rolls, seeing them as an implied form of second-class membership in the Hall of Fame. "The baseball writers of America," said *The Sporting News*, "insist that there have been shining exemplars of their profession who should be elected to the Hall of Fame, and they insist that the committee has full authority to do so."[9]

There were other specific complaints about the Honor Rolls:

1. Many people believed that some umpires should have gained election to the Hall as full members. The various committees had not selected any umpires between 1936 and 1946, and many felt that Tommy Connolly and Bill Klem, in particular, deserved full membership. It appears that the Hall of Fame had yet to come to grips with the umpires' contributions and their relationship to the game.

2. The committee honored six writers from New York, but one each from Chicago and St. Louis, and none at all from Detroit, Cleveland, Cincinnati, or other longtime major league cities. Ten of the 12 selected writers came from the eastern seaboard.

3. The committee overlooked many deserving writers. One might think that two Chicagoans, Ring Lardner and Hugh Fullerton, would have been among the first selections. None of the Spinks from St. Louis and *The Sporting News* made it, either, and other ignored writers included Fred Lieb and Grantland Rice.

4. Two of the executives on the committee, Ed Barrow and Bob Quinn, named themselves to the Honor Rolls. No matter how deserving they may have been, it always causes controversy when people honor themselves. The committee also named two of its own recently deceased members, Harry Cross and Sid Mercer, while bypassing the eminently qualified Grantland Rice, who replaced Cross on the committee in April 1946.

5. Many people questioned why the various committees in the 1930s overlooked Harry Wright, the first baseball manager and the man who, more than anyone else, created professional baseball. Wright managed the undefeated Cincinnati Red Stockings in 1869, won four National Association pennants with Boston from 1872 to 1875, and won two of the first three National League flags in 1877–78. Not only did the committee fail to elect Wright to the Hall of Fame, it also did not put him on the Honor Rolls. Many believed that Harry Wright deserved full Hall of Fame selection as much as John McGraw and Connie Mack, who at the time were the only two Hall of Famers elected mainly as managers.

6. Miller Huggins had a fine career as a second baseman from 1904 to 1916, after which he became manager of the New York Yankees. From 1921 to 1928, Huggins led the Yankees to six pennants and three World Series titles. Huggins, who died in 1929, finished third in the 1946 BBWAA balloting, and the men who came in first, second, fourth, fifth, and sixth were all named to the Hall of Fame by the Permanent Committee. Huggins, unexplainably, was relegated to the Honor Rolls. It appears that the Hall had not yet come to grips with the contributions of managers, either.

Table 1. BBWAA Hall of Fame election totals
(198 votes needed for election)

Year	Electee	Votes	Elector
1946	Frank Chance	150	P.C.
	Johnny Evers	110	P.C.
	Miller Huggins	106	Honor Roll
	Ed Walsh	106	P.C.
	Rube Waddell	87	P.C.
	Clark Griffith	82	P.C.
	Carl Hubbell	75	1947 BBWAA
	Frank Frisch	67	1947 BBWAA
	Mickey Cochrane	65	1947 BBWAA
	Lefty Grove	61	1947 BBWAA

The Permanent Committee, already reeling from the negative reception accorded the Honor Rolls, received a great deal of criticism for its choices of 11 players to full Hall membership at that same 1946 meeting. The committee enshrined three pitchers (Ed Walsh, Jack Chesbro, and Rube Waddell) who did not win 200 major league games, while passing over 300-game winners Tim Keefe, John Clarkson, Pud Galvin, Mickey Welch, and Kid Nichols. The comparison of Nichols to Chesbro, Walsh, and Waddell is especially illuminating:[10]

Table 2. Comparison of Waddell, Walsh, and Chesbro, all of whom were selected by the Permanent Committee, with Nichols.

Pitcher	W–L	%	ShO	HoF?
Kid Nichols	361-205 (+156)	.634	48	No
Rube Waddell	193-143 (+50)	.574	50	Yes
Ed Walsh	195-126 (+69)	.607	57	Yes
Jack Chesbro	198-132 (+68)	.600	35	Yes

Nichols, though he played in the major leagues at an earlier date than the other three, was still living in 1946. This makes the failure of his candidacy unusual, since Hall of Fame voting committees have often shown a preference for candidates who are still alive and able to enjoy the honor.

In addition, the previous committee had selected Charley (Old Hoss) Radbourn to the Hall in 1939 but ignored John Clarkson, a pitcher from the same era with almost identical credentials. The Permanent Committee also bypassed Clarkson when it selected 21 other players to the Hall in 1945 and 1946.

Table 3. Comparison of Charley Radbourn (HoF 1939) and John Clarkson.

	G	IP	W–L	%	ShO	HoF?
Clarkson	531	4536.3	328-178 (+150)	.648	37	No
Radbourn	528	4535.3	309-195 (+114)	.613	35	Yes

Clarkson, who won 19 more games than Radbourn and lost 17 fewer, did not receive a plaque in Cooperstown until 1963.

These and other inconsistencies in the Permanent Committee's selection process contributed to the lack of acceptance of the Honor Roll concept. Because the committee had made several highly criticized Hall of Fame choices in 1946, columnists and commentators across the nation considered the Honor Rolls to be not much of an honor. The committee had lowered the standards of the Hall of Fame with some of its more questionable selections, which made the Honor Rolls appear even less of an honor than they were intended to be. *The Sporting News* led the critical charge, calling the Honor Roll selections "mere appendages to the star wagon" and suggesting that the Rolls were a "convenient depository" for borderline Hall candidates.[11]

The Hall of Fame held an induction ceremony on June 13,

1946, to unveil the plaque of Commissioner Kenesaw M. Landis, who died in November 1944 and was elected to the Hall of Fame one month later. The ceremony for the 11 old-time players elected by the Permanent Committee in April 1946 and the four modern players selected by the BBWAA in 1947 was held in Cooperstown on July 21, 1947. Eight of the 15 men were still living at the time, but only the 66-year-old Ed Walsh appeared at the ceremony and received his plaque.[12]

As for the Honor Rolls, no transcript of the 1946 ceremony or the 1947 ceremony exists, and Hall of Fame archivists do not know if the 39 honorees were mentioned on either date. *The New York Times* did not mention the Honor Rolls or the 39 men named to the Rolls, and do not indicate that the Honor Rolls played a part in the proceedings at either ceremony. The archives of the Hall also contain no evidence that any formal Honor Rolls were ever displayed at the Cooperstown museum, and it appears that the Rolls themselves never took physical form.

After the hail of criticism subsided, the Honor Roll concept utterly disappeared from public view. Ken Smith's book, *Baseball's Hall of Fame*, devoted a whole chapter to the Honor Rolls of Baseball in its 1947 edition, but when the book was reissued several times in subsequent years the Honor Rolls were dismissed in one paragraph. Smith, in the 1974 edition of the book, listed the 39 honorees, but wrote, "the committee found itself in a hopelessly large field and there were never any additions to the original thirty-four [sic]."[13]

The Honor Rolls were quickly forgotten in the following years, and died a lonely death as the Permanent Committee, which had inducted 21 players and 39 Honor Roll recipients in a span of only 13 months, went into hibernation for the next three years. In 1949, the committee met again and inducted two deserving pitchers, Mordecai (Three-Finger) Brown, another beneficiary of the "death effect," and the previously ignored Kid Nichols, who was fortunately still alive at the time. The committee members added no new names to the Honor Rolls, and no mention of the Rolls can be found in the newspapers or in *The Sporting News*. When umpire Bill Klem died in September 1951, no mention of the Honor Rolls was made in his obituary in *The New York Times*, although Klem had won the honor only five years earlier.[14]

In 1953, the Permanent Committee split into two groups. The trustee function of the committee passed to the Board of Trustees, and the election function became the province of a new 11-man Veterans Committee. This panel met on September 28, 1953, in the offices of Commissioner Ford Frick, and in less than one hour it elected six men to the Hall of Fame. Three of the new inductees—umpires Bill Klem and Tommy Connolly, and executive Ed Barrow—were promoted from the Honor Rolls, though none of the newspaper reports at the time mentioned that fact. A fourth inductee was the long-overlooked Harry Wright. In future years, four of the five managers on the Honor Rolls have been elected to the Hall, as well as an additional umpire (Billy Evans), but news reports of their selections to the Hall of Fame made no mention of their past Honor Roll status.

The Veterans Committee did not address the issue of sportswriters and their place in the Hall of Fame at any time during the 1950s. With the Honor Rolls almost totally forgotten, the writers remained outside of Cooperstown until the early 1960s, with the establishment of a new honor for writers. Significantly, the recognition was (and still is) bestowed not by the Veterans Committee, but by a vote of the BBWAA itself.

The writers finally gained recognition in 1962 with the introduction of the J. G. Taylor Spink Award, given "for meritorious contributions to baseball writing." This is what is often referred to as the "writers' wing" of the Hall, although the so-called "wing" is actually a single plaque, listing all the recipients, as part of a display in the museum library. Spink himself was the first recipient, followed by Ring Lardner in 1963 and Hugh Fullerton in 1964. All three of these men had been passed over by the Honor Rolls.[15] To date, the only Honor Roll writers to win the Spink Award have been Sid Mercer (1969) and Tim Murnane (1978). However, the Hall of Fame regards the honored writers as a separate entity. The Hall of Fame web site clearly states that the Spink Award winners are "honorees," not "inductees," a word they reserve for full members of the Hall.[16]

Conclusion

Despite the criticism—much of it deserved—of the Honor Rolls of Baseball, the concept might have been a successful one if it had been implemented differently. The idea of a second level of honor for the Hall of Fame is a worthy one, although it is probably too late to attempt at this time, more than 65 years after the Hall first opened its doors in 1939.

Unfortunately, the idea for the Honor Rolls came too late. From 1937 to 1946 the Permanent Committee and its predecessors made several selections to the Hall of Fame that would have fit much better on an Honor Roll than with a plaque on the wall implying that the individual was the equal of a Babe Ruth. Roger Bresnahan, elected to the Hall by the Permanent Committee in 1945, played an important role in defining the catching position and in developing catching equipment. If the Honor Rolls had been instituted before 1945, perhaps his contributions would have been more appropriately recognized on an Honor Roll of contributors to the game. The same might be said of Candy Cummings, elected in 1939 mostly for inventing the curveball, Tommy McCarthy, selected in 1946 for contributions to strategy, and the previously mentioned Morgan Bulkeley.

By the time the Honor Roll emerged from the 1946 committee meeting, the Hall had already established a lower level of accomplishment as a qualification for enshrinement. In putting plaques on the wall for such lesser lights as Bresnahan, Bulkeley, McCarthy, and others, the Hall had created what Bill James has called "a second tier of Hall of Famers who stretched the definition of greatness so far that any reasonable version of equity could never be achieved without honoring hundreds and hundreds of players."[17] The Honor Rolls, then, appeared to many as an even more inferior level of honor, lower than the previous Hall selections

had established up to that point. It made the Honor Rolls look like an unwanted "Array of Almosts" who didn't quite measure up to the real Hall inductees, questionable as some of them might be.

The concept might have proved successful if the trustees of the Hall of Fame had created a scheme for the Honor Rolls before the first election in January 1936. Hand-in-hand with a concerted effort to identify the game's greatest players and contributors, the two-level system of recognition might have worked.

Notes

1. The Honor Rolls were sometimes called the Honor Roll, implying that each of the four classes of honorees existed on the same roll. Ken Smith, in his book *Baseball's Hall of Fame* (1947), used the term Honor Rolls or Rolls of Honor. *The New York Times* (April 24, 1946) employed the term Honor Rolls, but the 1947 *Sporting News Official Baseball Guide and Record Book* used the singular form, as did the weekly *Sporting News* itself.
2. James A. Vlasich, *A Legend for the Legendary: The Origin of the Baseball Hall of Fame* (Bowling Green, Ohio: Bowling Green State University Popular Press, 1990), pages 49–50.
3. Some sources state that the committee selected 10 old-timers at the suggestion of Commissioner Landis, who had foreseen a possible stalemate in the upcoming 1945 BBWAA voting.
4. Bill James, *The Politics of Glory: How Baseball's Hall of Fame Really Works* (New York: Macmillan Publishing Company, 1994), page 44.
5. Ken Smith, *Baseball's Hall of Fame* (New York: Grosset and Dunlap, 1947), page 213.
6. Ken Smith, *Baseball's Hall of Fame 5th edition* (New York: Grosset and Dunlap, 1974), page 64.
7. *The Sporting News*, May 2, 1946.
8. Ibid.
9. Ibid.
10. Statistics in this article come from the Baseball Reference web site at http://www.baseball-reference.com.
11. *The Sporting News*, May 2, 1946.
12. *The New York Times*, July 22, 1947.
13. Smith, *Baseball's Hall of Fame 5th edition*, page 71.
14. *The New York Times*, September 17, 1951.
15. The next three Spink Award winners - Charles Dryden (the 1965 winner), Grantland Rice (1966), and Damon Runyon (1967) - had also been overlooked for Honor Roll recognition in 1946.
16. For a list of Spink Award winners, see the Hall of Fame web site at http://www.baseball-halloffame.org.
17. James, page 157.

Bibliography

Carter, Craig, editor. *Daguerreotypes, 8th edition* (St. Louis, Missouri: The Sporting News Publishing Company, 1990).

Ivor-Campbell, Frederick, with Tiemann, Robert L. and Rucker, Mark, editors. *Baseball's First Stars* (Cleveland, Ohio: Society for American Baseball Research, 1996).

James, Bill. *The Politics of Glory: How Baseball's Hall of Fame Really Works* (New York: Macmillan Publishing Company, 1994).

Smith, Ken. *Baseball's Hall of Fame* (New York: Grosset and Dunlap, 1947, 1974).

Spink, J. G. Taylor, editor. *The Sporting News Official Baseball Guide and Record Book* (St. Louis, Missouri: The Sporting News Publishing Company, 1947).

Turkin, Hy, and Thompson, S. C. *The Official Encyclopedia of Baseball, Revised Edition* (New York: A. S. Barnes and Company, 1955).

Vlasich, James A. *A Legend for the Legendary: The Origin of the Baseball Hall of Fame* (Bowling Green, Ohio: Bowling Green State University Popular Press, 1990).

MEMBERS OF THE HONOR ROLLS

Writers

Tim Murnane was an Irishman who played in the National Association from 1871 to 1875 and in the National League from 1876 to 1878; he stole the first base in NL history in 1876. He also played for and managed the Boston Union Association club in 1884, then became a sportswriter. He wrote for the *Boston Globe* from 1887 till his death in 1917. He liked to put humor in his writing; he once wrote, "Pitcher [Harley] Payne contorts himself into the Chinese laundry symbol for 33 cents before the delivery of the ball." Some say that Murnane virtually invented the modern baseball newspaper column.

Francis Richter founded *Sporting Life* in Philadelphia in 1883, three years before *The Sporting News* opened for business in St. Louis. Richter was also instrumental in the return of the National League to Philadelphia that same year. Richter criticized the NL monopoly on baseball and supported the Players Association in 1890. He was so independent that during World War I, Major League Baseball gave financial assistance to *The Sporting News*, but refused to do the same for *Sporting Life*, which ceased publication shortly afterward.

Bill Slocum was one of the first writers to appear regularly on radio, and **Harry Cross**, president of the New York chapter of the BBWAA, served on the Permanent Committee before he died three weeks before the 1946 election. **William Hanna** received credit for bringing a literary quality to baseball writing.

Irving E. Sanborn, of the *Chicago Tribune*, exposed the story of ballplayers avoiding the military draft and accepting money for easy work in shipyards and defense plants during World War I. **Sid Mercer** was a longtime writer for the *New York Journal* and the later *Journal-American,* involved in many controversies with John McGraw. The Player of the Year award, given annually by the New York chapter of the BBWAA, is still called the Sid Mercer Memorial Award. **Joe Vila**, of the *Brooklyn Eagle* and the *New York Sun*, was the first writer to use a typewriter at ringside of a prizefight. He also created the football play-by-play story in the late 1880s.

George Tidden (New York), **Frank Hough** (Philadelphia), **John B. Sheridan** (St. Louis), and **Walter Barnes** (Boston) were all influential early sportswriters in their respective cities.

Managers

Frank Selee and **Ned Hanlon** managed all 10 NL pennant winners in the 1891–1900 decade, each winning five. Hanlon built the famous Baltimore Orioles team that won the flag from 1894 to 1896, then moved to Brooklyn and won in 1899 and 1900. Selee built two great teams, managing the Boston Beaneaters from 1890 to 1901 and then moving to the Chicago Cubs. He stepped down as Cubs manager in 1905 due to illness, just before Frank Chance led the club to four pennants in five seasons.

Bill Carrigan caught for the Boston Red Sox and managed the team from 1913 to 1916, winning World Series titles in 1915 and 1916. Carrigan introduced Babe Ruth to the majors, and Ruth said in his autobiography that Carrigan was the greatest manager he ever had. Carrigan then went into the banking business and returned as Red Sox manager from 1927 to 1930.

John Montgomery Ward threw a perfect game as a pitcher, then moved to shortstop when his arm gave out. He captained the New York Giants to pennants in 1888 and 1889, and founded the short-lived Players League in 1890. **Miller Huggins**, a former National League infielder, won six pennants and three World Series titles with the New York Yankees in the 1920s.

 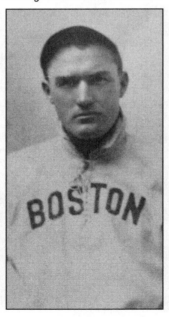  

L to R: Ned Hanlon, Bill Carrigan, Ed Barrow, and John T. Brush

L to R: Bill Klem, Bill Dinneen, Bob Emslie, and Silk O'Loughlin

Executives

Ed Barrow was the president of the Paterson, NJ, minor league club when he discovered Honus Wagner and sold him to the Louisville National League team in 1897. Barrow managed the Detroit Tigers, served as president of the International League, then succeeded Carrigan as Red Sox manager and won the 1918 World Series. He then became business manager of the Yankees and built that team into a dynasty.

Nicholas Young was known to all as "Uncle Nick" during his term as National League president from 1885 to 1903. He did his best to stay out of controversies, preferring instead to make flowery public pronouncements and busy himself with league statistics. Young, who became the league's first secretary in 1876, sometimes added hits to pad the averages of favorite players like Cap Anson, and for that reason the individual player statistics from the 1870s through the 1890s don't always add up to the league totals evenly.

Arthur Soden owned the Boston National League club from 1877 to 1906, while **Barney Dreyfuss** owned the Pittsburgh Pirates from 1900 to 1931 and **August Herrmann** ran the Cincinnati Reds from 1902 to 1927. **John E. Bruce** served as secretary of the National Commission when Herrmann chaired that body in the early 1900s. **Charles H. Ebbets** owned the Brooklyn Dodgers from 1898 to 1925 and built Ebbets Field, while **J. A. Robert (Bob) Quinn** was president and general manager of the Red Sox, Dodgers, and Braves.

Ernest S. Barnard was the second president of the American League (1927–1931), and **John A. Heydler** was president of the National (1918–1934).

John T. Brush, as primary owner of the Cincinnati Reds (1890–1902) and New York Giants (1902–1912), played a major role in the war between the leagues of 1901–1903. He refused to let his Giants play a post-season series against the American League champion in 1904, but Brush reversed course in 1905 and helped create the modern World Series.

Umpires

Tim Hurst was one of the most colorful umpires. He used an aggressive style and rough language to keep order on the field, and battled many players, managers, and even fans. His career as an umpire ended in 1909 when he spit on and spiked Philadelphia Athletics second baseman Eddie Collins. Hurst explained, "I don't like college boys."

Bill Klem umpired in the National League for 36 seasons, appearing in a record 18 World Series, and **Tommy Connolly** served for four years in the National League and 31 in the American. Connolly umpired the first game in American League history on April 24, 1901, at Chicago. Both men gained election to the Hall of Fame in 1953.

Bill Dinneen was a fine pitcher, winning 170 major league games and three more in the 1903 World Series, before he turned to umpiring. **Honest John Gaffney** and **Honest John Kelly** were the two leading umpires of the 19th century, while **Thomas Lynch** gave up his umpiring duties to become president of the National League from 1910 to 1913. **Billy Evans** was a great umpire, baseball's first general manager (for Cleveland in 1928), and the author of a widely read book on baseball rules called *Knotty Problems*.

Bob Emslie was an umpire for more than 30 years, best remembered for officiating the 1908 "Merkle's Boner" game between the Giants and Cubs. **Jack Sheridan** was an outstanding umpire who worked in four World Series from 1905 to 1910, and **Silk O'Loughlin** was famous for his bellowing "Strike Tuh" call.

Which Great Teams Were Just Lucky?

team's season record is massively influenced by luck. Suppose you take a coin and flip it 162 times to simulate a season. Each time it lands heads, that's a win, and when it lands tails, that's a loss. You'd expect, on average, to get 81 wins and 81 losses. But for any individual season, the record may vary significantly from 81–81. Just by random chance alone, your team might go 85–77, or 80–82, or even 69–93.

Suppose you were able to clone a copy of the New York Yankees, and play the cloned team against the real one. (That's hard to do with real players, but easy in a simulation game like APBA.) Again, on average, each team should win 81 games against each other, but, again, the records could vary significantly from 81–81, and the difference would be due to luck.

As it turns out, the range and frequency of possible records of a .500 team can be described by a normal (bell-shaped) curve, with an average of 81 wins and a standard deviation (SD) of about six wins. The SD can be thought of as a "typical" difference due to luck—so with an SD of six games, a typical record of a coin tossed 162 times is 87–75, or 75–87. Two-thirds of the outcomes should be within that range, so if you were to run 300 coin-seasons, or 300 cloned-Yankee seasons, you should get 200 of them winding up between 75 and 87 wins.

More interesting are the one-third of the seasons that fall outside that range. If all 16 teams in the National League were exactly average, you'd nonetheless expect five of them to wind up with more than 87 wins or with fewer than 75 wins. Furthermore, of those five teams, you'd expect one of them (actually, about 0.8 of a team) to finish more than 2 SDs away from the mean—that is, with more than 93 wins, or more than 93 losses.

This is a lot easier to picture if you see a real set of standings, so Table 1 shows a typical result of a coin-tossing season for a hypothetical National League where every team is .500.

In this simulated, randomized season, the Mets in the East and Diamondbacks in the West were both really .500 teams—but, by chance alone, the Mets finished ahead of Arizona by 27 games!

As it turns out, this season is a little more extreme than usual. On average, the difference between the best team and the worst team will be about 24 games, not 27. Also, there should be only one team above 93 wins (we had two), with the next best at 89.

PHIL BIRNBAUM is editor of *By the Numbers*, SABR's Statistical Analysis newsletter. A native of Toronto, he now lives in Ottawa, where he works as a software developer.

Table 1. Simulated NL season where each team is .500

	W	L	GB	Luck
Mets	94	68	- -	+13
Nationals	82	80	12	+1
Phillies	78	84	16	-3
Braves	77	85	17	-4
Marlins	70	92	24	-11
Brewers	84	78	- -	+3
Cardinals	83	79	1	+2
Pirates	82	80	2	+1
Reds	80	82	4	-1
Cubs	79	83	5	-2
Astros	78	84	6	-3
Padres	93	69	- -	+12
Dodgers	89	73	4	+8
Giants	84	78	9	+3
Rockies	75	87	18	-6
Diamondbacks	67	95	26	-14

Real Seasons

So far this is just an intellectual exercise because, of course, not every team is a .500 team. But even teams that aren't .500 have a standard deviation of around six games, so a similar calculation applies to them.

For instance, suppose you have a .550 team, expected to win 89 games. That's eight games above average. To get a rough idea of the distribution of wins it will actually get, you can just add those eight games to each row of Table 1. So, if our .550 team plays 16 seasons, in an extremely lucky season it'll finish 102–60, and in its unluckiest season it will go only 75–87—still a swing of 27 games (although, as we said, 24 is more typical). It's even possible that those two seasons will be consecutive, in which case the team will have fallen from 102 wins down to 75 in one season—and only because of luck!

If, in an average season, one team will drop 12 or more games out of contention for no real reason, and some other team will gain 12 games, it's pretty obvious that luck has a huge impact on team performance.

Which brings us to this question: is there a way, after the fact, to see how lucky a team was? The 1993 Philadelphia Phillies went 97–65. But how good were they, really? Were they like the top team in the chart that got 13 games lucky, so that they really should have been only 84–78? Were they like the bottom team in the chart that got 14 games unlucky, so that they were really a 111–51 team, one of the most talented ever? Were they even more extreme? Were they somewhere in the middle?

This article presents a way we can find out.

Luck's Footprints

A team starts out with a roster with a certain amount of talent, capable of playing a certain caliber of baseball. It ends up with a won-lost record. How much luck was involved in converting the talent to the record?

There are five main ways in which a team can get lucky or unlucky. Well actually, there are an infinite number of ways, but they will leave evidence in one of five statistical categories.

1. **Its hitters have career years, playing better than their talent can support.** Alfredo Griffin had a long career with the Blue Jays, A's, and Dodgers, mostly in the 1980s. A career .249 hitter with little power and no walks, his RC/G (Runs Created per Game, a measure of how many runs a team would score with a lineup of nine Alfredo Griffins) was never above the league average.

Griffin's best season was 1986. That year he hit .285, tied his career high with four home runs, and came close to setting a career high in walks (with 35). He created 4.16 runs per game, his best season figure ever.

In this case, we assume that Alfredo was lucky. Just as a player's APBA card may hit .285 instead of .249 just because of some fortunate dice rolls, we assume that Griffin's actual performance also benefited from similar luck.

What would cause that kind of luck? There are many possibilities. The most obvious one is that even the best players have only so much control of their muscles and reflexes. In *The Physics of Baseball*, Robert Adair points out that swinging one-hundredth of a second too early will cause a hit ball to go foul—and one-hundredth of a second too late will have it go foul the other way! To oversimplify, if Griffin is only good enough to hit the ball randomly within that .02 seconds, and it's a hit only if it's in the middle 25% of that interval, he'll be a .250 hitter. If one year, just by luck, he gets 30% of those hits instead of 25%, his stats take a jump.

There are other reasons that players may have career years. They might, just by luck, face weaker pitchers than average. They may play in more home games than average. They may play a couple of extra games in Colorado. Instead of ten balls hit close to the left-field line landing five fair and five foul, maybe eight landed fair and only two foul. When guessing fastball on a 3–2 count, they may be right 60% of the time one year but only 40% of the time the next.

I used a formula, based on his performance in the two seasons before and two seasons after, to estimate Griffin's luck in 1986. The formula is unproven, and may be flawed

for certain types of players—but you can also do it by eye. Here's Alfredo's record for 1984–1988:

Year	Outs (AB-H)	Batting runs	RC/game
1984	318	-28	2.46
1985	448	-20	3.43
1986	425	-5	4.16
1987	364	-16	3.52
1988	253	-22	2.15

Leaving out 1986, Griffin seemed to average about −22 batting runs per season. In 1986, he was −5: a difference of 17 runs. The RC/G column gives similar results: Griffin seemed to average around three, except in 1986, when he was better by about one run per game. 425 batting outs is about 17 games' worth (there are about 25.5 hitless at-bats per game), and 17 games at one run per game again gives us 17 runs.

The formula hits almost exactly, giving us 16.7 runs of "luck." That's coincidence, here, that the formula gives the same answer as the "eye" method—they'll usually be close, but not necessarily identical.

Griffin is a bit of an obvious case, where the exceptional year sticks out . Most seasons aren't like that, simply because most players usually do about what is expected of them. The formula will give a lot of players small luck numbers, like 6 runs, or −3, or such. Still, they add up. If a team's 14 hitters each turn three outs into singles, just by chance, that's about 28 runs—since it takes about 10 runs to equal one win, that's 2.8 wins.

And, of course, the opposite of a career year is an off year. Just as we measure that Alfredo was lucky in 1985, he was clearly unlucky in 1984, where his 2.46 figure was low even for him.

2. **Its pitchers have career years, playing better than their talent can support.** What's true of a hitter's batting line is also true of the batting line of what the pitcher gives up. Just as a hitter might hit .280 instead of .250 just by luck, so might a pitcher give up a .280 average against him instead of .250, again just by luck.

Using Runs Created, we can compute how many runs per game the pitcher "should have" given up, based on the batting line of the hitters who faced him (this stat is called "Component ERA"). And, just as for batters, a career year (or off-year) for a pitcher will stick right out.

Here's Bob Knepper, from 1980 to 1984:

Year	IP	ERA	Component ERA
1980	215.1	4.10	4.13
1981	156.2	2.18	2.26
1982	180	4.45	4.14
1983	203	3.19	3.62
1984	233.2	3.20	3.28

Leaving out 1982, Knepper seemed to average a CERA of about 3½. But in '82, he was at 4.14. That's about .7 runs per game, multiplied by exactly 20 games (180 innings), for about 14 runs lost due to random chance.

The formula sees it about the same way, assigning Knepper 17 runs of bad luck.

A pitcher's record necessarily includes that of his fielders—and so, whenever we talk about a pitcher's career year, that career year really belongs to the pitcher and his defense, in some combination.

3. It was more successful at turning base runners into runs. The statistic "Runs Created," invented by Bill James, estimates the number of runs a team will score based on its batting line.

Runs Created is pretty accurate, generally within 25 runs a season of a team's actual scoring. But it's not exactly accurate, because it can't be.

Run scoring depends not just on the batting line, but also on the timing of events within it. If a team has seven hits in a game, it'll probably score a run or two. But if the hits are scattered, it might get shut out. And if the hits all come in the same inning, it might score four or five runs.

The more a team's hits and walks are bunched together, the more runs it will score. That's the same thing as saying that the better the team hits with men on base, the more runs it will score. Which, again, is like saying the better the team hits in the clutch, the more runs it will score.

But several analyses, most recently a study by Tom Ruane of 40 years worth of play-by-play data, have shown that clutch hitting is generally random—that is, there is no innate "talent" for clutch hitting aside from ordinary hitting talent. So, for instance, a team that hits .260 is just as likely to hit .280 in the clutch as it is to hit .240 in the clutch.

And if that's the case, then any discrepancy between Runs Created and actual runs is due to luck, not talent.

And so when the 2001 Anaheim Angels scored 691 runs, but the formula predicted they should score 746, we chalk the difference, 55 runs, up to just plain bad luck.

4. Its opposition was less successful in turning base runners into runs. If clutch hitting is random, it's random for a team's opposition, too. So when the 1975 Big Red Machine held its opponents to 70 fewer runs than their Runs Created estimate says they should have scored, we attribute those 70 runs to random chance. The Reds' pitchers were lucky, to the tune of seven wins.

5. It won more games than expected from its Runs Scored and Runs Allowed. The 1962 New York Mets achieved the worst record in modern baseball history, at 40–120. That season they scored only 617 runs and allowed 948—both figures the worst in the league.

There's another Bill James formula, the Pythagorean Projection, which estimates what a team's winning percentage should have been based on their runs scored and runs allowed. By that formula, the Mets should have been 7.6 games better in the standings than they actually were—that is, they should have been 47–113.

Any difference between expected wins and actual wins has to do with the timing of runs—teams that score lots of runs in blowout games will win fewer games than expected, while teams that "save" their runs for closer games will win more than their projection. But studies have shown that run timing, like clutch hitting, is random. Teams don't have a "talent" for saving their runs for close games, and therefore any difference from Pythagorean Projection is just luck.

So seven of the Mets' 1962 losses were the result of bad luck, and based on this finding they weren't quite as bad as we thought. Of course, 47–113 is still pretty dismal.

Putting It All Together

Earlier, we mentioned the 1993 Phillies. How lucky were they? Let's take the five steps, one at a time:

1,2: Career Years or Off-Years

Everything came together in 1993, as individual Phillies hitters had career years, to the tune of a huge 131 runs.

Lenny Dykstra had a monster year, hitting 19 home runs (his previous high was 10) with a career-high .305 average. He was 37 runs better than expected. Rookie Kevin Stocker was lucky by 19 runs—he hit .324, but would never break .300 again. John Kruk and Pete Incaviglia were a combined 33 runs better than expected. Of the hitters, only Mickey Morandini, at −9, had an off-year of more than three runs.

Pitchers were lucky by 39 runs, led by Tommy Greene, who had the best year of his career, 37 runs better than expected. Otherwise the staff was fairly level:

Batter	Luck (runs)	Pitcher	Luck (runs)
Dykstra, Lenny	37	Greene, Tommy	37
Stocker, Kevin	19	Mulholland, Terry	24
Kruk, John	17	West, David	9
Incaviglia, Pete	16	Jackson, Danny	9
Daulton, Darren	11	Andersen, Larry	5
Chamberlain, Wes	11	Pall, Donn	4
Eisenreich, Jim	10	Williams, Mitch	3
Pratt, Todd	7	Williams, Mike	2
Batiste, Kim	6	Mauser, Tim	2
Hollins, Dave	5	Brink, Brad	2
Amaro, Ruben	5	Mason, Roger	1
Jordan, Ricky	1	Thigpen, Bobby	−1
Millette, Joe	0	DeLeon, Jose	−2
Bell, Juan	−2	Davis, Mark	−3
Thompson, Milt	−3	Green, Tyler	−7
Duncan, Mariano	−3	Ayrault, Bob	−9
Manto, Jeff	−3	Foster, Kevin	−9
Morandini, Mickey	−9	Schilling, Curt	−10
		Rivera, Ben	−16

3. Runs Created by Batters

The Phillies scored 24 more runs than expected from their batting line.

4. Runs Created by Opposition

The Phillies' opponents scored almost exactly the expected number of runs, exceeding their estimate by only one run.

5. Pythagorean Projection

Scoring 877 runs and allowing 740, the Phillies were Pythagorically unlucky. They should have won 3.1 more games than they did—at 10 runs per win, that's about 31 runs worth. Adding it all up gives:

Career years/off years by hitters	+131 runs
Career years/off years by pitchers	+ 39 runs
Runs Created by batters	+ 24 runs
Runs Created by opposition	- 1 run
Pythagorean projection	- 31 runs
TOTAL	+162 runs (16 wins)
Actual record	97-65
Projected record	81-81

We conclude that the 1993 Phillies were a dead-even .500 team that just happened to get lucky enough that it won 97 games and the pennant.

This shouldn't be that surprising. The Phils finished last in the division in 1992, and second last in 1994, with mostly the same personnel. You can argue, if you like, that the players caught a temporary surge of talent in 1993, which they promptly lost after the season. But the conclusion that they had a lucky year makes a lot more sense.

The Best and Worst "Career Years"

Which players had the worst "off-years" between 1960 and 2001? Here's the chart:

1986	TOR	Stieb, Dave	-60
1999	SEA	Fassero, Jeff	-56
1997	CHA	Belle, Albert	-53
1997	OAK	Brosius, Scott	-50
1973	PIT	Blass, Steve	-50
1980	CHN	Lamp, Dennis	-48
1962	CHN	Santo, Ron	-47
1997	CHN	Sosa, Sammy	-45
1961	CHA	Baumann, Frank	-45
1971	HOU	Wynn, Jimmy	-45

It's an interesting chart, but also shows a limitation of the formula—it can't distinguish between players who were lucky, and players who had a real reason for their performance problem.

Take Steve Blass, for example. His well-documented collapse in 1973 was not because he was just unlucky, but that he suddenly was unable to find the strike zone. While succumbing to "Steve Blass disease" is, I guess, a form of bad luck, it's not really the kind of luck we're investigating, which assumes that the player has his normal level of talent, but things just don't go his way. If you're doing an analysis of the 1973 Pirates, you might want to subtract out those 50 runs, based on the known understanding that they weren't really bad luck.

Dave Stieb in 1986—the worst "unlucky" season of the past 40 years—is another interesting case. Stieb was arguably the best pitcher in the AL in 1984 and 1985; he was legitimately bad in 1986, but went back to excellent in 1987 and 1988. What happened in 1986? Bill James suggested that Stieb had lost a little bit of his stuff, and was slow to accept his new limitations and pitch within them. I looked over a couple of game reports in the Toronto Star from that year, and the tone seemed to be puzzlement at Stieb's bad year—there was no suggestion that Stieb was injured or such.

Here are the luckiest years:

1972	PHI	Carlton, Steve	63
1961	DET	Cash, Norm	60
1980	OAK	Norris, Mike	60
1963	CHN	Ellsworth, Dick	58
1993	TOR	Olerud, John	58
1986	TEX	Correa, Ed	54
1970	LAN	Grabarkewitz, Billy	54
1991	BAL	Ripken Jr., Cal	52
1999	OAK	Jaha, John	51
2001	CHN	Sosa, Sammy	50

Steve Carlton's awesome 1972 season, when he went 28–10 for a dismal .378 team, comes in as the luckiest of all time. Norm Cash is second, for his well-documented cork-aided out-of-nowhere 1961 (note that the system is unable to distinguish luck from cheating). And it's interesting that Sammy Sosa appears on both lists.

You would expect that the luckiest season of all-time would be one like Cash's, where an average player suddenly has one great year. But, instead, Carlton's 1972 is a case where a great player has one of the greatest seasons ever. Of course, it's a bit easier for a pitcher to come up with a big year than a hitter, because there's a double effect—when his productivity goes up, his impact on the team is compounded because he gets more innings (even if only because he's not removed in the third inning of a bad outing). On the other hand, a full-time hitter gets about the same amount of playing time whether he's awesome or merely excellent.

Again, you can visit these cases to see if you can come up with explanations other than luck—Mike Norris, for instance, is widely considered to have been mortally overworked by Billy Martin in 1980, destroying his arm and, in that light, perhaps 60 runs is a bit of an overestimate.

Lucky and Unlucky Teams

The lists of players are interesting but probably not new knowledge—even without this method, we were probably aware that Norm Cash had a lucky season in 1961. On the other hand, which were the lucky and unlucky teams? I didn't know before I did this study. Not only didn't I know, but I didn't have a trace of an idea.

Table 2 shows the 15 unluckiest teams from 1960–2001.

The unluckiest team over the last 40 years was the 1962 New York Mets—the team with the worst record ever. This is not a coincidence—the worse the team, the more likely it had bad luck, for obvious reasons.

Most of the Mets' problems came from timing—poor hitting in the clutch, opponents' good hitting in the clutch, and poor hitting in close games. That poor timing cost them about 15 wins. Bad years from their pitchers cost them another seven wins, which was partially compensated for by two wins worth of good years by their hitters.

On the other hand, the 1979 Oakland A's had good timing—seven games of good luck worth. But their players had such bad off-years that it cost them 27 games in the win column. Of their 33 players, only five had lucky years of any size. The other 28 players underperformed, led by the 2–17 Matt Keough (43 runs of bad luck), off whom the opposition batted .315.

The 1995 Blue Jays were actually the unluckiest team by winning percentage—they were –196 runs in a shortened 144-game season. They wound up tied for the worst record in the league when in reality their talent was well above average.

But the 1998 Mariners could be considered the most disappointing of these 15 teams. Their talent shows as good enough to win 95 games, surely enough for the post-season—but they had 19 games worth of bad luck, and finished 76–85. It's not on the chart, but the Mariners were unlucky again the next season, by 13 games this time—they should have been a 92-win wild-card contender in 1999, but again finished down the pack at 79–83.

Table 2. The 15 unluckiest teams, 1960–2001

Team	Season	Career Year Hitters (Runs)	Career Year Pitchers (Runs)	Pythagoras Luck (runs)	Batting RC Luck	Opposition RC Luck	Total Luck (runs)	Actual W	Actual L	Luck-Adjusted W	Luck-Adjusted L
NYN	1962	24	-71	-76	-21	-62	-206	40	120	61	99
OAK	1979	-132	-142	42	23	7	-203	54	108	74	88
CLE	1987	-46	-83	2	-29	-40	-196	61	101	81	81
TOR	1995	-72	-50	-24	-43	-6	-196	56	88	76	68
SEA	1998	-35	-55	-49	-63	10	-192	76	85	95	66
PHI	1961	-53	-38	-69	9	-37	-188	47	107	66	88
CHN	1962	-75	-67	-7	-23	-12	-185	59	103	77	85
COL	1999	-61	-178	12	-22	68	-181	72	90	90	72
KC1	1964	-11	-162	-6	-23	24	-178	57	105	75	87
DET	1996	-67	-146	-13	38	9	-178	53	109	71	91
PIT	1985	-10	-54	-61	-17	-29	-171	57	104	74	87
DET	1960	-115	25	-47	-16	-8	-161	71	83	87	67
CLE	1985	-62	-57	-76	50	-15	-161	60	102	76	86
CHA	1970	-31	-89	-43	9	-7	-161	56	106	72	90
ATL	1977	-55	-151	19	20	8	-160	61	101	77	85

Table 3. The 15 luckiest teams, 1960–2001

Team	Season	Career Year Hitters (Runs)	Career Year Pitchers (Runs)	Pythagoras Luck (runs)	Batting RC Luck	Opposition RC Luck	Total Luck (runs)	Actual W	Actual L	Luck-Adjusted W	Luck-Adjusted L
SEA	2001	127	116	49	-21	3	273	116	46	89	73
NYA	1998	88	84	32	9	8	220	114	48	92	70
PIT	1960	77	67	18	-1	29	191	95	59	76	78
OAK	1992	81	18	67	0	20	186	96	66	77	85
SLN	1985	94	56	-11	16	29	183	101	61	83	79
LAN	1962	115	13	41	60	-49	180	102	63	84	81
NYA	1961	51	57	43	17	9	178	109	53	91	71
SFN	1993	64	67	30	6	11	178	103	59	85	77
SLN	2000	68	78	27	-23	24	174	95	67	78	84
NYA	1963	45	52	26	29	21	173	104	57	87	74
NYN	1969	-2	60	65	33	16	172	100	62	83	79
NYN	1986	74	47	31	12	5	169	108	54	91	71
CLE	1995	31	83	54	-27	26	167	100	44	83	61
SLN	1987	30	-2	27	60	52	166	95	67	78	84
CIN	1995	99	66	1	-9	9	166	85	59	68	76

TORONTO BLUE JAYS

Dave Stieb

The luckiest team (Table 3), by a runaway margin, was the 2001 Seattle Mariners, who won 116 games. And they did most of it through career years. Of the lucky runs, 127 came from the hitters (in this study, second only to the 1993 Phillies), and the pitchers contributed 116 of their own (fifth best). Thirteen separate players contributed at least one lucky win each—Bret Boone (40 runs), Freddy Garcia (38), and Mark McLemore (23) topped the list. Only one player was more than 10 runs unlucky (John Halama, at -11). Despite all the luck, the Mariners were still an excellent team—with average luck they would have still finished 89–73.

The 1998 Yankees are considered one of the best teams ever, and it's perhaps surprising that they emerge as the second luckiest team. Like the 2001 Mariners, the '98 Yankees got most of their luck from their players' performances—about eight games each from their hitting and pitching. In talent, they were 92–70, which is still a very strong team. Indeed, of the 15 luckiest teams, the 1998 Yankees show as the best.

The Miracle Mets of 1969 were 17 games lucky, but this time most of their luck was timing luck—10 wins in Runs Created, and about two wins in Pythagoras. Still, they were a respectable 83–79 team in talent.

The worst of these lucky teams was the 1960 Pirates. Bill Mazeroski's famous game 7 home run brought the World Series championship to a team that, by this analysis, was worse than average, at 76–78. The 97–57 Yankees, whom they beat, had been eight games lucky themselves, but were still the most talented team in the majors that year, at 89–65.

The Best Teams Ever

Which teams were legitimately the best, even after luck is stripped out of their record? Perhaps not surprisingly, the list is dominated by the "dynasty" teams:

Table 4. The best teams, 1960–2001

Team	Season	Actual W	Actual L	Talent W	Talent L
BAL	1969	109	53	102	60
ATL	1998	106	56	102	60
ATL	1997	101	61	100	62
BAL	1970	108	54	99	63
LAN	1974	102	60	98	64
CIN	1975	108	54	98	64
NYA	1977	100	62	98	64
ATL	1993	104	58	98	64
SEA	1997	90	72	98	64
ATL	1995	90	54	87	57
BAL	1971	101	57	95	63
CIN	1977	88	74	97	65
NYA	1997	96	66	97	65
OAK	2001	102	60	97	65
BOS	1978	99	64	98	65

The 1969, '70, and '71 Orioles all appear in the top 15, as do four Braves teams from the '90s. The ill-fated victims-of-Bucky-Dent 1978 Red Sox come in at number 15. (The list may not appear to be in the correct order because of rounding—but it is.)

The 1975 Reds make the list, but the 1976 Reds don't (they came in at number 42). Interestingly, the unheralded 1977 Reds, whose nine games of bad luck dropped them to 88–74, appear at number 12. The 1978 Reds, with a projected talent of 96–65, were 21st. This suggests the Big Red Machine stayed big and red longer than we thought, but bad luck made it seem the talent had dissipated.

I've never heard the 1974 Dodgers described as among the best of all time, but they're fifth on the list. It was Steve Garvey's first full season, and the Dodgers had a solid infield and legitimately strong pitching staff.

Arguably the biggest surprise on this list isn't the presence or absence of any particular team, but that only three teams over the last 40 years were talented enough to win 100 games. This is legitimate—if there were lots of 100-game teams, we'd see a substantial number getting moderately lucky and winning 106 games or more. Also, it's consistent with a different study I did back in 1988, which found that, theoretically, a team that wins 109 games is, on average, only a 98-game talent. But there is no assurance that this is correct—it's possible that my algorithm for "career years" overestimates the amount of luck and underestimates the amount of talent. Table 5 lists the worst teams ever.

With expansion, it's a lot easier to create a team that loses 100 games than a team that wins 100 games. The 100-game loser list is 23 teams long.

Interesting here is the repeated presence of the expansion San Diego Padres, with four teams in the top 15 abysmal list. It's actually worse than that—the 1970 team finished 19th, and the 1974 Padres were 29th. For six consecutive years San Diego fielded a team in the bottom 30. That they have not been recognized as that futile a team probably stems from the fact that, unlike the expansion Mets, they never had enough bad luck to give them a string of historically horrific records. From 1970 to 1973, their luck was positive each year.

Table 5. The worst teams, 1960–2001

Team	Season	Actual W	L	Talent W	L
NYN	1965	50	112	54	108
TOR	1977	54	107	54	107
TEX	1972	54	100	54	100
SDN	1969	52	110	57	105
SEA	1977	64	98	57	105
SDN	1971	61	100	58	103
NYN	1964	53	109	58	104
SDN	1973	60	102	59	103
NYN	1963	51	111	59	103
WS2	1961	61	100	59	102
HOU	1963	66	96	60	102
HOU	1964	66	96	60	102
SDN	1972	58	95	57	96
HOU	1962	64	96	60	100
FLO	1993	64	98	61	101

Missing from Table 5 are the 1962 Mets—as we saw, they really should have been 61–99, for 19th worst ever.

The bottom 14 teams are all from the '60s and '70s, suggesting—or confirming—that competitive balance has improved in recent decades.

How often does the best team win?

In 1989, a Bill James study found that because of luck, a six- or seven-team division will theoretically be won by the best team only about 55% of the time.

I checked the actual "luck" numbers for all 96 division races in 1969–1993 (excluding 1981), and found that 59% (57 of 96) were won by the most talented team—very close to Bill's figure.

Of the 39 pennant races that went to the "wrong" team, the most lopsided was the 1987 National League East. The Cardinals finished first by three games—but were only a 78-game talent, fully 16 games worse than the second-place Mets.

Also of note: the 1989 Mets should have finished 15 games ahead of the Cubs instead of six back. The 1992 White Sox should have won the division, beating the A's by 14 games, instead of finishing third. And the hard-luck Expos were the most talented team in the NL East in 1979, 1980, 1981, 1982, and 1984. They made the post-season only in 1981. In 1982, they were good enough to have finished first by 11 games.

In his 1989 article, Bill James speculated that a sub-.500 team could conceivably win the World Series, though it was unlikely. He wrote, "Did we see it in '88?" For the record, the 1988

Dodgers come out as an 82–80 team—close but not quite. The '82 Cardinals came the closest in the four-division era—they won the Series with 81.2-game talent.

But the 1960 Pirates fit the bill. Without luck, they were 76–78. Nineteen games of good fortune pushed them to 95–59, the World Series, and set the stage for Bill Mazeroski's heroics. Table 6 shows every World Series team from 1960 to 2001.

Table 6. World Series winners, 1960–2001

Year	Team	Talent	Luck (games)	Actual
1960	Pirates	76-78	+19.1	95-59
1961	Yankees	91-71	+17.8	109-53
1962	Yankees	92-70	+3.6	96-66
1963	Dodgers	90-72	+8.9	99-63
1964	Cardinals	82-80	+10.6	93-69
1965	Dodgers	89-73	+8.1	97-65
1966	Orioles	89-72	+8.5	97-63
1967	Cardinals	87-74	+14.4	101-60
1968	Tigers	92-70	+10.7	103-59
1969	Mets	83-79	+17.2	100-62
1970	Orioles	99-63	+8.7	108-54
1971	Pirates	96-66	+1.5	97-65
1972	A's	90-65	+2.7	93-62
1973	A's	94-68	-0.2	94-68
1974	A's	94-68	-4.0	90-72
1975	Reds	98-64	+9.9	108-54
1976	Reds	95-67	+7.3	102-60
1977	Yankees	98-64	+2.2	100-62
1978	Yankees	97-66	+2.9	100-63
1979	Pirates	86-76	+11.8	98-64
1980	Phillies	86-76	+5.2	91-71
1981	Dodgers	66-44	-2.9	63-47
1982	Cardinals	81-81	+10.8	92-70
1983	Orioles	85-77	+13.4	98-64
1984	Tigers	95-67	+8.7	104-58
1985	Royals	84-78	+7.4	91-71
1986	Mets	91-71	+16.9	108-54
1987	Twins	81-81	+3.5	85-77
1988	Dodgers	82-79	+12.3	94-67
1989	A's	94-68	+5.3	99-63
1990	Reds	86-76	+5.4	91-71
1991	Twins	88-74	+6.8	95-67
1992	Blue Jays	95-67	+1.4	96-66
1993	Blue Jays	88-74	+7.0	95-67
1995	Braves	87-57	+3.3	90-54
1996	Yankees	94-68	-1.8	92-70
1997	Marlins	93-69	-0.5	92-70
1998	Yankees	92-70	+22.0	114-48
1999	Yankees	96-66	+1.9	98-64
2000	Yankees	95-66	-8.4	87-74
2001	D-Backs	91-71	+0.7	92-70

Table 6 makes it evident that, to win the World Series, it's not enough to be good—you have to be lucky, too. Of the 41 champs, 35 had a lucky season. Of the six unlucky teams, only the '74 A's and the 2000 Yankees were unlucky by more than three games.

Before 1969, all the winning teams were lucky, some substantially. Between 1969 and 1993, in the four-division era, luck was a little less important. Since 1995, the champions were, on the whole, only marginally lucky (with the exception of 1998).

Table 7. Luckiest and unluckiest seasons for every Major League team, 1960–2001

LUCKIEST SEASON					UNLUCKIEST SEASON				
Team	Year	Talent	Luck (games)	Actual	Team	Year	Talent	Luck (games)	Actual
Angels	1986	76-86	+15.8	92-70	Angels	1996	85-76	-15.4	70-91
D-Backs	1999	84-78	+16.4	100-62	D-Backs	2000	90-73	-4.5	85-77
Braves	1991	81-81	+12.8	94-68	Braves	1977	77-85	-16.0	61-101
Orioles	1964	82-81	+15.0	97-65	Orioles	1967	90-71	-14.1	76-85
Red Sox	1995	76-68	+ 9.8	86-58	Red Sox	1965	78-84	-15.5	62-100
White Sox	1983	83-79	+15.8	99-63	White Sox	1970	72-90	-16.1	56-106
Cubs	1984	80-81	+16.1	96-65	Cubs	1962	77-85	-18.5	59-103
Reds	1995	68-76	+16.6	85-59	Reds	2001	77-85	-10.7	66-96
Indians	1995	83-61	+16.7	100-44	Indians	1987	81-81	-19.6	61-101
Rockies	2000	79-83	+ 3.0	82-80	Rockies	1999	90-72	-18.1	72-90
Tigers	1961	86-76	+14.7	101-61	Tigers	1996	71-91	-17.8	53-109
Marlins	1995	59-85	+8.5	67-76	Marlins	1998	63-99	-8.5	54-108
Houston	1986	80-82	+16.1	96-66	Houston	1975	78-83	-13.9	64-97
Royals	1971	73-88	+12.3	85-76	Royals	1997	79-82	-11.7	67-94
Dodgers	1962	84-81	+18.0	102-63	Dodgers	1992	74-88	-11.5	63-99
Twins	1965	92-70	+10.5	102-60	Twins	1964	95-67	-16.0	79-83
Brewers	1982	83-79	+11.8	95-67	Brewers	1977	78-84	-11.2	67-95
Expos	1994	61-53	+12.7	74-40	Expos	1969	66-96	-13.9	52-110
Yankees	1998	92-70	+22.0	114-48	Yankees	1982	89-73	-10.3	79-83
Mets	1969	83-79	+17.2	100-62	Mets	1962	61-99	-20.6	40-120
A's	1992	77-85	+18.6	96-66	A's	1979	74-88	-20.3	54-108
Phillies	1993	81-81	+16.2	97-65	Phillies	1961	66-88	-18.8	47-107
Pirates	1960	76-78	+19.1	95-59	Pirates	1985	74-87	-17.1	57-104
Padres	1996	78-84	+13.3	91-71	Padres	1990	84-78	- 9.4	75-87
Mariners	2001	89-73	+27.3	116-46	Mariners	1998	95-66	-19.2	76-85
Giants	1993	85-77	+17.8	103-59	Giants	1972	81-74	-11.5	69-86
Cardinals	1985	83-79	+18.3	101-61	Cardinals	1990	83-79	-13.1	70-92
Devil Rays	2000	70-91	-1.3	69-92	Devil Rays	1998	66-96	-2.8	63-99
Rangers	1986	76-86	+11.1	87-75	Rangers	1985	75-86	-13.2	62-99
Blue Jays	1993	88-74	+7.0	95-67	Blue Jays	1995	76-68	-19.6	56-88

This makes sense—back in the one-division league, one lucky team could blow away nine others. Now that team eliminates only three or four others, and even then, those other teams have a shot at the wild card. And the lucky team now has to win three series against superior opponents, instead of just one, which increases the chance that a legitimately good team, instead of just a lucky one, will now come out on top.

Before the wild card, champions with talent in the 80s were very common. But from 1996 to 2001, every World Series winner was over 90.

Table 7 lists the luckiest and unluckiest seasons for every major league team from 1960–2001. The Blue Jays and the Red Sox have had success over the years, but never had a huge season of 108 victories or something and ran away with the division. That seems to be because they never had the kind of awesome luck you need to have that kind of record. The Jays were never more than seven games lucky, and Boston never more than 9.8.

For the flip side, look at San Diego—they were never unlucky by more than 9.4 games. As noted earlier, perhaps this spares them a reputation as the worst expansion team ever—with a bit of bad fortune, their record could have rivaled the Mets for futility.

And the negative sign in Tampa Bay's "best luck" column is not a misprint—in the first four years of their existence, they were unlucky all four years.

Finally, take a look at the Twins. Their luckiest season immediately followed their unluckiest. As a result, they went from below .500 in 1964 to 102 wins in 1965—even though they actually became a worse team!

Summary

What can we conclude from all this? First, luck is clearly a crucial contributor to a team's record. With a standard deviation of six or seven games, a team's position in a pennant race is hugely affected by chance—seven wins is easily the difference between a wild-card contender and an also-ran.

Second, you have to be lucky to win a championship. As we saw, 85% of world champions had lucky regular seasons.

Third, teams with superb records are likely to have been lucky. Very few teams are truly talented enough to expect to win 100 games. The odds are low that the 2005 White Sox (99–63) and Cardinals (100–62) are really as good as their record.

Despite all this, it should be said that while luck is important, talent is still more important. The SD due to luck was 7.2, but the SD due to talent was 8.5. It's perhaps a comfort to realize that talent is still more important than luck—if only barely.

LUCK: THE ALGORITHM

This is the algorithm to calculate a player's career-year or off-year luck for a given season. The procedure is arbitrary. I used it because it seems to work reasonably well, but it no doubt can be improved, probably substantially. But, hopefully, any reasonable alternative algorithm should give similar results in most cases.

Of course, any algorithm should sum roughly zero, since over an entire population of players the luck should even out.

BATTERS: A batter's luck is calculated in "runs created per 27 outs" (RC/27). To calculate a batter's luck for year X:

1. Take the player's average RC27 over six years: two years ago counted once, last year counted twice, next year counted twice, and two years from now counted once. Weight the average by "outs made" (hitless AB + CS + GIDP) so that seasons in which a batter had more playing time will have a higher weight. Adjust each RC27 for league and park.

2. Add a certain number of "outs made" at the league average RC27:
   – if the player had more than 2,100 outs made in the six seasons, add 100 league-average outs made;
   – if the player had fewer than 1,200 outs made in the six seasons, add 900 league-average outs made; and
   – if the player had between 1,200 and 2,100 outs made, subtract that from 2,100 and add that number of league-average outs made.

   The purpose of this step is to regress the player to the mean. Just as a player who goes 2-for-4 in a game probably isn't a .500 hitter, a player who hits .300 in 1,200 outs made is probably less than a .300 hitter. This adjusts for that fact.

3. If the player had fewer than 1,600 outs made over the six seasons (not including those added in step 2), subtract 0.0006 for each out made under 1,600. In addition, if the player had less than 800 outs made over the six seasons, subtract another .0006 for each out made under 800.

   The purpose of this step is to recognize that players with fewer plate appearances are probably less effective players.

4. Add .09 if the player had more than 1,600 outs made (not including those added in step 2).

5. This gives you the player's projected performance, expressed in RC27. To figure the luck, subtract it from the actual RC27, multiply by outs made, and divide by 27. So if a player projects to 4.5, his actual was 5.5, and he did all that in 270 outs that year, then (1) he was lucky by 1.0 runs per game; (2) he was responsible for 10 games (270 outs divided by 27); so (3) he was "lucky" by 10 runs.

PITCHERS: A pitcher's luck is calculated in "component ERA" (CERA), which is the number of runs per game the opposition should score based on its batting line against him. To calculate a pitcher's luck:

1. Take the player's average CERA over six years: two years ago, last year counted twice, next year counted twice, and two years from now counted once. Weight the average by "outs made" (IP divided by three) so that seasons in which a pitcher had more playing time will have a higher weight. Adjust each CERA for league and park.

2. Add a certain number of "outs made" at the league average CERA:
   – if the player had more than 900 outs made in the six seasons, add 900 league-average outs made;
   – if the player had fewer than 400 outs made in the six seasons, add 400 league-average outs made; and
   – if the player had between 400 and 900 outs made, add that number of league-average outs made.

3. Temporarily add this year's outs made to the total of the six seasons (not including those added in step 2). If that total is less than 1,200, add 0.0006 for each out made under 1,200.

4. Add .35.

5. If the player started more than 70% of his appearances, add .1.

6. If the player had more than 300 outs made this year, but fewer than 300 outs made total in the six seasons from step 1, ignore the results of the previous five steps, and use the league/park average CERA instead. (That is, assume he's an average pitcher.)

7. This gives you the player's projected performance, expressed in CERA. To figure the luck, subtract the actual CERA, multiply by outs made, and divide by 27. So if a player projects to 3.50, his actual was 4.50, and he did all that in 270 outs that year, then (1) he was unlucky by 1.0 runs per game; (2) he was responsible for 10 games (270 outs divided by 27); so (3) he was "unlucky" by 10 runs.

Spreadsheets of every team and player can be found at www.philbirnbaum.com

Unsolved Photo Mysteries

My Mom started me on my never-ending search for the perfect sliding photos back in 1947. A regular part of every summer day was spent going through the newspapers, searching for sliding photos, then identifying the players without looking at the caption below the photo. I became quite adept at looking for key elements and in doing so spurred a life-long love affair for photos of sliding action.

Over the past 50 years I have studied thousands of photos of sliding action looking for information and clues about the photograph. Who are the players, the umpire, and the stadium, when it happened and why it happened. In most cases the information, while occasionally wrong, is attached to the back of the photograph. But with the following photos the information has been detached from the back and I had to start from scratch.

Last year I wrote an article in the *Baseball Research Journal* in which I shared this identification process on a number of misidentified photos. I showed how I came up with the players involved, the date and the inning. The keys to identifying a photo are to recognize the teams, the players, the umpire, the stadium, the year, and then spend a lot of hours in a library. I was gratified at the response to the BRJ article.

Even with a lot of solid research, there are some photos that are true mysteries that require special assistance. In the article last year, for example, I included a photo of a 1932 Yankees' game, the details of which had eluded me for years. Several SABR members came to the rescue in late 2004. Encouraged by that feedback, I put together a group of mystery photographs that have frustrated me for years because I haven't been able to identify them. I know something about them, but not enough, and I am looking for some help.

What follows are nine photos where there is just not enough information available to solve the mystery—but first, the now-identified 1932 photo:

GEORGE MICHAEL is the Emmy Award-winnng host of *The George Michael Sports Machine*, the longest-running sports show in syndication. The show made its national debut in September, 1984. Since that time, George Michael has won over 30 Emmys, including the national Emmy for "Best Sports Show Host." George and his Emmy Award-winning sportswriter wife Pat Lackman live in Comus, Maryland. The Michaels own a 160-acre ranch, where they have produced several world-champion quarter horses.

SOLVING THE 1932 YANKEES MYSTERY

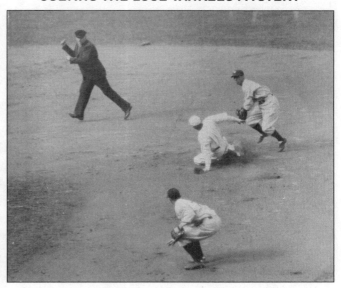

WHAT WE KNEW

1. It's the Yankees.
2. The photo was taken before April 18,1932 (a date stamped on back of the photo reads May 18, 1932).
3. A clean infield indicates that it is early in the game.
4. The Yankee in the foreground is Jack Saltzgaver, who played in the early games of 1932 against the Athletics and Red Sox.
5. From other photos, I know the shortstop is Lyn Lary.

WHAT WE DIDN'T KNOW

1. Whether the Yankees were playing the Athletics or the Red Sox (both teams wore similar uniforms in 1932).
2. The identity of the runner.

THE ANSWER

Several SABR members pointed to a key clue; the "sock" on the runners left sleeve which is barely distinguishable. Now knowing the runner is a Red Sox player, I studied the early 1932 games for the Yankees and Red Sox and found the play on April 16, 1932. The umpire is Bill Dinneen. Dave Smith of Retrosheet verified the facts: "In the first inning of April 16, 1932, Max Bishop was forced at second base."

CASE CLOSED

#1: THE SENATORS MYSTERY

This photo is very frustrating because there are only a few clues.

WHAT WE KNOW

1. The location is Griffith Stadium in Washington, D.C.
2. The crowd indicates a sellout game.
3. The catcher appears to be Muddy Ruel.
4. The socks worn by the Senators pitcher appear to match Senators uniforms from 1924 or 1925.

WHAT WE DON'T KNOW

Who is the pitcher? Is it Allan Russell? Who is the umpire? Who is the runner? Does the runner play for the Red Sox? Or is he wearing a Browns uniform?

I rate this photo as a "10" on the difficulty scale because we can't see the runner's face or the front of his uniform.

#2: THE DODGERS MYSTERY

This is a photo that is more than 80 years old, with no identification other than the fact that it is a "Pacific & Atlantic" photo. After a lot of research, it still remains a mystery.

WHAT WE KNOW

1. The only road uniform that matches up with what the catcher is wearing is one for the Phillies.
2. The runner appears to be out as the catcher has the ball in his hand.
3. The undisturbed chalk line tells us that it was early in the game or it was a very low scoring game.
4. The runner plays for Brooklyn. The Dodgers wore this style uniform from 1918 to 1922.
5. The location is Ebbets Field.

WHAT WE DON'T KNOW

Who is the Dodger runner? Who is the Phillies catcher?

If we can determine who the players are, then this photo will be a library research project to determine when the game was played, and when the play happened.

#3: THE HOOPER MYSTERY

Every once in a while comes a photo that is absolutely confounding. This is such a photo.

WHAT WE KNOW

1. This is a clear photo of Harry Hooper of the Red Sox sliding into third base at Fenway Park. Also, the Red Sox uniform with a solid white hat was worn from 1912 to 1920. If Hooper is wearing a pinstripe uniform, it is from the 1912–1915 period, but it is not clear that the uniform features pinstripes.

2. The white above the stripe on the stocking was worn from 1912 to 1919.

WHAT WE DON'T KNOW

For what team does the third baseman play?

There is no known uniform from 1912–1919 that matches the one he is wearing. Also, *who is he?* Some researchers believe they see a Yankee "N.Y." lettering on the first-base coach's uniform—the Yankees wore this type of home uniform in 1915 and 1916.

This photo rates a "10" on the difficulty scale because we don't have a clear view of the front of the uniform.

#4: A JACKIE ROBINSON MYSTERY

The difficulty in identifying this photo is in trying to figure out who the runner is being forced at second base.

WHAT WE KNOW

1. Jackie Robinson playing second base in a home uniform. So the game is obviously being played at Ebbets Field.

2. The Phillies uniform is pre-1950. Since Robinson played second base in the 1948 and 1949 seasons, this photo must have been taken during that period.

WHAT WE DON'T KNOW

Who is the Phillies runner sliding into second base? Identifying this photo seems to require the expertise of a researcher who *really* knows the Phillies.

#5: THE CUBS MYSTERY

I have had this photo for more than 10 years, and have never been able to confidently identify the Cubs second baseman. Many Cubs experts have looked at this photo without a definitive identification.

WHAT WE KNOW

1. The second baseman is a Chicago Cub at Wrigley Field.

2. The runner is wearing a pre-1951 Cardinals uniform (The Cardinals wore the striped sleeve up to 1951). Whitey Kurowski wore #1 for the Cardinals at this time, and since there is no health patch on his sleeve, the photo must have been taken between 1946 and 1950.

WHAT WE DON'T KNOW

Who is the Cubs second baseman?

The Cubs never wore their stockings like this between 1946 and 1950, which seems to contradict the health patch conclusion; so *what year was this photo taken?* If anyone can pinpoint the year of of the photo—and the identity of the Cubs second baseman—research can then be completed.

#6: THE DiMAGGIO MYSTERY

This is one of those photos in which a missing fact has halted the research as to when the action took place.

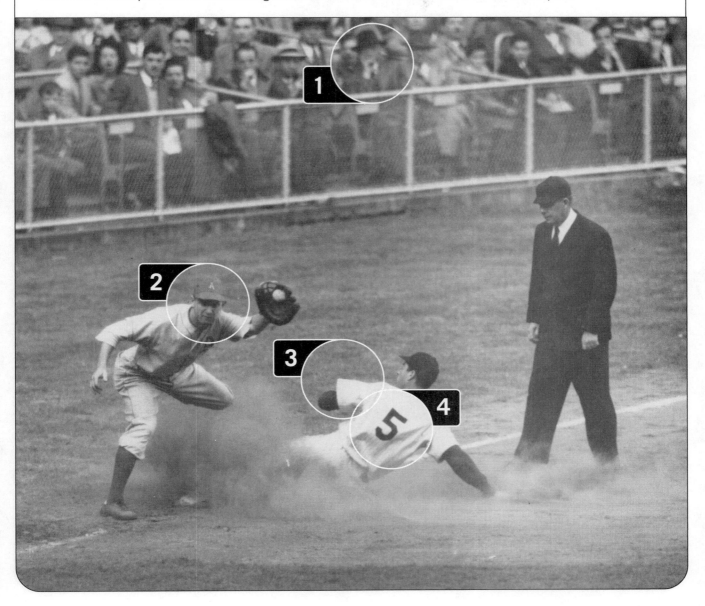

WHAT WE KNOW

1. The clothing worn by the fans indicate chilly weather, so the game may have been played in Spring or Fall.
2. The Athletics third baseman is Hank Majeski.
3. Since there are no patches on the players' sleeves, this photo must have been taken between 1946 and 1950.
4. The runner sliding into third base is Joe DiMaggio; since he's wearing the home whites, the game was played in Yankee Stadium.

WHAT WE DON'T KNOW

Who is the umpire?

Until the umpire can be positively identified, it is not possible to say with certainty when this play took place. Joe DiMaggio looks like he was safe on the play, but when it happened remains a mystery.

#7: THE GIANTS MYSTERY

This photo requires the knowledge of someone who really knows the prewar New York Giants.

WHAT WE KNOW

1. The Cubs infielder is Dick Bartell.
2. The patch on the Cubs uniform indicates that this photo was taken in 1939.
3. The uniforms indicate it is a home game for the Giants played at the Polo Grounds.
4. The clean dirt on the base paths indicates the play happened early in the game. The runner is obviously out on a force out.

WHAT WE DON'T KNOW

Who is the Giants runner?

Once the runner has been identified, it is then possible to go through game accounts and determine when the play occurred.

#8: THE CARDINALS MYSTERY

There are almost as many clues as there are questions in this photo. Yet after years and years of research, its identification has eluded me.

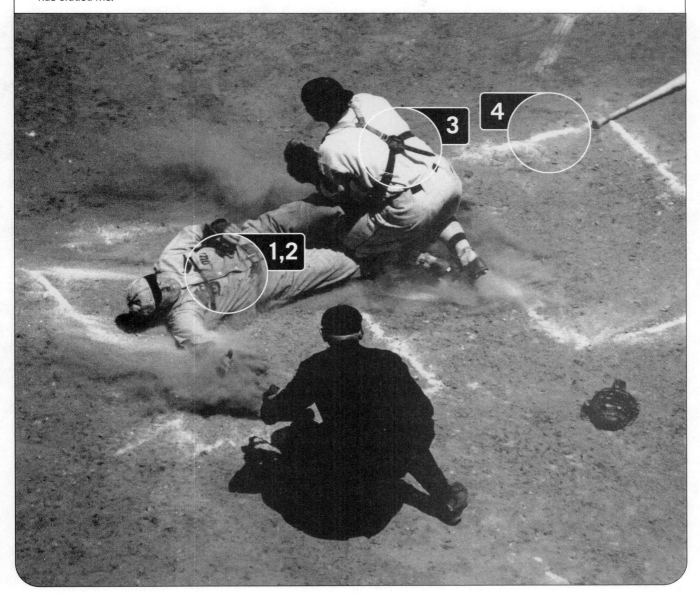

WHAT WE KNOW

1. The uniforms indicate that the Cardinals are playing the Braves in Boston.
2. It is 1930 or 1931. The Cardinals had "St. Louis" on their uniform as opposed to "Cardinals" in 1930 and 1931.
3. The Braves started wearing numbers on their uniforms in 1932, so this photo is pre-1932.
4. The undisturbed batters-box chalk marks indicate this is early in the game 1930–1931.

WHAT WE DON'T KNOW

Who is the Cardinals runner? Who is the Braves catcher? Who is the umpire?

Once we have this information, it will be possible to research the Cardinals–Braves games in 1930 and 1931 to determine how, and when, this play occurred.

#9: THE RED SOX MYSTERY

So much about this photo is obvious, but so much about this photo is unknown.

WHAT WE KNOW

1. The umpire is George Moriarty.
2. The uniforms indicate that the Yankees are playing the Red Sox at Fenway Park.
3. Because there are no patches on the sleeve, it is probably from 1938, 1940, or 1941.

WHAT WE DON'T KNOW

Who is the Red Sox runner? Who is the Yankees first baseman?

Until the players in this photo are positively identified, the research on when this play occurred is at a standstill. If you are a detective and think you can help solve these cold-case mysteries, I need your assistance. Send any information to: George Michael, 1201 Sugarloaf Mountain Road, Comus, MD 20842 or email George.Michael@nbc.com.

SCOTT A. SCHLEIFSTEIN

A Small, Yet Momentous Gesture

Bruce Markusen's *Baseball's Last Dynasty: Charlie Finley's Oakland A's*, an entertaining account of the club that dominated the American League West in the early to mid 1970s, has the following piece of trivia about the 1972 A's team: "Later in the year, when terrorists murdered several Israeli athletes during the Olympic Games, [Ken] Holtzman, [Mike] Epstein and Reggie Jackson wore black armbands in tribute to those who had been slain."[1] Fascinated, I wanted to find out as much as I could about this gesture.

Why?

Why did this interest me so? As a fellow Jew, I deeply admired Ken Holtzman and Mike Epstein for choosing to don the black armbands. In this "enlightened" age of moral ambiguity, when celebrity is too often and too easily mistaken for character, their act impressed me in its sincerity and visibility. Surely, no one would have faulted Holtzman or Epstein if they chose *not* to acknowledge the tragedy at the Munich Olympics. After all, they were baseball players, not statesmen or rabbis. Furthermore, Major League Baseball had already officially recognized the Olympic tragedy with the observance of a moment of silence prior to all major league games on September 6, 1972.[2] Beyond this, on the job, both Holtzman and Epstein faced the unique pressures of a hotly contested pennant race. Notwithstanding all this, Holtzman and Epstein remembered what was truly important—their Jewish identity. Through their actions Holtzman and Epstein powerfully and unequivocally affirmed the significance of their faith as an integral part of their lives. In this way the black armbands augmented as well as honored the legacy of Jewish ballplayers Hank Greenberg and Sandy Koufax, who refused to play on Yom Kippur.[3]

Reggie Jackson's participation was more of a puzzle. Not being Jewish, why did Jackson choose to do this? If the decision of Holtzman and Epstein to wear the black armband can be fairly characterized as "unanticipated," for Reggie to do so is well-nigh unfathomable.

SCOTT A. SCHLEIFSTEIN has been a baseball fan all his life and has made it his personal mission to visit every major league ballpark. When not following the fortunes of the New York Yankees from Yankee stadium or another ballpark, Scott finds time to practice promotion marketing law in New York.

Growing up in central New Jersey in the late 1970s, I loved the New York Yankees, and Jackson was part-man, part-myth to me. I marveled at Reggie's seemingly limitless self-confidence, his strong sense of conviction as well as his amazing feats in clutch situations. Who could forget his electrifying performance in the 1977 World Series against the Los Angeles Dodgers?[4]

The Game

On September 6, 1972, the Oakland A's played the Chicago White Sox at Chicago's Comiskey Park. Coming into the game, the A's led the American League's West Division by three games over the second-place White Sox. This two-game series would directly and significantly impact the pennant race,[5] as a White Sox sweep would reduce the A's lead to only one game. Conversely, if the A's took both games, their lead would swell to five games, and if they split the series, the lead would remain at three games.[6] Major League Baseball's playoff format in the 1970s amplified the games' importance: in each league the winner of the West Division would meet the winner of the East Division in a best three-of-five game series to determine which team would represent the league in the World Series. Unlike today, there was no "wild card" playoff berth. A lot was on the line here, and, if anything, the pressure was on the A's to win. In 1971, the A's won the American League West handily by 16 games, only to be swept by the American League East winners, the Baltimore Orioles, in the American League Championship series.[7]

A's manager Dick Williams started southpaw Ken Holtzman, who had a record of 15–11 coming into the game. Tom Bradley (13–12) was the White Sox starter. Reggie Jackson started in center field and batted fourth; Mike Epstein played first base and hit fifth.

For the record, Oakland won by the count of 9–1. Despite a shaky first inning in which he yielded a run, Holtzman notched a complete-game victory.[8] Epstein went 3-for-4, with two runs scored, while Jackson was 3-for-5 (one of the hits being his 23rd home run of the season), with three runs scored and one RBI. Holtzman was hitless.

Players' Reflections

In a telephone conversation on September 14, 2004, Mike Epstein spoke to me about the incident, cautioning that his memories may have become blurred by the passage of over 30 years. He did recall seeing a television news report of the massacre of the

Israeli Olympic contingent prior to the game on September 6. "We [Epstein and Holtzman] walked around town for hours" and were "in shock."[9] Epstein did not remember whether the idea came from himself or Ken Holtzman, but the two players agreed that wearing the black armband "was the right thing to do" and "expressed solidarity [with the Jewish people]."[10]

After the game Epstein explained his actions to the press as follows: "It hit us like a ton of bricks. Of course, Ken and I are Jewish, but I'd feel the same way if it was any other team. The Olympics are supposed to foster international brotherhood."[11]

Ken Holtzman

Ken Holtzman's memory was consistent with that of Epstein's. In a telephone call on September 7, 2004, Holtzman emphasized to me that wearing the armband "was the appropriate thing to do" and that the two players "decided on their own" to do it.[12] For his part, although a reporter described him as "still shaken" by the massacre of the Israeli Olympic contingent, Holtzman declined to discuss the tragedy in post-game interviews.[13]

The reasoning behind Reggie Jackson's participation is unclear. Ron Bergman's account of the game in the September 7, 1972 edition of the *Oakland Tribune* attributes this quote to Jackson: "I don't think the Olympics should go on after those killings. I know that if somebody assassinated a couple of our players here in Chicago - some nut who didn't want us to win - I wouldn't want to play the rest of the season, World Series, playoffs, nothing."[14]

Since attempts to arrange an interview with Jackson proved unsuccessful, I can only guess as to his intent. Holtzman indicated that neither he nor Epstein knew beforehand that Jackson would also wear a black armband.[15] When discussing his tenure with the Oakland A's in his autobiography (*Reggie: The Autobiography*), Jackson does not specifically address this episode.[16]

Still, at the risk of engaging in pop psychology, Jackson's autobiography seems to contain several clues as to his mindset. In various places Jackson seems to go out of his way to show respect for Jews and the Jewish faith generally. Perhaps most tellingly, in discussing the underlying rancor and bile in the New York Yankees clubhouse in 1977, Jackson relays how one day, in March, several of his teammates as well as the manager at the time (Billy Martin) "were making Jewish jokes about [Ken] Holtzman." Jackson added that he found the incident "disturbing" and "walked away."[17] True, Jackson did not intercede on Holtzman's behalf. However, such a confrontation might have been too much to expect, as Jackson himself was not accepted by his new teammates: from Jackson's perspective, he "wasn't one of *them*."[18]

At another point of the book, Jackson recalls that, as a youth living in the suburbs of Philadelphia, "a lot of my friends were Jewish."[19] Beyond this, Jackson looks to "Jewish people," among other ethnic groups, as a paradigm in combating the racism inherent in American society.[20]

Perhaps, when taken together, these statements signify a special sensitivity on Jackson's part toward the Jewish people; perhaps not. Maybe, as an African American man who was stung by racism and hate in his own life,[21] Jackson felt compelled to make a public statement by wearing the armband.

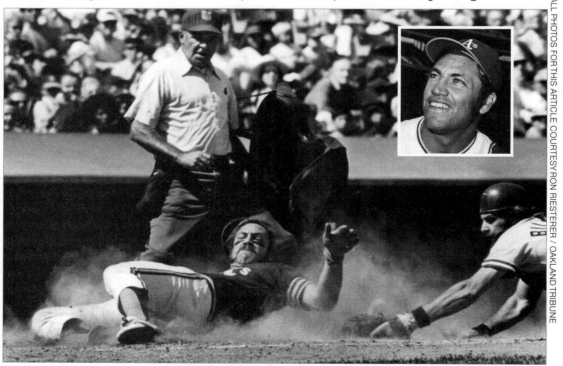

Mike Epstein sliding, inset

Reggie Jackson

During our conversation Epstein expressed skepticism as to Jackson's motives, suggesting that "Reggie capitalized on it,"[22] in an attempt to garner more attention for himself from the media. To this point, Epstein added that, unlike Jackson, he and Holtzman harbored no such ulterior motives.

When queried as to the reaction of their Oakland A's teammates to their actions, Holtzman commented that they "understood," "being intelligent guys."[23] My interview with A's third baseman Sal Bando confirmed Holtzman's generous assessment of his teammates. Although he did not specifically remember "the stripe,"[24] Bando thanked me for sharing a draft of this article with him. Bando reflected that, if asked to do so, he "would have worn one"[25] and wondered aloud, "Why didn't the rest of us [also wear a black armband]?"[26]

Notwithstanding his reputation as a hard-nosed, no-nonsense baseball man,[27] A's skipper Dick Williams supported the players' decision to wear the armbands. "I thought [White Sox manager] Chuck Tanner showed some class by not saying anything about the armbands. There could have been a flareup because Kenny [Holtzman] is a pitcher and he was wearing one. I'm all for it. I understand. I don't see how the Olympics can go on. I think the killings were a terrible thing, a terrible thing."[28] Williams added that, if requested to do so, he also would have worn a black armband.[29]

Every once in a while a person or act weaves together the various, seemingly unrelated strands of your life into a beautiful whole, ultimately renewing your faith in your convictions. Learning of the powerful gesture of Ken Holtzman, Mike Epstein, and Reggie Jackson on September 6, 1972, touched me in this extraordinary way. Judaism, Zionism, and baseball all seemed to dramatically and magically coalesce, if only for a single moment.

Notes

1. Bruce Markusen, *Baseball's Last Dynasty: Charlie Finley's Oakland A's* (Indianapolis, IN: Masters Press, 1998), at p.108.

2. United Press, "Baseball Observes Moment for Israelis," *San Francisco Chronicle*, September 7, 1972, p. 63.

3. For a discussion of Sandy Koufax's decision not to pitch Game 1 of the World Series on October 6, 1965 as it fell on Yom Kippur, see Jane Leavy's *Sandy Koufax: A Lefty's Legacy* (New York: HarperCollins Publishers Inc., 2002), at pp. 181–185. More recently, Arizona Diamondbacks' outfielder Shawn Green, when he was on the Los Angeles Dodgers, chose not to play in a crucial late season game against the San Francisco Giants on Yom Kippur 2004 (i.e., September 25, 2004), as he had the previous year. See "Grand Slam by Feliz Lifts Giants' Postseason Hopes," *The New York Times*, September 26, 2004, p.5 (Sports Section).

4. In Game 6, Jackson hit home runs against three different Dodger pitchers, all on their first offering. See Ron Smith, *The Sporting News Chronicle of Baseball* (New York: BDD Illustrated Books, 1993), at p. 271.

5. A's third baseman Sal Bando and Ken Holtzman each separately acknowledged the importance of the Game to the *Chicago Tribune's* Bob Logan. While asserting that the series was not "decisive," Bando allowed that "Still, we couldn't let them beat us two straight here." Holtzman noted that "this was a big series" for the A's. Bob Logan, "Games Aren't Decisive Yet, Explains Oakland's Bando," *Chicago Tribune*, September 7, 1972, Section 3 at p. 1.

6. The White Sox and A's split the series, with the White Sox winning the second game 6 - 0. See www.baseballlibrary.com.

7. Smith, *The Sporting News Chronicle of Baseball*, at pp. 236–237.

8. In critiquing his pitching performance for Bob Logan of the *Chicago Tribune*, Holtzman indicated that after some "early control trouble," he had "good stuff." Logan, "Games Aren't Decisive Yet, Explains Oakland's Bando," *Chicago Tribune*, September 7, 1972, Section 3 at p. 1.

9. Telephone interview with Mike Epstein, conducted by Scott A. Schleifstein, September 14, 2004.

10. Ibid.

11. Thomas Rogers, "Personalities: A Chin Is Exposed," *The New York Times*, September 8, 1972, at p.24.

12. Telephone Interview with Ken Holtzman, conducted by Scott A. Schleifstein, September 7, 2004.

13. Logan, "Games Aren't Decisive Yet, Explains Oakland's Bando," *Chicago Tribune*, September 7, 1972, Section 3 at p. 1.

14. Ron Bergman, "Athletics Greedy for More," *Oakland Tribune*, September 7, 1972, at p.37.

15. Telephone Interview with Ken Holtzman, September 7, 2004.

16. Jackson with Lupica, *Reggie - The Autobiography*, Chapters 4 & 5, pp. 66 - 101.

17. Ibid., p.149.

18. Jackson with Lupica, *Reggie - The Autobiography*, at p.149. Elsewhere, Jackson notes that 1977 "would turn out to be the worst year of my life" and "If I'd had any idea what it was going to be like in New York, I never would've signed. To this day, with all I accomplished on the field in New York - and off the field - I wouldn't have signed with them in a million years." As if the reader still harbored any doubts on this point, Jackson adds "I wish I had worn Dodger blue." See *Reggie - The Autobiography*, at p. 149, 151 and 152. Quite contradictorily, Jackson currently works for the New York Yankees. Somehow, over the past twenty years, Jackson must have drastically changed his feelings toward the Yankees.

19. Ibid., p.134.

20. Ibid., pp.129–130

21. See Chapter 3 of *Reggie - The Autobiography* (pp. 56 - 65), where Jackson describes the racism he encountered playing for the A's minor league affiliate in Birmingham, Alabama.

22. Telephone interview with Mike Epstein, September 14, 2004.

23. Ibid. Reggie Jackson, in his autobiography *Reggie - The Autobiography*, confirms Holtzman's assessment of the sophistication of their teammates on the 1972 Oakland A's. As further discussed below, in describing the anti-Semitic behavior of certain members of the 1977 New York Yankees, Jackson contrasted the small-mindedness of the Yankees clubhouse with the relatively more-enlightened thinking of the A's teams on which he had played: "It [anti-Semitic jokes] just hadn't been done in Oakland. It felt strange. Disturbing." Reggie Jackson with Mike Lupica, *Reggie - The Autobiography* (New York: Villard Books, 1984), at p.149.

24. Email communication from Sal Bando to Scott A. Schleifstein, on March 26, 2005.

25. Telephone interview with Sal Bando, March 29, 2005.

26. Ibid.

27. In *Reggie - The Autobiography*, Jackson alternately describes Williams as "macho" and "tough" (p.96).

28. Bergman, "Athletics Greedy for More," at p.37.

29. Ibid.

The Best Post-Season Ever
"Wild" Bill Serena's 1947 Batting Feats

You can whiffle all you want about Reggie Jackson's 18 post-season home runs. Big deal—it took him 77 games and 281 at-bats to reach that mark. More impressive is Mantle's 18 in 65 games and 230 at-bats—all hit in the World Series. I am even more impressed by the Babe's 15 in the 36 games and 118 at-bats where he was not playing as a pitcher. Give him Mickey's 230 at-bats and the Babe hits 29 homers. Give him Reggie's 281 at-bats, and he hits 36 (or, conversely, Mr. October hits eight in the Babe's 118 at-bats). All this is conjecture, however. To find the best post-season ever, read on . . .

For the Lubbock Hubbers of the West Texas–New Mexico League, 1947 was a banner year. Under the leadership of their playing manager, Carl "Jack" Sullivan, they stormed through their season, finishing a torrid 99–41 and setting league records in wins, games ahead of the second-place team (14), and finishing with the second-best winning percentage in league history, .707, a mere one percentage point behind the record set a year earlier by Abilene (97–40).

The Hubbers finished second in batting at .315 and first in slugging with a .533 mark. Their on-base percentage was a robust .398 figure, they hit 210 home runs, scored runs at 8.9 per game, and allowed the fewest runs per game, 5.7. This means they scored over three runs a game more than they surrendered, a sure recipe for a .700 season.

In Table 1 you will notice that six of the league's eight teams hit over .300 and had an on-base percentage of over .400, and that six had slugging averages of .500 or better. The Hubbers pounded out 596 extra-base hits, a mighty 4.25 per game. Just how good was the hitting in the '47 edition of the WT–NML? A .355 batting average would have gotten you 10th, as would 140 runs, 129 RBI, 44 doubles, and 187 hits. All this in just a 140-game season!

Conversely, how bad was the pitching? Well, a 4.96 ERA would have gotten you the 10th and final spot on the league's top 10 charts. Eleven qualifying pitchers, on the other hand, had ERAs over 6.00—and two were over 9.00. One pitcher, "Wild" Bill Hair of Borger, has his own chapter in the It's Better to Be Lucky Than Good encyclopedia. He compiled a 9.21 ERA, allowing 19.5 BR/9,

and gave up a cool 11 runs total every nine innings and yet he finished the season at 15–13.[1]

The starting eight for Lubbock consisted of first baseman Virgil Richardson, second baseman–manager "Jack" Sullivan, third baseman Jack McAlexander, shortstop Bill Serena, left fielder Pat Rooney, center fielder Jack Cerin, right fielder Ernest "Zeke" Wilemon, catcher Cliff Dooley, and outfielder/catcher Clem "Co" Cola.

The First Round of Playoffs

In round one, the heavy lumber of Lubbock unlimbered on the hapless staff of the Lamesa Lobos. It was a mismatch.

Game one was played at Lubbock to a crowd of about 5,000. The hitting stars for the Hubbers were Jack Cerin, who went 2-for-4 with a home run and three RBI, and catcher Dooley, who hit two triples and added three RBI of his own. Our Bill was 2-for-4 with two runs and an RBI. The game, which took a seemingly interminable one hour and 37 minutes, ended in an 8–1 Lubbock victory. Paul Hinrichs, who had gone 18–5 on the year and who had led the league in ERA with a 3.34 mark, went the distance for the win.

Game two was the closest in the series, with Lubbock squeaking by 7–5. Cerin had another good game, hitting two doubles and driving in another run. Serena went 2-for-3 with a solo homer. This game dragged on for two hours and 19 minutes.

The slumbering (they had hit only .298 for the first two games with a measly 15 runs) Lubbock bats finally awoke in game three, with the Hubbers smacking 20 hits and with 18 runs scurrying across the plate. Richardson and Wilemon each cracked four hits (with Wilemon scoring four runs), and Dooley hit three doubles and drove in three runs. Serena's bat also woke up, as he had a double and two home runs, plating four runs. Pitcher Heinz added three RBI in his own cause.

Game four for the Lobos was, unfortunately, more of the same—only worse, with Lubbock trouncing them, 23–3, before around 1,000 dispirited Lobo lovers. It was close for three innings, both teams having scored once in the first. But the Hubbers scored 11 times in the middle three stanzas and 11 more times in the final three to put a halt to any Lobo dreams of a big championship series payday.

Cerin, Rooney, and Sullivan each collected four hits, with Cerin and Rooney also adding four runs apiece. Dooley added two more doubles (giving him five for the four games series), and drove in

JAMIE SELKO lives where the pyramid meets the eye. His wife and six children, who share the same coordinates on the space-time continuum but not the same reality, make sure that he is not allowed to run with sharp objects.

Table 1. West Texas–New Mexico team batting

	G	AB	H	R	OR	TB	2B	3B	HR	RBI	BB*	SB	BA	SA	OB%	RPG	ORPG
Albuquerque	138	4989	1601	1096	926	2494	264	121	129	973	618	60	.321	.500	.432	7.9	6.7
Lubbock	140	5023	1582	1247	794	2675	309	77	210	1116	808	115	.315	.533	.398	8.9	5.7
Pampa	139	4948	1536	1004	975	2226	323	32	101	862	596	62	.310	.450	.413	7.2	7.0
Borger	140	5034	1547	1117	1336	2597	337	49	205	901	730	67	.307	.516	.412	8.0	9.5
Amarillo	140	4986	1529	1135	889	2552	318	42	207	1039	770	59	.307	.512	.426	8.1	6.4
Lamesa	139	4889	1472	1032	1066	2236	311	36	127	895	766	111	.301	.457	.409	7.4	7.7
Clovis	139	4984	1445	927	1422	2127	278	34	112	827	702	61	.290	.427	.391	6.7	10.2
Abilene	139	4845	1345	882	1032	2005	265	34	109	764	759	102	.278	.414	.376	6.3	7.4
League	**1114**	**39698**	**12057**	**8440**	**8440**	**18912**	**2405**	**425**	**1200**	**7377**	**5749**	**637**	**.304**	**.476**	**.413**	**7.6**	**7.6**

Table 2. Lubbock hitting

	G	AB	H	R	TB	2B	3B	HR	RBI	BB*	SB	BA	SA	OB%
Virgil Richardson, 1B	99	368	124	107	244	31	1	29	113	93	4	.337	.663	.471
Carl "Jack" Sullivan, 2B	125	516	183	140	315	36	18	20	120	59	18	.355	.610	.421
Bill Serena, SS	137	506	189	183	421	43	9	57	190	146	26	.374	.832	.514
Frank McAlexander, 3B	90	350	115	81	175	22	4	10	65	50	2	.329	.500	.413
Ernest "Zeke" Wilemon, OF	106	448	152	97	233	32	5	13	96	50	10	.339	.520	.406
Jack Cerin, OF	120	505	150	126	236	24	4	18	101	46	8	.297	.467	.356
Pat Rooney, OF	111	439	144	116	202	21	11	5	60	80	5	.328	.460	.432
Cliff Dooley, C	121	449	142	114	244	33	6	19	102	60	22	.316	.543	.397
Clem Cola, UT	103	337	110	85	211	19	5	24	91	99	3	.326	.626	.479
The Regulars		**3918**	**1309**	**1049**	**2281**	**261**	**63**	**195**	**938**	**683**	**98**	**.334**	**.582**	**.433**
The Team	**140**	**5023**	**1582**	**1247**	**2675**	**309**	**77**	**210**	**1116**	**808**	**115**	**.315**	**.533**	**.398**

*Includes HBP

four runs, giving him 10 RBI, the same number Cerin (who had six in this game) had. Serena was 3-for-6 with three runs, two RBI, and a homer. Only the starting eight (Cola made no appearances in this series) and the pitchers played. The starters compiled the following stats: 62–138 for a .449 BA, an .812 SA, and a .596 OB%. They hit 12 doubles, four triples, and 10 home runs, scored 53 runs, and drove in 49. (If one includes the pitchers, the averages fall a bit to .416, .727, and .491). Lubbock scored 56 runs—14 a game— and gave up 18 (4.5). The Hubbers drew 22 walks while going down on strikes only 12 times (their pitchers walked 16 and struck out 36 (including nine by Jerry Ahrens in game three and 14 by Eulis Rosson in the clincher).

The Championship Series vs. Amarillo

The headline after the first game against the Gold Sox read, "Hey, this ain't Lamesa." It certainly appeared that that was correct, as Lubbock fell, 7–0, behind the four-hit pitching of Bill Lonergan. Lonergan had led the WT–NM in Ks with 216 (in 196 innings) and finished fourth in ERA with a 3.99 mark. His 11.46 BR/9 (base runners per nine innings) had just beaten out the Hubbers' Hinrichs for the league lead in that department.

Amarillo finished second, 14 games behind Lubbock, during the regular season, and boasted the second stingiest staff in their league. It also featured a one–two punch straight out of Minor League Heaven—"Bad" Bob Crues and big (6'5", 235, one of the two or three largest players in baseball at the time) Joe

Bauman. Crues hit 52 homers and drove in 178 runs for the Gold Sox in 1947, and the next year he would hit 69 homers and drive in an incredible 254 runs. He added 45 doubles amongst his 210 hits for 427 total bases in '47, and had a .772 slugging average. Bauman slugged .727 thanks to 38 homers and 45 doubles of his own. He walked 151 times, and compiled a .526 on-base percentage. Seven years later Joe would launch 72 homers in a 140-game season playing for the Roswell Rockets in the Longhorn League.

The estimated 5,000 Hubber fans in attendance at the game must have been disappointed to see their hometown heroes fall in such a stunning fashion. All they could do was hope that tomorrow would be a better day.

And better day it was, as the Hubbers evened the series at a game apiece, winning 6–4 behind three home runs, one each by Cerin, Dooley, and our Bill, and despite 11 K's, courtesy of Gold Sox starter Tom Spears. Spears had been a surprise starter, as he finished the season with a 12–10 record despite an ERA of 6.24. Serena got only the one hit, and pulled off a rarity afield. He played the entire game at short and had no official fielding chances.

The headline for game three, played before the second-largest crowd in Amarillo baseball history, 4,230 fans, read, "Sox Allee Samee Like Clovis," no doubt in reference to Lubbock's five doubles (three by Serena) and five homers en route to a 21–11 rout of Amarillo.

The Hubbers collected 23 hits, five by Bill, who added a homer to his doubles, giving him four extra-base hits for the day. He had four RBI, but was topped in that department by manager Sullivan's five. Richardson, who hit a pair of homers in the game, scored five runs. Leonard Heinz, who had become the first 20-game winner for Lubbock since Pat Ralsh did so in 1940, struck out 10 before being lifted in the seventh when he weakened and allowed five runs to score.

Attendance was down for game four of the series in Amarillo, the reason stated as being the high school football game between the Amarillo Sandies and the Childress Bobcats, so the home-town fans missed out on a thrilling 13–8 Gold Sox win (Amarillo came from behind twice, 3–0 in the first and 5–3 in the third, and Lubbock drew to within one, 8–9, in the fifth. Serena was 1–4 with two runs and a double, and he also had an RBI. The game, which featured 21 runs, 23 hits, 11 walks, and four errors, lasted one hour and 58 minutes.

The Hubber bats awoke for the last game in Amarillo, pounding out 20 hits and scoring 16 runs (oddly, they went down 10 times on strikes but drew not a single walk). Amarillo was victimized by six errors, and the game, which produced 23 runs (Amarillo scored seven times), 32 hits, those six Gold Sox errors, and eight walks by Lubbock pitchers, took three hours and one minute to play.

No Lubbock player got more than three hits (four got that number), and only Rooney scored as many as three runs. Leadoff man McAlexander had four RBI. Serena was 2-for-6 with two home runs and three RBI in the rout, which actually it wasn't, as the game was tied 7–7 after regulation. After a scoreless 10th, which featured Amarillo loading the bases with one out in the bottom of the inning but not being able to score, the Hubbers exploded for nine runs in the top of the 11th, including a grand slam by McAlexander.

The final game of the series was played before 5,200 fans in Lubbock. This one was another extra-inning thriller, one which found the home team down by two after one, and 3–4 after six. It was a sloppy game, with seven errors, including four by the winners. There were no standout performances by any Hubbers, as only Sullivan had as many as three hits. Serena had a solo homer. To show his appreciation of his team's efforts, club president Sam Rosenthal sent the team on what was called a "two day scenic junket" through New Mexico at the club's expense.

So, how did Serena fare during the championship round and in the playoffs overall? He hit only .370 in round two, but still managed to eke out a 1.074 slugging average. I believe that he received either three or four walks, which would give him an on-base percentage of either .433 or .452. Nine of his 10 hits were for extra bases, including five home runs. In the six games, he scored nine times and drove in 10 runs. He made two errors and fielded .935.

The team hit .327 and slugged .558 during the Amarillo series, averaging nine runs a game. Their on-base percentage was .374. They did manage to compile 28 extra-base hits for the six games, including 16 home runs. Manager Sullivan tied Serena for the series RBI lead with 10. (Big Joe Bauman hit .400 for the series with two doubles, three home runs (for an .840 slugging aver-

age), and 12 RBI. Bob Crues hit .560 with ten runs and ten RBI. He slugged .960, thanks to two doubles and three home runs).

Serena ended his year-long assault against WT–NM pitching with the following numbers:

G	AB	H	R	TB	2B	3B
147	551	207	201	470	47	9

HR	RBI	BB	BA	SA	OB%
66	218	155	.376	.853	.513

The Battle for the Class C Championship of Texas

In 1946, the various officials in the West Texas–New Mexico and East Texas league had decided to have a playoff to determine the Class C champion of Texas. The first such contest was an oily affair indeed, with the Pampa Oilers of the WT–NML emerging victorious over the Henderson Oilers in four straight games. The East Texas League changed its name to the Lone Star League for the 1947 season, and the Kilgore Drillers emerged as the champs, earning the right to face Lubbock.[2]

Kilgore, with a record of 78–60, had won the pennant in a very close race with Longview, Marshall, and Tyler. They defeated Tyler four games to none in the first round of the play-offs and then knocked off Marshall, four games to two, for the Lone Star championship.

Kilgore averaged .288 for the season with a .401 slugging average, a .372 on-base percentage, and 71 homers. They had averaged 6.7 runs a game during the season, and had four regulars who hit over .300. The Drillers had three players with over 100 runs and one player, Irv J. Clements (who was also their home run leader with 15), had at least 100 RBI. The Drillers' best pitcher, Robert Ross, finished the season 20–9 with a 3.88 ERA.

In what the *Lubbock Avalanche* called the "Little Dixie Series" the Hubbers won game one, 14–1, before a home crowd of 3,300 fans. Len Heinz handcuffed the Drillers on eight hits and a single walk, and the Hubs played flawless defense. Their hitters, meanwhile, had 14 hits and took advantage of two Driller errors and seven walks to score their runs.

A new face appeared in the Lubbock lineup, as "Co" Cola took over in left for Wilemon. Manager Sullivan had an excellent game, going 3-for-4 with four runs. The "California Clipper," as Serena was referred to in the paper, was 3-for-5 with a homer and six RBI. A three-run homer with two outs in the first was his feature blast.

Game two was "more of the same," as the *Avalanche* head-line read. A disappointing crowd of 3,000 turned out to see Royce "Buster" Mills, described as "chunky" and "a handy little fellow in the clutch" come through in relief to earn a 14–8 victory. The game had 26 hits, five errors, 12 walks, and three pitching changes,.

The Hubbers fell behind 5–0 in the first inning, and after six frames were down 8–3. All eight starters had at least one RBI for Lubbock, and they smacked eight extra-base hits, six doubles, a triple, and a home run by Serena (referred to as "Bambino" Bill in the game write-up).

Top: The Lubbock team. Bottom: Winning Hubbers with trophy.

The Hubbers prevailed in game three, 10–1, at home in front of approximately 3,100 fans in a game which took two hours and two minutes. The Drillers committed six more errors in this one, giving them 10 in the first three games (Lubbock was not that much better with six errors themselves). For the second day in a row, manager Sullivan contributed a double and a triple to the Lubbock cause. Serena had two hits, one a solo homer, drew the only Driller walk, and scored two runs. Wilemon was back in the lineup as Cola gave catcher Dooley a break.

From Lubbock the series was moved to Kilgore for however many games remained to be played to determine the Class C champion of Texas. Finances and distance dictated that the 2–3–2 format with which we are familiar was not feasible. It was almost 480 miles from ballpark to ballpark, and the bus ride would have taken 12 hours. By comparison, only one drive in the WT–NML was over 180 miles from Lubbock, that being the trip to Albuquerque, 320 miles away.

The reporters for the *Avalanche* were perspicacious in noting that the change in elevation from Lubbock to Kilgore would have an effect on the Hub hitters and give a marked advantage to curveball pitchers, an advantage absent in the high lonesome of West Texas: Lubbock sat at 3,195 feet, Kilgore at 333. The Hub hitters had undoubtedly benefited from the fact that they played in parks that averaged 3,436 feet above sea level (the lowest elevation in the league was found at Abilene, which at 1,791 feet was the only league town under 3,000 feet other than Lamesa, 2,997). The average Lone Star team sat at 411 feet, and only two towns (Jacksonville at 513' and Tyler at 558') were located even 500 feet above sea level.[3]

Sure enough, game four was a different kettle of fish, with the Hubbers going down 10–2 and managing to push only six hits past the defense. It was Lubbock's turn to be embarrassed afield also, as they committed five errors (two by Serena) to the Drillers' none. The Hubs went down 10 times via the K route in this one, and managed only two extra-base hits (a double by Richardson and a homer by Cola), whereas they had been averaging almost seven a game at home. Our Bill was a weak 1-for-4.

Apparently, the Hubs adjusted before game five, because they won that one in a walk, 8–1, to win the "Little Dixie Series," four games to one. Dooley was back in the lineup and had three doubles. Leadoff man McAlexander corralled four RBI. In his last game of the season, Bill "The California Clipper" Serena was 2-for-5, and one of those was his 70th homer of the year.

Lubbock hit .358, slugged .630, had a .432 on-base percentage in their final series, and smacked another 26 extra-base hits (15 doubles, two triples, and nine homers). While drilling the Drillers they averaged nine runs, while their pitchers surrendered only 4.2 runs per game. Their fielding was nothing to write home about, .923 with 16 errors (Serena fielded a very poor .829 with six errors, four of them in the two Kilgore games). Kilgore's field work was not much better at .923 with 14 errors.

Post-season Overview

The Lubbock non-pitchers hit .369 in their 15 post-season games, they had a .646 slugging average, and garnered a .436 on-base percentage They scored 152 runs, slammed 38 doubles, seven triples, and 35 home runs. Manager Sullivan scored 23 runs, drove in 22, and hit five doubles and four triples. Cerin scored 19 runs, drove in 16, and popped six homers to match his six doubles. Richardson hit seven homers and chalked up 18 RBI. Dooley hit nine doubles, two triples, four homers, and drove home 24 runs. None of these above-mentioned efforts are shabby, especially considering the fact that they were compiled over only 15 games and the fact that they were rung up not only on the cream of the opposition in their own league but also against the champion of another circuit.

Serena was 28-for-67 for a .418 batting average. I figured his on-base percentage with 12 walks (he may have had more, I am almost certain he did not have fewer), which comes out to .506, a pretty impressive figure. His slugging average is what reaches out and grabs you—71 total bases, good for a 1.060 mark. He scored 26 runs in those 15 games, drove in 28, and smashed 13 homers.

Serena's numbers got him promoted to Dallas of the Texas League in 1948, and then on to Buffalo the same year. His combined average was under .250. In 1949 he was back in Dallas, where he hit 28 homers, earning a promotion to the Chicago Cubs at the end of the year. He had a few bright moments in his six big league seasons, but none shone brighter than his 1947 post-season.

Notes

1. If I ever can find microfiche of Hair s season (which I have been trying to find for about ten years), I'd love to do an article on him also.

2. The Class C Championship series for the bragging rights in the Lone Star state would have one more edition. In 1948, the Amarillo Gold Sox, led by Bob Crues and his 69 homers and 254 RBI, would beat the Kilgore Drillers, led by manager Joe Kratcher's .433 batting average, four games to two. Thus, the WT–NML won all three of the series with a total of 12 wins against only three losses, an .800 winning percentage. In 1949, the Lone Star league reverted to the East Texas league, and no further Class C Championships were contested.

3. I asked stats legend Bill Weiss, whom I was fortunate enough to meet at a SABR convention and who was gracious enough to join us for lunch, about the stats in the WT–NML, and whether the park size or the altitude had the greater affect I was surprised when he told me that, in his opinion, it was mostly because of the type of ball in use in the league.

4. If you add his season stats to his post-season ones, Serena played in 152 games. His totals are 573 AB, 217 hits, 209 runs, 492 TB, 47 doubles, 9 triples, 70 home runs, 218 RBI, 159 walks, 27 steals, a .379 BA, an .859 SA, and a superb .514 on-base percentage.

Teams With Three 20-Game Winners

In the baseball season just concluded, Dontrelle Willis of the Florida Marlins, Chris Carpenter of the St. Louis Cardinals, Roy Oswalt of the Houston Astros and Bartolo Colon of the Los Angeles Angels were baseball's only 20 game winners. In 2004, Curt Schilling won 21 games for the Boston Red Sox, Johan Santana won 20 for the Minnesota Twins, and Roy Oswalt won 20 for the Houston Astros. No other pitcher won as many as 20 games in Major League Baseball. In a climate where wins are spread thin among pitching staffs populated by five starters, swingmen, middle relievers, setup men, and closers, a pitcher who wins 20 games during a single season has become a rarity.

Even more unusual is a team that fields multiple 20-game winners. In 2002, Red Sox Pedro Martinez and Derek Lowe were both 20-game winners, as were Diamondbacks Curt Schilling and Randy Johnson. There have been no such duos since.

Will we ever again see a staff with three 20-game winners during the same season? It has never been commonplace, but it is certainly not unprecedented. Since 1901, 23 teams have fielded staffs with at least three 20-game winners in a single season, eight from the NL, 14 from the AL, and one from the short-lived Federal League. It has not happened, however, since the 1973 Oakland Athletics garnered 21 wins each from Catfish Hunter and Ken Holtzman, and 20 from Vida Blue. Between 1901 and 1920, 15 teams had three pitchers notch at least 20 wins in the same season. Since then only eight have done so, and none have done so in over 30 years.

Although the A's with their three aces won the 1973 World Series over the New York Mets, fielding three 20-game winners is not a guarantee for a championship. In fact, of the 24 teams that have accomplished the feat since 1901, only 13 have won pennants, and of the 19 that played during a season in which there was a World Series, only five won the title. Two teams have had four 20-game winners on the roster, but neither won the World Series, and in fact, the 1920 White Sox did not even win the pennant, finishing two games behind the Indians. The 1971 Baltimore Orioles, with Dave McNally winning 21 and Pat Dobson, Mike Cuellar, and Jim Palmer victorious in 20 each, lost the World Series to the Pittsburgh Pirates, who had no 20-game winners. Of

TIM CONNAUGHTON is an attorney who lives in Troy, Michigan with his wife and two sons. His work has also been published in *The National Pastime* and *Motor City Sports Magazine*.

course, as expected, it's difficult to post a losing record with three 20-game winners on a staff, and no such team has ever finished worse than third.

The best winning percentage for a team with three 20-game winners in the 20th century was .741, posted by the 1902 Pirates, who were 103–36, and not only had three 20-game winners, but five pitchers with at least 15 wins to their credit. The worst winning percentage was .558, by the 1920 New York Giants, who finished in second place, seven games behind Brooklyn. The most successful franchise in history, the New York Yankees, has never finished a regular season with three 20-game winners, while the long-suffering fans of the Indians may be surprised to learn that Cleveland has had three 20-game winners in a single season five times, more than any other franchise.

Only two pitchers have been members of a staff with two other 20-game winners on the roster in three separate seasons. Christy Mathewson won at least 20 for the 1904, 1905, and 1913 New York Giants, and Early Wynn did the same for the Indians in 1951, 1952, and 1956. All of those teams fielded two additional 20-game winners.

The 23 teams since 1901 with at least three 20-game winners are listed below, with some noteworthy information on each.

1901 Philadelphia Phillies   83–57 (.593), Second place
The first team of the 20th century to do it, but just barely. The Phillies' Al Orth, Red Donahue, and Bill Duggleby each won exactly 20 games in 1901. Orth and Duggleby lost 12 apiece, while Donahue dropped 13.

1902 Pittsburgh Pirates   103–36 (.741), First place
The Pirates lapped the field in the National League in 1902. The newly founded American League had a detrimental impact on many NL clubs, luring quality players to the new league. The Pirates, however, remained unaffected, keeping their players almost without exception. The previous season's closest competition, the Phillies noted above, lost key offensive players in Elmer Flick and Ed Delahanty, as well as two of their three 20-game winners, Al Orth and Red Donahue, to the AL. Their third 20-game winner, Duggleby, jumped to the A's but returned to the Phillies in May. The Pirates' Jack Chesbro led the team, and the National League, with 28 wins, while Jesse Tannehill and Deacon Phillippe notched 20 each. The rotation had unusual depth for the time period. While many teams relied very heavily on their top two or three

pitchers, the Pirates, in addition to their three workhorses, also had Ed Doheny and Sam Leever with 16 and 15 wins respectively, while losing only four and seven respectively.

1903 Boston Americans   91–47 (.659), First place

Boston was led by Cy Young, who at age 36 led the league in wins (28), and winning percentage (.757). Bill Dinneen was 21–13, and Long Tom Hughes chipped in with 20 wins against only seven defeats. Boston beat Pittsburgh in the first ever American League versus National League World Series, five games to three. Young and Dinneen combined to pitch an astounding 69 of 71 World Series innings, while Hughes threw only two innings.

1903 Chicago Cubs   82–56 (.594), Third place

The 1903 Cubs' staff was one of only four with at least three 20-game winners without a Hall of Famer among them. Bob Wicker, who began the season with St. Louis, was 20–9. Jack Weimer finished 20–8, and Jack Taylor led the staff with 21 wins, but also lost 14. Taylor, Weimer, and Wicker combined for a 61–31 record, a winning percentage of .663. By comparison, the rest of the staff won only about 45% of its decisions, for a combined record of 21–25.

1904 Boston Americans   95–59 (.617), First place

The Americans repeated the feat in 1904, but Jesse Tannehill replaced Long Tom Hughes in the triumvirate. Tannehill finished the year with a 21–11 mark while Cy Young notched a 26–16 record and Dinneen was 23–14. Young, Dinneen and Tannehill combined for nearly 1,000 innings pitched, as only five men took the mound all season for Boston. The workload didn't seem to wear down the staff, as the team finished with a 2.12 ERA. New York Giants' ownership and management apparently felt that, in spite of the results of the prior year's fall classic, the competition in the AL was far inferior and not worthy of a postseason matchup with the NL champs, who also boasted three 20-game winners.

1904 New York Giants   106–47 (.693), First place

While their record suggests they were the superior team, we'll never know in light of the Giants' refusal to play Boston in the 1904 World Series. Not only did the Giants have three 20-game winners, but two of their hurlers, Joe McGinnity and Christy Mathewson, won at least 30. McGinnity led the team with 35 wins against only eight losses, and also paced the NL with 408 innings pitched and a 1.61 ERA. Mathewson recorded a typically brilliant season, with a record of 33–12, while Dummy Taylor rounded out the trio with 21 wins and 15 losses.

1905 New York Giants   105–48 (.686), First place

The Giants beat the A's in five games in the 1905 World Series, and did not give up a single earned run in the entire series. The lone loss came in game two, when the A's scored three unearned runs off McGinnity. The other four contests were Giants shutouts, three of them complete-game whitewashes by Christy Mathewson,

who finished the regular season 31–9 with an ERA of 1.28 and 32 complete games. McGinnity was 22–16 for the Giants, while Red Ames won 22 and lost only eight.

1906 Cleveland Naps   89–64 (.582), Third place

The first of five Cleveland teams to have three 20-game winners on the staff, the 1906 Naps couldn't crack the top two in the AL in spite of their hurlers. Bob Rhoades was 22–10, while Hall of Famer Addie Joss finished one of many great seasons with a record of 21–9. Otto Hess won 20, but also lost 17 for Cleveland. All three pitchers compiled ERAs less than 2.00, and the team ERA, a miniscule 2.09, led the league.

1907 Chicago White Sox   87–64 (.576), Third place

The '07 White Sox found themselves in a similar position as the '06 Naps, third place. While Doc White, Ed Walsh, and Frank Smith all had fine seasons and the Sox finished 23 games over .500, Chicago had difficulty winning when anyone else toed the rubber. White (27–13), Walsh (24–18), and Smith (23–11) accounted for 74 of the team's 87 wins, almost 84% of their total victories.

1907 Detroit Tigers   92–58 (.613), First place

The Tigers were two Ed Siever wins away from having four 20-game winners in 1907. In spite of the depth of starting pitchers, they were swept by the Cubs in the World Series. This trio, like those of the 1901 Phillies and 1903 Cubs, was devoid of Hall of Fame pitchers. Wild Bill Donovan finished 25–4, while Ed Killian and George Mullin posted records of 25–13 and 20–20 respectively.

1913 New York Giants   101–51 (.664), First place

Another great Giants team of the early 20th century, this squad was led by Mathewson yet again. He finished the regular season with a mark of 25–11 and led the National League with a 2.06 ERA. This would be the last time in his career that he would team with two other 20-game winners. Rube Marquard (23–10) and Jeff Tesreau (22–13) enjoyed stellar regular seasons, but couldn't help Mathewson in the World Series, which the Giants dropped to the Athletics four games to one. While Mathewson continued his regular season brilliance in the post-season, Marquard posted an ERA of 7.00, and Tesreau an unimpressive 6.48. Neither won a game in the fall classic.

1915 St. Louis Terriers (FL)   87–67 (.566), Second place

During the second and final season of the ill-fated Federal League, the Terriers finished just behind Chicago in a pennant race in which a half game separated first place from third. Eddie Plank, nearing the end of his Hall of Fame career, posted the last of his eight 20-win seasons, with a record of 21–11. Dave Davenport (22–18) and Doc Crandall (21–15) also finished as 20-win winners.

1920 Chicago White Sox   96–58 (.623), Second place

The White Sox made history becoming the first 20th-century major league team to produce four 20-game winners. Two of those, Lefty Williams (22–14) and Eddie Cicotte (21–10), were removed from the team with about two weeks left in the season for their part in the previous year's infamous "Black Sox scandal." The others were Red Faber, who led the team in wins with 23, against 13 losses, and Dickie Kerr (21–9). The rest of the staff garnered only nine wins as Chicago lost a tight race to Cleveland.

1920 Cleveland Indians   98–56 (.636), First place

The 1920 version was the only Cleveland team among the five noted here to win a pennant, and the club also went on to win the World Series that fall. Jim Bagby led the team with a 31–12 record, while Stan Coveleski posted a mark of 24–14 and Ray Caldwell was 20–10. Bagby, who had several solid seasons prior to 1920, played only three more years, and never won more than 14 games again. The team also had a lefty, Duster Mails, who won only seven games, but never suffered a defeat that season, and posted a 1.85 ERA. His success continued in the World Series, when he threw over 15 innings without allowing an earned run, including a complete-game shutout in game six against Brooklyn.

1920 New York Giants   86–68 (.558), Second place

All of the other Giants' 20-win trios led teams to seasons of more than 100 victories. This team, however, recorded the lowest winning percentage of any team with three or more 20-game winners. Four seasons removed from Christy Mathewson's departure, this trio boasted no Hall of Fame pitchers. Fred Toney and Art Nehf led the staff with 21 wins each against 11 losses for Toney and 12 for Nehf. Jesse Barnes completed the campaign at 20–15.

1923 Cincinnati Reds   91–63 (.591), Second place

The Reds were led by a brilliant season from Dolf Luque, who paced the league in wins (27), winning percentage (.771), ERA (1.93), and shutouts (6). Pete Donahue compiled a 21–15 mark, and Eppa Rixey was 20–15.

1931 Philadelphia Athletics   107–45 (.704), First place

This formidable Athletics team featured standout Lefty Grove as the team's ace. Grove won 31 and lost only four. George Earnshaw was 21–7 and Rube Walberg notched 20 wins against 12 defeats. They were heavily favored to trounce the Cardinals in the World Series, but St. Louis center fielder Pepper Martin stole the show, batting .500 against the A's vaunted staff, with 12 hits, five RBI, and a series-high five runs scored. The rest of the Cardinals hit just .205, but it was enough to take the series from Philadelphia in seven games.

1951 Cleveland Indians   93–61 (.604), Second place

After 20 years without a major league team having three 20-game winners in the same season, Cleveland broke through with

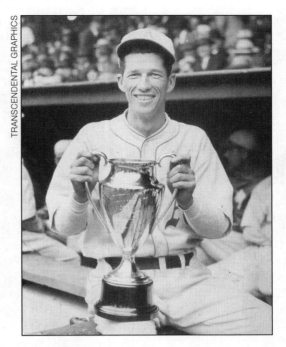

Lefty Grove (top) and Dolf Luque

NATIONAL BASEBALL HALL OF FAME, COOPERSTOWN, NY

Early Wynn

1956 Cleveland Indians   88–66 (.571), Second place

For the third time in six seasons the Indians could have sent three 20-game winners to the mound in the post-season. The problem was, they missed the post-season again, yielding to the Yankees for the fifth time in six seasons. Wynn, Herb Score, and Lemon all won exactly 20 games. Wynn and Score lost nine, while Lemon dropped 14.

1970 Baltimore Orioles   108–54 (.667), First place

The 1960s came and went without a trio of 20-game winners on one team in one season. The Orioles reversed that trend in 1970 with two 24-game winners in Mike Cuellar and Dave McNally, and 20 wins from a young Jim Palmer. They made quick work of their post-season opposition, sweeping the Minnesota Twins in the ALCS and beating Cincinnati four games to one in the World Series. The trio combined for a post-season record of 5–0, and the Orioles' staff got 60 runs of support in eight games.

1971 Baltimore Orioles   101–57 (.639), First place

Pat Dobson joined the Orioles staff in 1971 and joined the 20-win club immediately. Along with Cuellar and Palmer, Dobson won 20, while McNally won 21, marking the fourth consecutive season in which he recorded at least 20 victories. As they had done the year before, they swept their foe in the ALCS, this time Oakland. They faced a Pittsburgh Pirates team with no 20-game winners in what certainly seemed like a mismatch, at least from a pitching standpoint. The Pirates' game one and two starters each failed to pitch beyond the fourth inning and Baltimore led the series 2–0. But Pittsburgh's Steve Blass and Nelson Briles combined to pitch 27 innings and allow only two earned runs, notching three victories between them. The Pirates won the series in seven games as Blass finished off Baltimore with a four-hit complete game. The combination of four 20-game winners had not happened since the 1920 White Sox, and has not happened since this 1971 Orioles staff accomplished the feat. It is highly unlikely to happen again.

the first of what would become three such staffs in a span of six years. The Cleveland teams of the late 1940s and the 1950s were blessed with great pitching, and this squad was no exception. Imagine a roster on which Bob Lemon was the fourth best pitcher, and you have the 1951 Indians. Bob Feller was 22–8, Mike Garcia 20–13, and Early Wynn, part of three such trios in his career, 20–13 also. Cleveland's team ERA of 3.38 led the American League. 1951 was the only season from 1948 to 1954 in which Lemon won less than 20 games, as he finished the campaign with 17 victories.

1952 Cleveland Indians   93–61 (.604), Second place

Not much changed for the Indians in 1952. They had three 20-game winners, a record of 93–61, finished in second place, and watched an American League team from New York beat a National League team from New York in the World Series. What did change was that Bob Feller gave way to Bob Lemon when Lemon finished 22–11, while Feller dipped to a disappointing 9–13. Wynn again had a big year, going 23–12, and Mike Garcia won twice as often as he lost, with a mark of 22–11.

1973 Oakland Athletics   94–68 (.580), First place

The 1973 Athletics were the last team to field three 20-game winners in the same season. In a pitching duel with Baltimore's vaunted staff, Oakland held Baltimore to only nine runs in the last four games of the ALCS, winning it three games to two. They then went on to best the Mets in the World Series in seven games. Catfish Hunter was 21–5 for Oakland, while Ken Holtzman also won 21 for the A's, losing 13 times. A young Vida Blue posted his second 20-win season, finishing 20–9. Rollie Fingers and his 22 saves and 1.92 ERA out of the bullpen assisted the trio.

1971 Baltimore Orioles pitchers (L to R) McNally, Cuellar, Palmer, and Dobson

During the last 30 plus years, only a few teams have even come close to fielding three 20 game winners in the same season. The 1985 Cardinals had two 20 game winners in John Tudor and Joaquin Andujar. Danny Cox managed 18 victories for St. Louis. The 1990 Athletics got 27 and 22 wins from Bob Welch and Dave Stewart respectively, while Scott Sanderson notched 17. Tom Glavine and Greg Maddux had typical stellar seasons in 1993, each winning at least 20 for the Braves. Steve Avery garnered 18 wins for that club. Surprisingly, Glavine, Maddux and John Smoltz never finished a season as teammates with 20 victories each in spite of their great years together in Atlanta. It seems that if a trio like that could not cross the threshold, it is unlikely to happen again. This year's 20 game winners had no teammates who equaled their accomplishment, never mind two such teammates. After Willis, the Marlins' biggest winners were Josh Beckett with 15 and A. J. Burnett with only 12. Mark Mulder and Jeff Suppan both fell four wins short of 20 for the Cardinals as the next closest for St. Louis. Astros Andy Pettitte and Roger Clemens were second and third on the club in wins, but totaled only 30 victories (Pettitte with 17 and Clemens with 13). John Lackey followed Colon on the Angels win leader board with 14. Los Angeles' Ervin Santana and Paul Byrd won 12 each. We are unlikely to see a trio of 20 game winners on the same team, unless there are changes in the way managers handle their pitchers. The managerial style utilized this post season by Ozzie Guillen might make the White Sox the leading candidate to have three teammates with 20 victories in the same year. They have the quality pitching to do it, with Mark Buehrle, Freddy Garcia, Jon Garland and Jose Contreras. If Guillen lets them stay in games like he showed a willingness to do this October, and their arms hold up, they have a chance, albeit a slim one.

World Series Winners and Losers
What's the Difference?

When the Boston Red Sox recorded the final out against the St. Louis Cardinals in the 2004 World Series, it concluded the 100th fall classic in Major League Baseball history. The outcomes of these 100 matchups have ranged from boringly predictable to totally shocking, with everything in between.

One hundred is a nice round number to use as the population basis for a statistical analysis of World Series winners and losers. With this wealth of data, certain burning questions might be addressed, and some surprising facts could emerge. What is it that differentiates the teams that win the World Series from those that lose? Is there a unique quality, a certain special ability, which the winners have and the losers do not? And more particularly, what the heck happened to the 1954 Indians?

Fundamentally, the ability to score and prevent runs is the best indicator of a team's success. Let us then create something that we will call the Team Strength Index. Here's how it works. In a given league in a given year, a normal distribution and standard deviation are created for *runs scored per game* and *runs allowed per game*, using the entire population of teams in the league as the statistical basis. The position of every team in the league on the two normal curves is located; in statistics, this position is called the *z-score*. The z-score is simply an indicator of how far a *given score* is from the *mean score.* Each team's two z-scores (for runs allowed and runs scored) are added together to form its TSI.

Eagle-eyed statistical purists will note that the term "normal distribution" snuck into the preceding paragraph before we even switched on the floodlights. In any collection of random data, a normal distribution can be calculated and imposed, creating an aesthetically pleasing bell curve out of what may be a data distribution mess. In reality, the numbers could be quite crooked. For an example league and year, the constituent teams might be clumped at the high and low ends of the range, with a no-man's land in the middle. Or, there might have been a few powerhouse teams at the top, with everyone else crowded together at the bottom. In any distribution, there is a degree of *skewness*, a statistical concept whose discussion is beyond the scope of this essay. Further, a data sample may more closely resemble any number

of other types of statistical distributions. Rigid use of the normal distribution in this study is a simplifying assumption put in place to keep us from ascending into the statistics methodology stratosphere and suffering from the attendant lightheadedness.

Another important assumption being made here is that by simply adding the two z-scores for runs scored and runs prevented, we are presuming that offense and defense are equally important. No attempt is being made to put a weighting factor on either side of the ledger. Scoring and preventing runs are two sides of the same team coin.

So how does the Team Strength Index work? Example: In a hypothetical league, each side scores an average of five runs per game. Thus, the mean of the normal curve for both *runs scored* and *runs allowed* is five. Standard deviations are computed, based on the entire population of teams in the league, and are found to be 0.75 in both cases (equivalence is never true in reality, but we're keeping it simple for the sake of argument here).

In this example, the team that the league sends to the Series happens to score an average of 6.5 runs per game and allow 3.5 runs per game during the regular season. Since they score at 1.5 runs better than the league average, their offensive component of the TSI (z-score) is equal to 1.5 divided by the standard deviation of 0.75, which is 2. Similarly, the defensive component is also 2 (the negative sign is reversed, since fewer is better). This gives our hypothetical squad a TSI of $2 + 2 = 4$.

The point of rating each World Series team in relation to the rest of the teams in its respective league is to make valid comparisons. The average number of runs scored per game has ebbed and flowed over the years as baseball has evolved, so directly comparing a team from 2004 to one from 1903 would be meaningless. The game has changed so much over time (the Deadball Era, the advent of the basket glove, the lowered pitching mound, the designated hitter, interleague play, steroids, etc.) that you can meaningfully compare a team only to its peers.

The one intangible variable in all this is the relative strength of the two leagues in a given year. We have to assume that, *over time,* the AL and NL have had a fairly even distribution of talent and ability between them. It's an assumption that has to be made for this study to have any meaning, even though in any year one can argue that league A is better than league B.

We now crunch the numbers for all 200 teams that have advanced to the Series, calculating a TSI for each one. The average World Series winner has a TSI of 2.259; losers show a TSI of 2.169.

KENT von SCHELIHA is a stress analysis engineer who works in the aerospace industry. He resides in Kirkland, Washington. His fantasy baseball team stinks.

M. BROWN.   J. PFEISTER.   A. HOFMAN.   C.G. WILLIAMS.   O. OVERALL.   E. REULBACH.   J. KLING.
H. GESSLER.   J. TAYLOR.   H. STEINFELDT.   J. McCORMICK.   F. CHANCE.   J. SHECKARD.   P. MORAN.   F. SCHULTE.
C. LUNDGREN.   T. WALSH.   J. EVERS.   J. SLAGLE.   J. TINKER.

CHICAGO NATIONAL LEAGUE BALL CLUB 1906

1906 Chicago Cubs

The winners are *only 4% stronger* than the losers on average. That's it. Further, the stronger of the two teams emerged victorious only 56% of the time. So in a short series (most World Series were best-of-seven), the stronger team has a barely better than 50/50 chance of winning it all.

Another interesting point: on average, teams that go to the Series are slightly better at preventing runs than scoring runs. This fact holds true for both winners and losers. Winners are about 7% better at preventing than scoring; for losers, that number is 6%. So while winners are slightly stronger overall than losers, both are skewed toward the run-prevention side of the equation. We might then conclude that strong pitching and defense will get you to the Series more reliably than strong hitting, but there's no advantage to be had once the Series begins.

Using the Team Strength Index, we can compare and rank all 200 teams. First, the monster teams:

Five Strongest Teams to Play in the World Series

Year	Team	TSI	Outcome
1998	New York Yankees	3.89	Winner
1927	New York Yankees	3.74	Winner
1917	New York Giants	3.70	Loser
1984	Detroit Tigers	3.69	Winner
1986	New York Mets	3.58	Winner

The '98 Yanks stand as the best team in history, edging out their legendary 1927 namesakes. With a TSI of 3.89, they were leaps and bounds ahead of what anyone else was doing in the AL that year. On the other side of the ledger:

Five Weakest Teams to Play in the World Series

Year	Team	TSI	Outcome
1987	Minnesota Twins	-0.33	Winner
1973	New York Mets	0.33	Loser
1985	Kansas City Royals	0.43	Winner
1906	Chicago White Sox	0.59	Winner
2003	Florida Marlins	0.66	Winner

The '87 Twins stand as the biggest anomaly in history. This is the only team out of the 200 that have played in the World Series to have been below average in its league in *both* scoring and preventing runs. They have the distinction of being the only World Series team with a negative TSI, perhaps proving that sometimes statistics don't tell the whole story. Furthermore, the fact that out of the five weakest teams, only one lost, suggests that once the World Series begins, *anything can happen.*

Consider now the biggest mismatches in history. We define mismatch as the largest difference in TSI between the teams for each World Series pairing in which the stronger team won.

Five Biggest Mismatches in World Series History

Year	Stronger	Weaker	TSI Difference
1984	Tigers	Padres	2.78
1998	Yankees	Padres	2.63
1927	Yankees	Pirates	1.92
1961	Yankees	Reds	1.91
1973	Athletics	Mets	1.86

Let us not shed a tear for the Padres. Even though they came up empty-handed in two trips to the Series, they were on the wrong side of the two most lopsided matchups ever. Against the Tigers in 1984 and the Yankees in 1998, they never had a chance. The Team Strength Index also allows us to rank the upsets:

Six Greatest Upsets in World Series History

Year	Winner	Loser	TSI Difference
1985	Royals	Cardinals	-2.63
1969	Mets	Orioles	-2.28
1987	Twins	Cardinals	-2.25
1906	White Sox	Cubs	-2.23
1990	Reds	Athletics	-1.88
1995	Braves	Indians	-1.88

The Miracle Mets of 1969 can be considered only the second most miraculous winners of the World Series, dethroned by the '85 Royals. Conspicuous by its absence from this list of upsets is the Giants' win over the Indians in 1954. Baseball lore often cites this as the biggest World Series collapse ever. Yet in spite of Cleveland's 111—43 regular season record, they were *merely an average World Series team*. Their TSI of 2.22 falls somewhere in the middle of the pack. While certainly an impressive squad, their ability to score and prevent runs does not indicate their eye-popping won-lost record. *Could they be the team in history that caught the most lucky breaks in the regular season?* Tellingly, their loss to the Giants ranks as only the 31st biggest upset.

By breaking out each team's run-scoring and run-preventing components of the TSI, we can establish which teams that played in the World Series relied mostly on offense or defense. Here are the teams that were the offensive powerhouses.

Five World Series Teams with the Strongest Offense

Year	Team	Run-Scoring Component	Outcome
1976	Cincinnati Reds	2.45	Winner
1975	Cincinnati Reds	2.35	Winner
1914	Philadelphia Athletics	2.30	Loser
1953	Brooklyn Dodgers	2.28	Loser
1993	Philadelphia Phillies	2.24	Loser

Yes, the Big Red Machine of the mid-70s certainly earned its reputation. Conversely, the teams that rode their defense (primarily pitching) to the World Series:

Five World Series Teams with the Strongest Defense

Year	Team	Run-Preventing Component	Outcome
1990	Oakland Athletics	2.51	Loser
1979	Baltimore Orioles	2.28	Loser
1923	New York Yankees	2.25	Winner
1981	New York Yankees	2.24	Loser
1998	New York Yankees	2.16	Winner

Curiously, being dominant either offensively or defensively does not consistently lead to a win in the World Series, as the last two tables seem to show. The most balanced team was the Yankees squad that won in 1938. Their TSI of 3.00 was comprised of identical run-scoring and run-preventing components of 1.50.

A few conclusions can be drawn from this study. As scholars of the game have long suspected, the World Series is simply too short for the stronger team to win consistently. While a best-of-31 series might favor victory for the stronger team, few baseball fans are going to have the patience and perseverance to watch the same two teams play each other night after night into December. And this is a good thing. The short series makes the outcome virtually unpredictable, giving hope to the underdog and riveting our attention for a week or so in October.

The fact that teams that go to the World Series are slightly stronger in pitching and defense than they are in hitting indicates something about the game itself. Many baseball people believe intuitively that pitching and defense can be relied upon more consistently than hitting. When the game is on the line, success is more likely to come from a timely strikeout or double play than it is from a clutch hit. The statistics here seem to support what managers already knew in their gut.

If you want to get to the Series, load up on pitching and be strong up the middle. That said, once you're there, *anything can happen*.

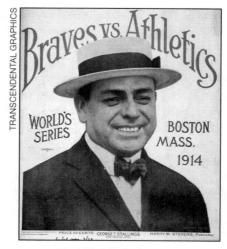

1914 World's Series program

Team Strength Indices for World Series Winners and Losers, 1903–2004 (stronger team in *italics*)

Year	Winner	z-OFF	z-DEF	TSI	Loser	z-OFF	z-DEF	TSI	Year	Winner	z-OFF	z-DEF	TSI	Loser	z-OFF	z-DEF	TSI
2004	*BOS*	1.88	0.85	2.74	STL	1.33	1.10	2.43	1953	*NYY*	1.70	1.15	2.86	BRO	2.28	0.50	2.78
2003	FLA	0.06	0.60	0.66	*NYY*	0.95	0.81	1.76	1952	*NYY*	1.23	1.25	2.48	BRO	1.64	0.68	2.32
2002	ANA	0.82	1.44	2.26	SF	1.20	1.30	2.50	1951	*NYY*	1.40	1.05	2.45	NYG	0.96	0.89	1.85
2001	*ARI*	0.81	1.18	2.00	NYY	0.26	0.76	1.02	1950	*NYY*	1.01	0.95	1.96	PHI	-0.15	1.48	1.33
2000	NYY	0.25	0.65	0.90	*NYM*	-0.04	1.00	0.96	1949	NYY	1.12	0.79	1.92	*BRO*	2.10	0.99	3.09
1999	*NYY*	0.71	1.84	2.55	ATL	0.48	1.52	2.00	1948	CLE	0.85	1.89	2.74	*BOB*	0.77	1.98	2.75
1998	*NYY*	1.73	2.16	3.89	SD	0.04	1.22	1.26	1947	*NYY*	1.66	1.36	3.03	BRO	0.76	0.64	1.40
1997	*FLA*	-0.07	0.85	0.78	CLE	1.04	-0.29	0.75	1946	*STL*	1.50	1.22	2.71	BOS	1.85	0.67	2.52
1996	NYY	-0.01	0.99	0.98	*ATL*	0.22	1.27	1.49	1945	DET	0.56	0.89	1.45	*CHI*	0.48	1.68	2.16
1995	ATL	-0.38	2.02	1.64	*CLE*	1.84	1.68	3.52	1944	*STL*	1.41	1.66	3.07	SLB	0.80	1.10	1.90
1993	TOR	1.24	0.39	1.63	*PHI*	2.24	-0.14	2.10	1943	NYY	1.22	1.23	2.45	*STL*	0.79	1.92	2.71
1992	TOR	1.24	0.32	1.56	*ATL*	1.20	1.53	2.73	1942	STL	1.32	1.56	2.88	*NYY*	1.51	1.46	2.96
1991	MIN	0.72	1.26	1.99	*ATL*	1.61	0.44	2.05	1941	NYY	1.25	1.43	2.67	*BRO*	1.62	1.10	2.72
1990	CIN	0.24	1.22	1.46	*OAK*	0.83	2.51	3.34	1940	*CIN*	0.32	1.90	2.22	DET	1.54	0.51	2.05
1989	OAK	0.42	1.69	2.11	SF	1.51	0.78	2.29	1939	*NYY*	1.91	1.62	3.53	CIN	1.02	1.21	2.23
1988	LA	0.00	1.31	1.31	OAK	1.35	1.54	2.89	1938	*NYY*	1.50	1.50	3.00	CHI	0.48	1.07	1.55
1987	MIN	-0.16	-0.18	-0.33	STL	1.15	0.77	1.92	1937	*NYY*	1.71	1.51	3.22	NYG	0.61	0.97	1.58
1986	*NYM*	2.05	1.53	3.58	BOS	0.90	0.88	1.77	1936	*NYY*	1.83	1.29	3.11	NYG	0.29	1.27	1.56
1985	KC	-0.94	1.37	0.43	*STL*	1.68	1.38	3.06	1935	*DET*	2.06	1.08	3.14	CHI	1.43	1.32	2.76
1984	*DET*	2.05	1.64	3.69	SD	0.54	0.38	0.92	1934	STL	1.36	0.80	2.16	*DET*	1.98	1.02	2.99
1983	*BAL*	1.10	1.23	2.32	PHI	0.68	0.92	1.60	1933	NYG	0.29	1.24	1.53	*WAS*	0.86	1.51	2.37
1982	STL	0.40	1.36	1.76	*MIL*	2.12	0.30	2.41	1932	*NYY*	1.36	1.11	2.47	CHI	0.16	1.58	1.75
1981	*LA*	0.45	1.56	2.01	NYY	-0.33	2.24	1.91	1931	*STL*	1.26	1.16	2.41	PHA	0.53	1.76	2.30
1980	PHI	1.46	0.35	1.80	KC	0.97	0.66	1.62	1930	PHA	0.89	1.10	1.99	STL	1.07	0.71	1.78
1979	PIT	1.41	0.77	2.18	*BAL*	0.18	2.28	2.46	1929	PHA	1.24	1.84	3.08	CHI	1.34	0.80	2.13
1978	NYY	0.70	1.56	2.26	*LA*	1.64	1.33	2.97	1928	*NYY*	1.73	0.76	2.49	STL	1.06	0.71	1.78
1977	NYY	1.02	1.31	2.33	*LA*	0.85	1.63	2.48	1927	*NYY*	1.89	1.84	3.74	PIT	1.15	0.66	1.81
1976	*CIN*	2.45	0.17	2.62	NYY	1.44	1.29	2.74	1926	*STL*	1.81	0.33	2.15	NYY	1.37	0.21	1.58
1975	*CIN*	2.35	1.08	3.43	BOS	1.96	-0.29	1.68	1925	*PIT*	1.97	0.69	2.66	WAS	0.46	1.49	1.95
1974	*OAK*	0.96	2.16	3.12	LA	1.76	1.35	3.11	1924	WAS	-0.50	2.05	1.55	*NYG*	1.79	0.63	2.42
1973	*OAK*	1.24	0.95	2.19	NYM	-0.93	1.26	0.33	1923	*NYY*	1.00	2.25	3.24	NYG	1.87	0.60	2.46
1972	*OAK*	1.18	1.44	2.62	CIN	1.27	0.74	2.02	1922	*NYG*	0.86	1.45	2.31	NYY	0.31	1.56	1.88
1971	PIT	1.97	0.60	2.57	*BAL*	1.77	1.48	3.25	1921	*NYG*	1.80	0.70	2.50	NYY	1.43	1.01	2.44
1970	BAL	1.88	1.42	3.31	CIN	0.71	0.87	1.58	1920	CLE	1.22	1.17	2.39	BRO	0.77	1.23	2.01
1969	NYM	-0.30	1.37	1.07	*BAL*	1.35	2.00	3.35	1919	*CIN*	1.27	1.17	2.44	CWS	1.46	0.58	2.04
1968	*DET*	2.00	1.17	3.17	STL	0.43	1.43	1.86	1918	BOS	0.52	1.48	2.00	*CHI*	1.25	1.75	3.00
1967	STL	1.19	1.02	2.21	BOS	1.77	-0.33	1.43	1917	CWS	1.70	1.24	2.94	*NYG*	1.56	2.14	3.70
1966	*BAL*	2.05	0.35	2.41	LA	-0.84	2.00	1.16	1916	BOS	-0.37	1.05	0.68	*BRO*	1.05	1.02	2.07
1965	LA	-0.53	1.93	1.40	*MIN*	2.15	0.49	2.63	1915	BOS	0.63	0.92	1.55	*PHI*	1.23	1.86	3.08
1964	STL	0.82	-0.02	0.79	*NYY*	1.09	0.84	1.93	1914	BOB	0.81	1.01	1.82	*PHA*	2.30	0.73	3.03
1963	LA	0.22	1.20	1.42	*NYY*	1.02	1.41	2.43	1913	PHA	2.15	0.13	2.29	*NYG*	0.65	1.78	2.43
1962	*NYY*	1.57	0.79	2.36	SF	1.57	0.52	2.09	1912	BOS	1.44	1.46	2.90	*NYG*	1.86	1.42	3.28
1961	*NYY*	1.44	1.51	2.95	CIN	0.27	0.77	1.04	1911	*PHA*	1.75	1.40	3.15	NYG	1.15	1.01	2.15
1960	*PIT*	1.42	1.11	2.53	NYY	1.50	0.88	2.38	1910	PHA	1.20	1.47	2.67	*CHI*	1.10	1.77	2.87
1959	LA	0.38	0.37	0.75	*CWS*	-0.18	1.60	1.42	1909	PIT	0.78	1.08	1.86	DET	1.32	0.02	1.34
1958	*NYY*	1.53	1.20	2.73	MIL	-0.10	1.84	1.74	1908	*CHI*	1.36	1.01	2.37	DET	0.48	0.65	1.13
1957	*MIL*	1.42	1.17	2.58	NYY	1.20	1.34	2.54	1907	*CHI*	1.57	1.80	3.37	DET	1.94	1.34	3.28
1956	*NYY*	1.52	0.82	2.34	BRO	0.89	1.06	1.95	1906	CWS	-0.64	1.23	0.59	*CHI*	0.83	1.99	2.82
1955	*BRO*	1.87	1.16	3.03	NYY	0.96	1.02	1.98	1905	*NYG*	1.30	1.64	2.95	PHA	0.65	1.12	1.77
1954	NYG	0.41	1.44	1.85	*CLE*	0.90	1.32	2.22	1903	BOS	1.65	-0.83	0.82	*PIT*	1.03	0.88	1.92

1,000 Extra-Base Hits
A Mark of Greatness?

Many things contribute to playing winning baseball, but one thing is certain. If a team doesn't score, they don't win. extra-base hits drive in runs and we measure sluggers by their extra-base hit performance. For home run hitters, 500 is the magic number. There is no consensus for extra-base hits but I chose to look at players with 1,000 or more extra-base hits.

Ken Griffey Jr.'s sixth-inning double off Kip Wells on August 28, 2005, gave the 1,000 EBH Club its 25th member. Table 1 gives the members of this exclusive club (*italics* denote players active in 2005).

Table 1. Members of the 1,000 XBH Club

Rank	Player	XBH	2B	3B	HR
1	Hank Aaron	1477	624	98	755
2	Stan Musial	1377	725	177	475
3	Babe Ruth	1356	506	136	714
4	*Barry Bonds*	1349	564	77	708
5	Willie Mays	1323	523	140	660
6	*Rafael Palmeiro*	1192	585	38	569
7	Lou Gehrig	1190	535	162	493
8	Frank Robinson	1186	528	72	586
9	Carl Yastrzemski	1157	646	59	452
10	Ty Cobb	1138	725	296	117
11	Tris Speaker	1131	792	222	117
12	George Brett	1119	665	137	317
T13	Ted Williams	1117	525	71	521
T13	Jimmie Foxx	1117	458	125	534
15	Eddie Murray	1099	560	35	504
16	Dave Winfield	1093	540	88	465
17	Cal Ripken	1078	603	44	431
18	Reggie Jackson	1075	463	49	563
19	Mel Ott	1071	488	72	511
20	Pete Rose	1041	746	135	160
21	Andre Dawson	1039	503	98	438
22	Mike Schmidt	1015	408	59	548
23	Rogers Hornsby	1011	541	169	301
24	Ernie Banks	1009	407	90	512
25	*Ken Griffey Jr.*	1002	430	36	536

Note: The sources for the statistics found in this article were Baseball-reference.com, MLB.com, and Lee Sinin's *Sabermetric Baseball Encyclopedia*. There is no consensus on Ty Cobb's career totals in doubles and triples. His doubles are listed as anything from 723 to 725, his triples from 295 to 297. For the purposes of this paper, I went with Lee Sinin's numbers.

It seems clear that 1,000 or more extra-base hits is a fairly substantial achievement. Andre Dawson is the only player on the list who is eligible for, but not in, the Hall of Fame. But as with any statistic that only counts something, it can be instructive to look at rates, not just raw numbers. After all, the fact that Richie Hebner hit 203 career home runs to Albert Pujols' 201 (so far) would not cause many to claim Hebner is the better home run hitter.

It is interesting to note the highest and lowest totals for each kind of hit among these players.

Table 2. Fewest/Most XBH Totals

	Fewest	Most
Doubles	Ernie Banks (407)	Tris Speaker (792)
Triples	Eddie Murray (35)	Ty Cobb (296)
Home runs	Speaker & Cobb (117)	Hank Aaron (755)

In Table 3, I will look at EBHAvg, the Extra-base Hit Average. This is calculated just as batting average is, EBH/AB.

Table 3. Extra-Base Hit Average (XBHAvg)

Rank	Player	XBHAvg
1	Babe Ruth	.161
2	Lou Gehrig	.149
3	Barry Bonds	.148
4	Ted Williams	.145
5	Jimmie Foxx	.137
6	Ken Griffey Jr.	.127
7	Stan Musial	.126
8	Rogers Hornsby	.124
9	Willie Mays	.12159
10	Mike Schmidt	.12153
11	Hank Aaron	.1195
12	Frank Robinson	.1185
13	Rafael Palmeiro	.114
14	Mel Ott	.113
15	Tris Speaker	.111
16	Reggie Jackson	.109
17	George Brett	.108
18	Ernie Banks	.107
19	Andre Dawson	.105
20	Ty Cobb	.100
21	Dave Winfield	.099
22	Eddie Murray	.0970
23	Carl Yastrzemski	.0965
24	Cal Ripken	.093
25	Pete Rose	.074

This view of the data makes a couple of interesting points. First, Babe Ruth is clearly in a class by himself. Also clear is the fact that Pete Rose's membership in this club is due mostly to the fact that he has nearly 1,700 more at-bats than anyone else in history. Interestingly, looking at this statistic rather than just the number of extra-base hits lends support to those who support Andre Dawson for the Hall of Fame. His EBHAvg is a good bit higher than that of Dave Winfield, Eddie Murray, and Carl Yastrzemski, all of whom were, like Dawson, viewed primarily as slugging run producers.

Another way to look at these data is by percentages of types of hits. In Table 3, we can see 2BAvg (2B/AB) and 2BPct (2B/EBH), with the sorting done by most doubles.

Table 4. Double Average (2BAvg) and Double Percentage (2BPct)

	2B	2BAvg	2BPct
Tris Speaker	792	.078	.700
Pete Rose	746	.053	.717
Stan Musial	725	.066	.527
Ty Cobb	725	.063	.637
George Brett	665	.064	.594
Carl Yastrzemski	646	.054	.558
Hank Aaron	624	.050	.422
Cal Ripken	603	.052	.559
Rafael Palmeiro	585	.056	.491
Barry Bonds	564	.062	.418
Eddie Murray	560	.049	.510
Rogers Hornsby	541	.066	.535
Dave Winfield	540	.049	.494
Lou Gehrig	535	.067	.450
Frank Robinson	528	.053	.445
Ted Williams	525	.068	.470
Willie Mays	523	.048	.395
Babe Ruth	506	.060	.373
Andre Dawson	503	.051	.484
Mel Ott	488	.052	.456
Reggie Jackson	463	.047	.431
Jimmie Foxx	458	.056	.410
Ken Griffey Jr.	430	.055	.429
Mike Schmidt	408	.049	.402
Ernie Banks	407	.043	.403

Lou Gehrig

Looking at the data again shows that Rose is on the elite end of the list due mostly to longevity. If we look only at 2BAvg, we see Rose in the middle of the pack.

Looking at 2BPct (Table 6) we see Rose at the top, meaning the large majority of his extra-base hits were doubles. In this regard, he is most like Tris Speaker, but Speaker's totals were accumulated in substantially fewer at-bats.

FRED WORTH is a professor of mathematics at Henderson State University and a lifelong Mets fan who, whenever he plays softball, still wears #24 in honor of his boyhood hero, Willie Mays.

Table 5. Double Average (2BAvg)

Tris Speaker	.078
Ted Williams	.068
Lou Gehrig	.067
Rogers Hornsby	.0662
Stan Musial	.0661
George Brett	.064
Ty Cobb	.063
Barry Bonds	.062
Babe Ruth	.060
Jimmie Foxx	.0563
Rafael Palmeiro	.0558
Ken Griffey Jr.	.055
Carl Yastrzemski	.054
Pete Rose	.0531
Frank Robinson	.0528
Cal Ripken	.0522
Mel Ott	.0516
Andre Dawson	.051
Hank Aaron	.050
Eddie Murray	.0494
Dave Winfield	.0490
Mike Schmidt	.0485
Willie Mays	.048
Reggie Jackson	.047
Ernie Banks	.043

Table 7. Triples

Ty Cobb	296
Tris Speaker	222
Stan Musial	177
Rogers Hornsby	169
Lou Gehrig	162
Willie Mays	140
George Brett	137
Babe Ruth	136
Pete Rose	135
Jimmie Foxx	125
Hank Aaron	98
Andre Dawson	98
Ernie Banks	90
Dave Winfield	88
Barry Bonds	77
Frank Robinson	72
Mel Ott	72
Ted Williams	71
Carl Yastrzemski	59
Mike Schmidt	59
Reggie Jackson	49
Cal Ripken	44
Rafael Palmeiro	38
Ken Griffey Jr.	36
Eddie Murray	35

Table 9. Triple Percentage (3BPct)

Ty Cobb	.260
Tris Speaker	.196
Rogers Hornsby	.167
Lou Gehrig	.136
Pete Rose	.130
Stan Musial	.129
George Brett	.122
Jimmie Foxx	.112
Willie Mays	.106
Babe Ruth	.100
Andre Dawson	.094
Ernie Banks	.089
Dave Winfield	.081
Mel Ott	.067
Hank Aaron	.066
Ted Williams	.064
Frank Robinson	.061
Mike Schmidt	.058
Barry Bonds	.057
Carl Yastrzemski	.051
Reggie Jackson	.046
Cal Ripken	.041
Ken Griffey Jr.	.036
Rafael Palmeiro	.03188
Eddie Murray	.03185

Table 6. Double Percentage (2BPct)

Pete Rose	.717
Tris Speaker	.700
Ty Cobb	.637
George Brett	.594
Cal Ripken	.559
Carl Yastrzemski	.558
Rogers Hornsby	.535
Stan Musial	.527
Eddie Murray	.510
Dave Winfield	.494
Rafael Palmeiro	.491
Andre Dawson	.484
Ted Williams	.470
Mel Ott	.456
Lou Gehrig	.450
Frank Robinson	.445
Reggie Jackson	.431
Ken Griffey Jr.	.429
Hank Aaron	.422
Barry Bonds	.418
Jimmie Foxx	.410
Ernie Banks	.403
Mike Schmidt	.402
Willie Mays	.395
Babe Ruth	.373

Table 8. Triple Average (3BAvg)

Ty Cobb	.026
Tris Speaker	.022
Rogers Hornsby	.021
Lou Gehrig	.020
Babe Ruth	.0162
Stan Musial	.0161
Jimmie Foxx	.015
George Brett	.0132
Willie Mays	.0128
Andre Dawson	.0099
Pete Rose	.00961
Ernie Banks	.00955
Ted Williams	.009
Barry Bonds	.0084
Dave Winfield	.0080
Hank Aaron	.0079
Mel Ott	.0076
Frank Robinson	.0072
Mike Schmidt	.0071
Reggie Jackson	.00497
Carl Yastrzemski	.00492
Ken Griffey Jr.	.0046
Cal Ripken	.0038
Rafael Palmeiro	.0036
Eddie Murray	.003

Table 10. Home Runs

Hank Aaron	755
Babe Ruth	714
Barry Bonds	708
Willie Mays	660
Frank Robinson	586
Rafael Palmeiro	569
Reggie Jackson	563
Mike Schmidt	548
Ken Griffey Jr.	536
Jimmie Foxx	534
Ted Williams	521
Ernie Banks	512
Mel Ott	511
Eddie Murray	504
Lou Gehrig	493
Stan Musial	475
Dave Winfield	465
Carl Yastrzemski	452
Andre Dawson	438
Cal Ripken	431
George Brett	317
Rogers Hornsby	301
Pete Rose	160
Ty Cobb	117
Tris Speaker	117

Table 11. Home Run Average (HRAvg)

Babe Ruth	.085
Barry Bonds	.077
Ted Williams	.0676
Ken Griffey Jr.	.0681
Jimmie Foxx	.06565
Mike Schmidt	.06561
Lou Gehrig	.062
Hank Aaron	.0610
Willie Mays	.0606
Frank Robinson	.059
Reggie Jackson	.057
Rafael Palmeiro	.05434
Mel Ott	.05433
Ernie Banks	.0540
Eddie Murray	.0444
Andre Dawson	.0441
Stan Musial	.043
Dave Winfield	.042
Carl Yastrzemski	.038
Cal Ripken	.0373
Rogers Hornsby	.0368
George Brett	.031
Tris Speaker	.0114
Pete Rose	.0113
Ty Cobb	.010

Table 12. Home Run Percentage (HRPct)

Mike Schmidt	.540
Ken Griffey Jr.	.535
Babe Ruth	.527
Barry Bonds	.525
Reggie Jackson	.524
Hank Aaron	.511
Ernie Banks	.507
Willie Mays	.499
Frank Robinson	.494
Jimmie Foxx	.478
Rafael Palmeiro	.4773
Mel Ott	.4771
Ted Williams	.466
Eddie Murray	.459
Dave Winfield	.425
Andre Dawson	.422
Lou Gehrig	.414
Cal Ripken	.400
Carl Yastrzemski	.391
Stan Musial	.345
Rogers Hornsby	.298
George Brett	.283
Pete Rose	.154
Tris Speaker	.1034
Ty Cobb	.1028

A couple of observations on these last charts are in order. Babe Ruth is surprisingly high on the list for rate of triples. Even looking at his triples as a percentage of extra-base hits shows Ruth was definitely not a one-dimensional hitter. Also, note that Rose is the only non–Deadball Era player with home runs in fewer than 3% of his at-bats.

In Table 12, we have the players and list their 2BPct, 3Bpct, and HRPct. Additionally, I have listed the difference between their highest and lowest percentage in order to see which players had their extra-base hits most evenly divided.

Table 13

	2B/XBH	3B/XBH	HR/XBH	Max Diff
Lou Gehrig	.450	.136	.414	.313
Jimmie Foxx	.410	.112	.478	.366
Rogers Hornsby	.535	.167	.298	.368
Andre Dawson	.484	.094	.422	.390
Willie Mays	.395	.106	.499	.393
Stan Musial	.527	.129	.345	.398
Ted Williams	.470	.064	.466	.406
Mel Ott	.456	.067	.477	.410
Dave Winfield	.494	.081	.425	.414
Ernie Banks	.403	.089	.507	.418
Babe Ruth	.373	.100	.527	.426
Frank Robinson	.445	.061	.494	.433
Hank Aaron	.422	.066	.511	.445
Rafael Palmeiro	.491	.032	.477	.459
Barry Bonds	.418	.057	.525	.468
George Brett	.594	.122	.283	.472
Reggie Jackson	.431	.046	.524	.478
Eddie Murray	.510	.032	.459	.478
Mike Schmidt	.402	.058	.540	.482
Ken Griffey Jr.	.429	.036	.535	.499
Carl Yastrzemski	.558	.051	.391	.507
Cal Ripken	.559	.041	.400	.519
Ty Cobb	.637	.260	.1028	.534
Pete Rose	.717	.130	.1537	.587
Tris Speaker	.700	.196	.1034	.597

Lou Gehrig is easily the most balanced of the 1,000 EBH Club. The least balanced are Rose and the Deadball Era players.

A Few Who Didn't Make It

Let's next look at some folks who haven't joined the club. The following table lists the only players with 600+ doubles, 200+ triples, or 500+ home runs who have not joined the 1,000 EBH Club (**bold italics** denote players active in 2005).

Table 14

600+ Doubles	2B	3B	HR	XBH
Nap Lajoie	657	163	82	902
Honus Wagner	640	252	101	993
Paul Molitor	605	114	234	953
Craig Biggio	604	52	260	916
Paul Waner	603	190	113	906

200+ Triples	2B	3B	HR	XBH
Sam Crawford	458	309	97	864
Honus Wagner	640	252	101	993
Jake Beckley	473	243	86	802
Roger Connor	441	233	138	812
Fred Clarke	361	220	67	648
Dan Brouthers	460	205	106	771

500+ Homers	2B	3B	HR	XBH
Sammy Sosa	355	44	588	987
Mark McGwire	252	6	583	841
Harmon Killebrew	290	24	573	887
Mickey Mantle	344	72	536	952
Willie McCovey	353	46	521	920
Eddie Mathews	354	72	512	938

Honus Wagner is the only player to end up on more than one of these lists. Not surprisingly, most of the players on the doubles and triples lists are from the Deadball Era. Mark McGwire deserves special mention, since more than two-thirds (69.3%) of his extra-base hits are home runs. Pete Rose and Tris Speaker are the only 1,000 EBH Club members with more than two-thirds of their extra-base hits being of any one kind, with each of them with doubles accounting for more than 70%.

Current Players

The following table gives the players who were active in 2005 and have 800 or more extra-base hits.

Table 15

	3B	3B	HR	XBH
Sammy Sosa*	355	44	588	987
Jeff Bagwell*	488	32	449	969
Craig Biggio	604	52	260	916
Larry Walker	471	62	383	916
Frank Thomas	447	11	448	906
Gary Sheffield	413	24	449	886
Luis Gonzalez	495	63	316	874
Manny Ramirez*	411	15	435	861
Juan Gonzalez	388	25	434	847
Jeff Kent	474	42	331	847
Steve Finley	425	112	297	834

Several of these players are unlikely to reach the 1,000 EBH Club based on their 2005 performance. While making clear that I make no claims to psychic power, those marked with an asterisk are ones I think will make it.

A few other current players deserve special mention as players who are strong candidates for the 1,000 EBH Club.

Table 16

	AB	2B	3B	HR	XBH	Age
Alex Rodriguez	6195	338	25	429	792	30
Jim Thome	5919	324	24	430	778	35
Carlos Delgado	5529	384	14	369	767	33
Todd Helton	4560	373	24	271	668	32
Vladimir Guerrero	4895	294	38	305	637	29
Albert Pujols	2954	227	11	201	439	25

Helton and Lou Gehrig are the only players in history with two 100+ extra-base hits seasons. Thome's chances of 1,000 extra-base hits are heavily dependent on his recovery from this season's injuries. Also, for Helton, Delgado, and Thome, their chances of joining the 1,000 EBH Club are dependent on having at least three more seasons with production similar to what they've had their last few full seasons. Their ages may be working against them. Guerrero has had some trouble with injuries. He will have to stay injury-free to make it. Rodriguez and Pujols are as close to guarantees as there are. Barring severe injuries, or pitchers suddenly figuring out consistent ways to get them out, they could threaten Aaron's leadership.

Conclusion

I think a strong case can be made for 1,000 EBH Club membership being an ironclad Hall of Fame qualification. It requires a long period of consistent production at a high level. Pete Rose, the weakest member of the club, will probably make the Hall of Fame if he is ever reinstated. Rafael Palmeiro may find his path to the Hall obstructed by this year's steroid scandal. But, considering the number of players Major League Baseball has seen, the number of members of the 1,000 EBH Club, and the strong role extra-base hits play in that all-important consideration of scoring runs, I think it can reasonably be called a mark of greatness.

ROBERT REYNOLDS, STEVEN DAY, & DAVID PACULDO

Deconstructing the Midas Touch
Gold Glove Award Voting, 1965–2004

Gold Glove Awards, first presented in 1957, are given annually to the best defensive players at each position in each league. Guidelines for Gold Glove Award voting now state that coaches and managers may vote for players in their league, but not for players on their own team. The guidelines do not suggest what characteristics the coaches and managers should consider in making their selections.

Using the non-strike player-seasons since 1965, we used regression models to predict award recipients by position based on plausible predictive variables, including fielding, offense, and reputation. The best-fitting models showed that defensive skills and having previously won a Gold Glove are strong predictors of winning another one in a current season. Measures of offensive skills and All-Star or post-season appearances are significant for some positions, in keeping with some better-known baseball stereotypes, such as the offensive role of third basemen. Number of wins and strikeouts also affect the chances of winning a Gold Glove as a pitcher.

The models achieve a satisfactory level of predictive ability, and we feel they improve upon previous work in this area, especially with the addition of models for pitchers and outfielders.

Introduction

The Gold Glove Award was conceived in 1957 when the Rawlings Corporation, the well-known manufacturer of baseballs and baseball equipment, presented awards for excellence in fielding to nine Major League Baseball players. Awards were given to players at each field position. Though separate at the beginning, the three awards for outfielders did not differentiate between field after 1960. Thus, in theory three left fielders could win the award in the same year. Since 1958, the Rawlings Corporation has awarded Gold Gloves annually to 18 players, nine each from the American and National Leagues. In 1985 Rawlings gave an extra Gold Glove in the American League when a tie in the voting resulted with Dwight Evans of the Boston Red Sox and Gary Pettis of the California Angels both winning a Gold Glove for outfield.

In 1957, a committee of sportswriters chose the recipients. From 1958 until 1964 the active players in the leagues voted for the winners. Since 1965, Gold Glove Awards have been determined by the votes of managers and coaches of all the teams in each of the major leagues. Voting rules state that managers and coaches may only vote for players in their own league, and may not vote for players on their own team. The rules, however, offer no guidance as to what criteria should be used in deciding for whom to vote. Thus voters are free to use whatever criteria they feel are relevant.

What criteria make a player more or less likely to win a Gold Glove? Conventional baseball wisdom has a glib answer: whoever won last year. While there is undoubtedly some truth to this, it falls far short of telling the whole story. There must be a basis upon which the managers decide for whom to vote other than repeat winners - if not, when a current batch of winners retires, no new ones could be selected. In this paper we sought to determine those accomplishments and attributes that have consistently distinguished Gold Glove winners from the rest of the players in Major League Baseball.

We are aware of only one previous analysis that attempted to identify the characteristics of Gold Glove winners.[1] In his 2005 study, Arthur Zillante tested the specific hypothesis that so-called "reputation effects" influence Gold Glove voting. Zillante's reputation variables include post-season appearances, All-Star appearances, and previous Gold Gloves won. While Zillante's work is thorough and often sensible, the current work represents an improvement in several important respects:

1. Zillante reported separate models for each infield position, but did not provide models for pitchers or outfielders. Here we present separate models for each infield position, including pitchers, and a model for outfielders collectively.

2. Zillante based his analyses on player-seasons from 1957 through 1999. The current work uses records from 1965 through 2004. This range is better suited to testing the Gold Glove voting patterns, as this is the entire period in which the award has been chosen by *only* managers and coaches. Before 1965, the award was chosen first by sportswriters and later by players, each of whom might have had very different standards for voting.

3. We exclude strike seasons that interrupted playing time. These irregular seasons could possibly skew the results by providing incomplete player-seasons, which may have been judged differently from other years.

4. We consider a wider range of predictor variables than did Zillante. We do not assume that the only variables that

might be significantly associated with winning a Gold Glove are those that reflect the conscious decision-making of the voters. Due to his specific hypothesis of reputation influencing voting, Zillante constrained himself to such assumptions. Here we recognize that while some variables may be explicitly considered by voters, others may be highly correlated with the intangibles of excellent defense. Thus we have the ability to identify a variable that may have a strong impact on a player's chance of winning a Gold Glove, even though coaches and managers may not explicitly consider it in their decision processes.

Thus in this paper we use logistic regression analysis and a healthy dose of common sense to find variables that best predict Gold Glove winners in non-strike seasons since 1965.

METHODS
Player Performance Data
The data for this research were taken from the 2005 version of the Lahman Database. This source contains information on Major League Baseball from 1871 to 2004. More information on the database may be found on the Baseball Archive web site.

Specifically, the data used in this study are drawn from the fielding, hitting, pitching, master, and award tables of the database. The raw data consist of one record for each player, in each position played, for each team, in each year in each of the major leagues. For example, Henry Aaron played both third base and outfield for the Milwaukee Braves in 1959; as such he has two fielding records for that year, one for each position. In the analysis, these records would act as two separate players, each with his own fielding records and Gold Glove outcome. Had he played third base for two different teams (in the same league) in the same year, however, those records would have been combined to create a single fielding record by adding the counting statistics. Thus "player-position-seasons" is the unit of analysis in our models; we will refer to them as "player-seasons" from here forward.

Table 1 shows the distribution of player-seasons by position

and in five-year intervals. The table also lists the minimum number of games played for any one player-season to be included in the analysis. The minimum-game threshold was chosen by selecting all player-seasons that had as many or more games played than the minimum number of games played among all the Gold Glove winners (for all years) at that position. A minimum number of games was chosen instead of a minimum number of innings because the information on innings played at each position other than pitcher is unavailable for records prior to 2000.

For every position except first base and outfield there are 74 total Gold Gloves used in the analyses. This corresponds to 10 awards in each five-year interval, except in the eras 1970–74, 1980–84, and 1990–94. In each of these eras a single strike year was dropped from the analysis, resulting in eight Gold Gloves in each of those eras.

The outfield model contains a total of 223 Gold Glove Awards, as the outfield records were analyzed as a group rather than by position. The outfield records were grouped because the records for some players in the 1960s list them only as having played outfield (instead of left, center, or right fields), and because each voter casts three votes for outfielders without identifying left, right, or center field.

The first base model included only 73 Gold Gloves instead of 74, because Rafael Palmeiro's 1999 Gold Glove was dropped from the analysis. Palmeiro's award in that season is widely regarded as a reward for his offensive accomplishments; we dropped it here because his low number of games played at first base (28) made his award a severe outlier.

Hitting information used in the analyses were the counting statistics of offense, including the numbers of all types of hits, at-bats, sacrifices, hit by pitch, and RBI. Batting average, slugging percentage, and on-base percentage were all excluded from the analyses due to the statistical error associated with small numbers of at-bats for some players.

Fielding information consisted of the standard statistics of fielding: number of games at each position, assists, putouts, errors, double plays, fielding percentage, and passed balls. In each

Table 1. Player-seasons of data by player positions and era

Years	P (G ≥ 23)[1]	C (G ≥ 87)[1]	1B (G ≥ 93)[1]	2B (G ≥ 118)[1]	3B (G ≥ 115)[1]	SS (G ≥ 114)[1]	OF (G ≥ 44)[1]
1965-69	979	94	91	65	69	64	488
1970-74	842	81	73	57	67	64	451
1975-79	1120	115	105	75	93	87	598
1980-84	957	93	89	74	67	71	494
1985-89	1229	111	108	90	90	87	616
1990-94	1103	97	87	64	66	66	517
1995-99	1572	130	115	88	89	96	682
2000-04	1676	131	126	92	94	100	696
All Years	**9478**	**852**	**794**	**605**	**635**	**635**	**4542**

[1]Minimum number of games for a player-season to be included in the analysis

of the models presented here, fielding percentage is expressed as a percent between 0 and 100 rather than as a decimal number between 0 and 1.

Pitching data included all counting statistics for pitchers, including ERA and opponents' batting average, though the latter two were not used for the same reasons that batting average and other offensive-rate statistics were not used. Offensive-rate measures (batting average, slugging, etc.) were excluded for pitchers (as for other positions). We decided to exclude these rate variables because they depended on the number of innings pitched and batters faced, information that was not always available; this led to uncertainty about the reliability of these variables due to the size of statistical error in the measurements of their effects.

All records had indicators of league, season (as calendar year), whether the player was an All-Star in that year, whether the player made the post-season in that year, and age in each season (as of July 1). We also calculated a number of variables, including career totals and average-per-game rates for each counting statistic. Variables were also created to indicate cumulative All-Star appearances, cumulative post-season appearances, and cumulative Gold Gloves won.

Gold Glove Distribution

Table 2 shows the distribution of all Gold Glove Awards in 1957–2004. There were only 251 original winners of the slightly more than 850 awards given in that interval. About half the winners have won one or two awards each. Among the half who have won three or more awards, most have won between three and five, though there are 48 players (18%) who have won six or more Gold Gloves. This is no doubt the source of many sportswriters' suggestions that the winner in any given year is whoever won the year before. In the absence of any other information, this is not a bad bet, and should be born in mind as the results from position-specific models are presented.

Statistical Analyses

We fit logistic regression models to the data, with the Gold Glove indicator as the outcome variable (yes/no). The logistic regression model fits the log (natural logarithm) odds of success for a binary variable (in this case win of a Gold Glove, yes or no) to a linear function of explanatory variables. The resultant parameter estimates can be used to calculate the probability of an event occurring based on the values of the explanatory variables for a given observation. Logistic regression is a robust method and is used widely in the health sciences. Further details on the methodology are available in standard statistics texts such as that of Hosmer & Lemeshow.

Stepwise selection of variables was used to determine which among the possible explanatory variables were most significant in predicting a Gold Glove win. Variables that were significant at the 5% level in the stepwise routine were initially retained. Linearity in the continuous variables was then tested using indicator variables and higher-order terms, and competing models were compared by way of the log likelihood tests and/or the Akaike Information Criterion.

We tested for significance of interaction terms, starting with each of the main effects crossed with each other. Significance in interaction variables represents an effect that is different for different values of main effects. For example, an interaction between putouts and league would indicate that the effect of number of putouts on a player's chances of winning a Gold Glove is different in the American and National Leagues.

All data were extracted from the Lahman database and analyzed using the SAS system for Windows.

RESULTS
Pitcher Model

Table 3 displays the model for predicting pitching Gold Gloves based on all player-seasons with at least 24 games. The model shows that for pitchers, a combination of defensive opportunities, reputation, and pitching prowess is highly predictive of winning a Gold Glove.

In the pitchers' model, defensive opportunities are represented by total chances per game. The value of this variable is calculated by dividing the total number of defensive chances in a season by the total appearances in that position in the season. In spite of the wide confidence interval associated with the odds ratio, this variable nonetheless has a strong and clear effect: accruing more putouts, assists, and even errors is a positive factor.

A previous win of a Gold Glove had a tremendous impact on a pitcher's chance of winning an award. As we shall see, this was true at every position, but the pitching Gold Glove winners' club is particularly hard to break into. Pitchers who have won previously are over 100 times more likely to win again as a pitcher who has not yet won. This is further reflected in the fact that once a player

Table 2. Distribution of the 856 Gold Gloves awarded 1957–2004

Total Gold Gloves won	1	2	3	4	5	6	7	8	9	10	11	12	13	14	16	Total
Players with this total	92	34	39	22	16	9	11	10	5	5	2	2	1	1	2	251

wins at least once, he is 1.36 times as likely to win another for each award he has won.

Table 3. Logistic model for pitchers

Variable	Odds Ratio	95% CI[1]
Total chances per game[2]	8.106	(3.516, 18.692)
Not yet won a Gold Glove	0.012	(0.005, 0.027)
Number of previous Gold Gloves	1.360	(1.187, 1.558)
Wins	1.208	(1.096, 1.331)
Strikeouts pitched	1.011	(1.004, 1.018)

[1]95% Confidence Interval

[2]Calculated as sum of chances in season divided by games played in season

Wins and strikeouts are, perhaps not surprisingly, significant predictors of award winning. For each win credited to him, a pitcher is 1.208 times as likely to win a Gold Glove, and for each strikeout posted he is 1.011 times as likely to win a Gold Glove. Thus a pitcher who has 100 strikeouts in a season is 1.73 times as likely to win a Gold Glove as a pitcher who has only 50 strikeouts ($1.011^{50} = 1.73$).

Catcher Model

The model for catchers relies on a broad mixture of variables: fielding measures, age, reputation, and offense. For catchers, at least 87 appearances in the season were required to be included in the analysis. The full model is displayed in Table 4.

Table 4. Logistic model for catchers

Variable	Odds Ratio	95% CI[1]
Assists	1.043	(1.021, 1.066)
Fielding percentage[2]	3.754	(1.923, 7.326)
Age	0.680	(0.597, 0.775)
Postseason appearances		
Current season	0.394	(0.173, 0.898)
Total career appearances	1.754	(1.373, 2.242)
Not yet won a Gold Glove	0.034	(0.015, 0.077)
Number of Hits in current season	1.020	(1.008, 1.032)
Sacrifice hits		
Three or fewer	0.259	(0.127, 0.526)
Four or more[3]	1.000	---

[1]95% Confidence Interval

[2]Calculated as fielding percentage as a decimal, multiplied by 100

[3]Odds ratio of 1.000 and no confidence interval denotes the reference group

Bob Gibson

ASSOCIATED PRESS

The table shows that for catchers, fielding percentage and the total number of assists in a season are related to winning the Gold Glove. It is somewhat surprising that passed balls, a special error unique to catchers, is not a significant factor in the model. Instead, errors hurt catchers' chances of winning by reducing their fielding percentages.

The offensive statistics included here are worth noting. While accumulating a higher number of hits improves the chances of winning an award, sacrifice hits have a threshold of three. A player who accrues three or fewer sacrifice hits suffers a severe penalty to his chances of winning a Gold Glove as compared to those who accrue four or more.

The reputation effects in this model relate to post-season appearances and whether or not the player has won a Gold Glove before. Notably, being in the post-season is a highly negative factor for winning a Gold Glove, but having been in many post-seasons is a positive factor. As expected, never having won a Gold Glove previously is a large negative factor.

First Base Model

The model for first base (Table 5) is based on player-seasons with at least 93 games, and contains fielding measures, age, and reputation. In particular, the chief skill of a first baseman, putouts, is highly significant, and a high number of putouts can substantially increase his chances of winning the Gold Glove. Fielding percentage matters as well, with each unit increase conferring an almost six-fold increase in the chances of winning. In this model, fielding percentage was expressed as a whole number, that is, the decimal fielding percentage multiplied by 100. To reduce the standard error on the parameter estimate (and thus the confidence interval of the odds ratio), these percents were rounded to the nearest whole number.

Table 5. Logistic model for first basemen

Variable	Odds Ratio	95% CI[1]
Putouts	1.003	(1.002, 1.005)
Fielding Percentage	5.879	(3.018, 11.450)
Age		
Younger than 31[2]	1.000	--
Each year over 31	0.345	(0.200, 0.595)
All-Star Appearances		
All-Star in previous season	3.552	(1.429, 8.826)
Total appearances (including current season)	0.691	(0.530, 0.899)
Gold Gloves		
Not yet won a Gold Glove	0.112	(0.044, 0.285)
Number of Gold Gloves won	1.839	(1.392, 2.431)

[1]95% Confidence Interval

[2]Odds ratio of 1.000 and no confidence interval denotes the reference group

Reputation effects in this model include All-Star appearance in previous season, the total number of career All-Star appearances, whether or not the player has won a Gold Glove, and the total number of Gold Gloves won. As expected, never having won a Gold Glove is a highly negative factor, and winning multiple awards

bestows an ever-increasing bonus. A surprising result came from the All-Star appearance variables; while going to the All-Star game is a large positive factor, each individual appearance is a negative factor. This finding is likely one of correlation rather than causation, as we can imagine no explanation why coaches or managers would (or should) discriminate against players who were All-Stars in the previous years.

A final important factor for first basemen is age. Once a player passes age 31, his chances of winning a Gold Glove decline precipitously. It is certainly possible to win a Gold Glove at age 31 and older, however, and it has happened a total of 20 times (27%).

Second Base Model

The model for second base is presented in Table 6. The model is based on all player-seasons with at least 118 appearances at the position.

Table 6. Logistic model for second basemen

Variable	Odds Ratio	95% CI[1]
Games played in season		
Under 141 games[2]	1.000	--
Each game over 141	1.109	(1.057, 1.166)
Fielding percentage	4.030	(2.083, 7.119)
Age		
Younger than 28[2]	1.000	--
Each year past 28	0.692	(0.583, 0.856)
Not yet won a Gold Glove	0.034	(0.019, 0.107)
All-Star appearance in current season	4.229	(1.687, 7.124)

[1]95% Confidence Interval

[2]Odds ratio of 1.000 and no confidence interval denotes the reference group

For second base, the number of games played is important. The chances of winning a Gold Glove are flat for those players who play only 141 games at second base. Thereafter, the chances rise by approximately 11% per game (odds ratio 1.109). This dramatic increase suggests that only full-time second basemen who log a substantial amount of playing time are serious contenders for a Gold Glove.

Fielding percentage is a strong predictor for this middle infield position. As one would expect (and has been seen in other models), the higher the fielding percentage, the higher the chances of winning a Gold Glove.

Age is again an important variable. The chances of a second baseman winning an award decline by more than 30% per year after age 28.

A player who has never won a Gold Glove is 0.034 times as likely to win as a player who has won previously. Being an All-Star makes a second baseman over four times as likely to win.

Third Base Model

The model for third basemen was fit to all player-seasons that had at least 115 games associated with them.

Among the fielding measures important for third base is assists. In the model, the chances of winning a Gold Glove are uni-

Brooks Robinson

ROBERT REYNOLDS is a Senior Consultant Data Analyst with Kaiser Permanente in Oakland, CA. He holds a Master of Public Health in Epidemiology and a Bachelor of Science in Psychology, both from the University of Arizona. On most nights between the months of April and October, he can be found in section 319 of SBC Park.

STEVEN DAY earned a Ph.D. in Statistics from the University of California, Riverside and two Master's degrees in Mathematics from the University of California, Davis. Dr. Day lives in Southern California and supports all Los Angeles baseball teams.

DAVID PACULDO is a Senior Researcher/Analyst affiliated with the Life Expectancy Project in San Francisco, CA. He is a graduate of the University of California, Irvine and holds a Master of Public Health from Dartmouth College. In addition to performing biostatistical research, he is a die-hard Chicago Cubs fan.

form until a player accrues at least 230 assists. After this number, the chances of winning a Gold Glove increase by 1.6% per assist. This is an enormous adjustment in light of the fact that a few full-time third basemen have tallied 400 or more assists in a season. Thus, for example, compared to a third baseman with 200 assists, a player with 400 assists is 23.92 times more likely to win a Gold Glove.

As in the other positions so far, fielding percentage is a significant factor. The chances of winning a Gold Glove almost double with each percent increase in fielding percentage.

For third base, a marker of long-term career consistency in fielding was also significant: the average putouts per game over the entire career of the player (up to and including the season in question). The chances of winning an award were flat for any career average under 8.4 putouts per game, and increase by almost four-fold for each unit change in this average after that.

Table 7. Logistic model for third basemen

Variable	Odds Ratio	95% CI[1]
Assists		
Fewer than 230 assists[2]	1.000	--
Each assist over 230	1.016	(1.007, 1.024)
Average putouts per game, career		
Under 8.4[2]	1.000	--
Each average putout over 8.4[3]	3.768	(1.756, 8.086)
Fielding percentage	1.914	(1.370, 2.674)
Age		
Younger than 23 years old	1.000	--
Each year over 23	0.875	(0.778, 0.985)
Not yet won a Gold Glove	0.022	(0.008, 0.055)
Post-season appearance in previous season	2.874	(1.259, 6.557)
Runs Batted In		
Fewer than 90 RBI[2]	1.000	--
90 or more RBI	10.070	(4.504, 22.516)

[1] 95% Confidence Interval
[2] Odds ratio of 1.000 and no confidence interval denotes the reference group
[3] Defined as total career putouts divided by total career games played

The third base model is influenced by reputation in much the same way as the other infield positions. Never having won a Gold Glove is a significant negative factor, making a player only 2.2% as likely to win the award.

An interesting finding in this model is that the number of Runs Batted In (RBI) significantly influences the chances of winning for players who have at least 90 of them. Though any causal explanations offered for this association would be purely speculative, RBI is a favorite offensive statistic of so-called "baseball men." Thus it seems probable that this is something explicitly considered by coaches and managers in the voting process.

Shortstop Model

The model for shortstop is based upon player-seasons with games totaling 114 or more. The model uses fielding measures, age, and reputation, and is displayed in Table 8.

The total defensive chances are significantly related to the odds of winning a Gold Glove for shortstops. For each defensive chance, the player is 1.010 times more likely to win a Gold Glove. In addition to this, each unit of fielding percentage makes the player almost four times as likely to win an award. These two together will greatly reward the player who reaches and successfully fields a large number of balls.

The chances of winning an award at shortstop increase linearly with age up to 28 years, after which the risk is flat. The chances increase at almost 9% per year until age 27. This model of age suggests improvement in the odds through the 20s, with a peak in the chances of winning at age 27. After age 27, the flat risk suggests that the chances of winning an award are governed by factors other than age. This effect is likely due to increasing reputation as an excellent fielder up to age 28, after which voters perceive an equalization of talent between Gold Glove candidates. Were this effect due to increasing skill, the risk should plateau at age 28, and then decline in lockstep with declining physical ability; instead, the chances remain constant indefinitely.

Table 8. Logistic model for shortstops

Variable	Odds Ratio	95% CI[1]
Total chances	1.010	(1.006, 1.014)
Fielding Percentage[2]	3.786	(2.403, 5.964)
Age		
Each year up to 27	1.085	(1.045, 1.126)
28 and older[3]	1.000	--
Not yet won a Gold Glove	0.198	(0.075, 0.487)
Number of previous Gold Gloves	1.325	(1.098, 1.598)
All-Star appearance in current season	2.598	(1.350, 5.003)
Postseason appearance	2.917	(1.386, 6.138)
Natural logarithm of stolen bases	1.851	(1.233, 2.778)

[1] 95% Confidence Interval
[2] Fielding percentage expressed as decimal fielding percentage multiplied by 100, rounded to the nearest whole number.
[3] Odds ratio of 1.000 and no confidence interval denotes the reference group

Reputation figures significantly into the chances of winning for shortstop (as it does for every position). Not yet having won a Gold Glove is detrimental to the chances of winning the first one. Having won before increases the chance of winning in a current season by 32.5% per award won. Being an All-Star increases the chances by roughly 260%, and making a post-season appearance makes a player almost 300% as likely to win an award.

Finally, one offensive measure significantly predicts Gold Glove winners at shortstop, that of the stolen base. In this model, an increase in one unit of the natural logarithm of the number of stolen bases in a season makes a player 1.851 times as likely to win an award. In essence this means that while a high number of stolen bases is good, it is subject to quickly diminishing returns, as it takes an exponential amount of stolen bases to continually raise the value of the natural logarithm. For example, it takes 3 stolen bases to get a score of 1.1, 7 stolen bases to score 2, and 20 stolen bases for a score of 3.

Luis Aparicio (top) and Ozzie Smith

Outfield Model

Table 9 displays the logistic model for outfielders. This model is based on roughly four times the number of player-seasons as the other models. The difference mostly stems from the fact that the three outfield positions were aggregated into one model, but may also be due to the fact that many teams keep a larger staff of outfielders for platooning. The model includes only those player-seasons that had a game count of 44 or more.

Table 9. Logistic model for outfielders

Variable	Odds Ratio	95% CI[1]
Putouts	1.011	(1.008, 1.014)
Fielding percentage	1.746	(1.366, 2.231)
Age		
Younger than 27[2]	1.000	--
Each year past 27	0.695	(0.611, 0.791)
Not yet won a Gold Glove	0.113	(0.068, 0.190)
Number of previous Gold Gloves won	2.016	(1.698, 2.393)
All-Star appearances		
Appearance in current season	4.408	(2.667, 7.286)
Total appearances	0.718	(0.629, 0.820)
Post-season appearance	1.459	(0.945, 2.253)
Runs		
Fewer than 26	1.000	--
Each past 26	1.022	(1.010, 1.034)
Natural Logarithim of Runs Batted In	2.915	(1.527, 5.564)
Calendar year[3]	0.971	(0.953, 0.989)

[1] 95% Confidence Interval
[2] Odds ratio of 1.000 and no confidence interval denotes the reference group
[3] Years since 1965

The fielding components to the model are putouts and fielding percentage, both of which are positive factors for winning an award. For each putout, the player is 1.011 times more likely to win a Gold Glove, while he is 1.746 times more likely to win for each unit increase in fielding percentage.

Age is important for outfielders as well. The chances are flat until age 27, after which they decline with age by approximately 30% per year.

The history of Gold Glove winnings is important; much like the other player positions, having won before is very helpful, with each additional award conveying more than twice the likelihood of winning again.

Total All-Star appearances and an All-Star appearance in the current season are both significant in the model. However, while an appearance in the current season is helpful, more appearances harm the chances of winning. To better understand this relationship, consider the following example: a player who appeared in the All-Star game twice before and also appears in the current season has an overall 1.63 times the chance of someone who has never gone to the All-Star game $[(0.718)^3*(4.408)]$. A player who has appeared three times overall but does not make the All-Star game in the current season has 0.370 times the chance of winning a Gold Glove $[(0.781)^3]$. It seems then that going to the All-Star game is a largely important factor for the first few appearanc-

es, but then the effect fades. When a repeat All-Star finally fails to make the All-Star game, it hurts his chances greatly.

Making a post-season appearance is also helpful; those who do it are almost 1.5 times as likely to win a Gold Glove.

Two offensive measures are significant in the model, and both help a player's chances of winning an award. For each run over the 26th, players' chances increase by 1.022 times. Each increase in the natural logarithm of RBI gives 2.915 times the chances of winning.

Finally, calendar year (expressed as number of years since 1965) is significant. Significance in this variable means that, on average, it is getting harder for all players to win a Gold Glove award each year that goes by. The chances of winning shrink at an average rate of 2.9% per year. In 2004, this reduction equates to $(0.971)^{40} = 0.308$. This means that players today are only 0.308 times as likely to win a Gold Glove as players were in 1965.

This is a logical finding, but ultimately not an important one. As awards are given every year, it does not matter how likely one is to win in comparison to players of years past; everyone who is eligible for a Gold Glove has the same chance, all other factors being equal. The term for calendar year would only then be important if we wanted to compare the performances of two players from two different years. The year term would allow us to standardize the chances of winning an award for historical players who had the benefit of playing in smaller leagues. We include the variable here because it makes an overall significant contribution to the model, and thus should not be ignored.

Prediction

Having constructed models for each position, we then tested the models by using the calculated probabilities from the models to rank the likelihood of winning a Gold Glove at each position, by league and by year.

To do this, we ranked the players in each league and each year based on their probabilities of winning according to the appropriate model. We then examined the percentage of Gold Glove winners who received a #1 ranking from the model. The results are listed in Table 10.

Table 10. Percentage of Gold Glove award winners correctly predicted by models

P	C	1B	2B	3B	SS	OF*
68.9	63.5	72.6	64.9	81.1	68.9	64.6

*Uses the top three rankings as predicted winners in each league and year.

Table 10 shows that most of the models correctly predicted the winner 60–70% of the time. The notable exception is the third base model, which achieved a correct prediction rate of 81%. The outfield model is considered to have correctly predicted the winner when the winner was ranked number one, two, or three, since three awards are given every year.

Discussion

As mentioned in the Introduction, the models reported here do not necessarily reflect the thought processes of the coaches and managers when voting for Gold Glove winners. Instead, the models reported in this paper may be thought of as the characteristics that historically have been most strongly associated with the winners of Gold Gloves at the various positions. These characteristics may be what sway coaches and managers when voting (consciously or subconsciously), or they may be characteristics that are highly correlated with the true attributes coaches rely on which are not accounted for directly here. Only a survey of the coaches and managers would be able to discern on what explicit criteria they cast their ballots.

Several general trends are common to all the models. The first and most important is the role of having previously won a Gold Glove. In every model presented, the indicator variable of not yet having won a Gold Glove is significant. Invariably it has a large effect, ranging from an odds ratio of 0.012 for pitchers to an odds ratio of 0.192 for shortstops (thus players who have won a Gold Glove before are from 5.21 to 83.33 times as likely to win one in the current season as a player who has not yet won). In models in which the total number of Gold Gloves won before is significant, its effects are large, acting as the expected complement to never having won a Gold Glove before. The odds ratios given in the models range between 1.360 and 2.016 *for each additional Gold Glove won*. Overall, the effect is dramatic. Those who have not won before are not likely to start winning, but those who have won are likely to keep winning. Indeed this may say as much about the inherent talent of the players as it says about the effect of reputation.

As would be suspected, fielding percentage is present in nearly all models, and in each case is associated with greater chances of winning a Gold Glove. The association of high percentage of successful fielding with winning a fielding award would be the first and most basic hypothesis possible; as such the presence of this variable in most of the models lends face validity to the models presented here.

Raw fielding totals also figure prominently in some models. Since we are not using more complex fielding metrics here, the raw fielding statistics may indirectly capture exceptional fielding by showing not only the proportion of error-free plays, but the larger number of such plays made. In other words, the best fielders not only get their glove on the ball more often than other men in the leagues, they turn those opportunities into successful outs more often too.

Age was a significant predictor in all but pitching models. Whether or not voters use this criterion when casting ballots is again debatable, but the usual sharp decline in the chances of winning past each position-specific age threshold seems to suggest that if this is not the case, age is at the very least linked to something important related to fielding, such as an age range that is the best balance of skill and athletic ability for performing at position. If the skill versus athletic ability explanation is true, age should be accounted for more carefully when evaluating or projecting the careers of position players, as large changes in ability may come suddenly with age.

Conspicuous by its absence is a lack of differences in variables between leagues for any of the awards. This is not entirely unexpected, however; in spite of league differences, players, coaches, and managers are constantly moving between leagues, keeping the culture of the major leagues uniform. With the advent of interleague play in the 1990s, the cultural similarity between the leagues could have only increased. Most important, what makes a great player in one league shouldn't be different from what makes a great player in the other (with the possible exception of pitchers who might also be great hitters, or designated hitters).

The article by Arthur Zillante fitted similar models to data from a different time period, and for fewer positions. Overall, the best of Zillante's models correctly predict winning a Gold Glove 50–65% of the time, varying by position. These models are based on offensive, defensive, and reputation effects, with the best results naturally coming from the models that keep only statistically significant predictors.

There may be two reasons that Zillante's models are less accurate than the models presented here. Zillante's models are in all cases much simpler than the current set; he has fewer variables, and often has raw counting statistics for fielding instead of rate statistics. Noticeably absent from his models are age terms, which here contribute substantially to most models.

Where there are similarities between the present study and Zillante's, the similarities are sometimes striking. The third base model in the current study has the same variables as the Zillante model, with the only differences between the models being different parameterizations of some variables, plus some additional variables in our model. Other models share common variables and similar odds ratio estimates.

The utility of the models presented here may be severely limited in time. The models have acceptable predictive value for the data used in this study, which span 1965 to 2004. This is not to say, however, that things will not change over time—slowly or rapidly. In an age in which long-standing records are being broken and the integrity of the players is under close scrutiny, it is tempting to think that the standards may change or that anything is possible. However, if history is our guide, the culture of baseball is slow to change, and the skills and other attributes common among winners of the Gold Glove Award will likely not change in the foreseeable future.

Notes

1. Zillante, A. (2005). *Reputation Effects in Gold Glove Award Voting.* Paper presented at the Public Choice Society 2005 Annual Meeting. Article available at www.pubchoicesoc.org/papers2005/zillante.pdf.

Consider Your Sources
Baseball and Baked Beans in Boston

Tim Wiles, director of research at the National Baseball Hall of Fame for the past 10 years, wrote an entertaining article, "The Joy of Foul Balls," in issue #25 of *The National Pastime*. At a recent SABR board meeting, Norman Macht read a couple of paragraphs aloud and the room convulsed with laughter for a few minutes. The story, in Tim's words, ran as follows:

On August 11, 1903, the A's were visiting the Red Sox, then playing in the old Huntington Avenue Grounds. At the plate in the seventh inning was Rube Waddell, the colorful southpaw pitcher for the A's, who was known to run off the mound to chase after passing fire trucks, and to be mesmerized whenever an opposing team brought a puppy onto their bench to distract him. Waddell lifted a foul ball over the right-field bleachers that landed on the roof of a baked-bean cannery next door.

The ball came to rest in the steam whistle of the factory, which began to go off. As it was not quitting time, workers thought there was an emergency and abandoned their posts. A short while later, a giant cauldron containing a ton of beans boiled over and exploded, showering the Boston ballpark with scalding beans. It is probably safe to say that this was the most dramatic foul of all time.

Certainly so! When laughter subsided, I remarked that I'd contributed a multi-part series of articles for the Red Sox magazine in 2003, recounting every game of the 1903 season, which culminated in the first victory in a modern World Series for the Boston Americans. (The team was not named the "Red Sox" until owner John I. Taylor designated that name on December 18, 1907, while selecting new uniforms for the 1908 season.) I'd not come across any mention of an explosion raining baked beans onto the crowd—it's the kind of thing you'd remember—but I certainly wanted to learn more.

I wrote Tim and asked him where he'd learned about this incident, and he referred me to Mike Gershman's book *Diamonds*. On page 70, there it was, a story the very respected Gershman titled, "The Great Beantown Massacre." Mike gave as his source Charles Dryden, whom he described as "for years Philadelphia's leading baseball writer." Dryden's rendition was even more dramatic:

In the seventh inning, Rube Waddell hoisted a long foul over the right-field bleachers that landed on the roof of the biggest bean cannery in Boston. In descending, the ball fell on the roof of the engine room and jammed itself between the steam whistle and the stem of the valve that operates it. The pressure set the whistle blowing. It lacked a few minutes of five o'clock, yet the workmen started to leave the building. They thought quitting time had come.

The incessant screeching of the bean-factory whistle led engineers in the neighboring factories to think fire had broken out and they turned on their whistles. With a dozen whistles going full blast, a policeman sent in an alarm of fire.

Just as the engines arrived, a steam cauldron in the first factory, containing a ton of beans, blew up. The explosion dislodged Waddell's foul fly and the whistle stopped blowing, but that was not the end of the trouble. A shower of scalding beans descended on the bleachers and caused a small panic. One man went insane. When he saw the beans dropping out of a cloud of steam, the unfortunate rooter yelled, "The end of the world is coming and we will all be destroyed with a shower of hot hailstones."

An ambulance summoned to the supposed fire conveyed the demented man to his home. The ton of beans proved a total loss. (Dryden's story ran in the *Philadelphia North American* on August 12, 1903.)

What a great story! Naturally, I wanted to learn more. I was surprised I hadn't come across such a dramatic event while reading 1903's daily game stories in the *Boston Herald*. I'd read all the usual books about the Red Sox and hadn't heard this one before. I couldn't find anything on ProQuest, which made me wonder even more. So I took myself off to the Microtext Reading Room at the Boston Public Library. Surely Dryden would not have been the only sportswriter to have noticed 2,000 pounds of boiling baked beans splattering the bleachers at the ballpark, or the dozen factory whistles shrieking alarm.

The *Boston Globe* had no mention of any such incident. The seventh inning was a particularly unremarkable inning, about the only inning not described in detail in the game account. The *Herald* noted, "Murphy opened the seventh by striking out and Monte Cross drew the first gift of his side, but it amounted to nothing as Powers was out to Dougherty and Waddell fouled to LaChance." Waddell did foul out, but one presumes that LaChance caught the ball somewhere in the vicinity of his position at first base. There was no mention of an earlier foul in the at-bat that went out of the grounds, or of baked beans cascading onto unwitting patrons of the park, or anything of the sort.

Dryden's piece seemed oddly comic, almost as though it had been written as comedy for a publication such as *The Onion*. There was a particular line that stood out to me: "One man went insane." Though one could imagine losing a grip on reality if suddenly and unexpectedly coated with scalding baked beans and molasses as sirens shrieked from all sides, there was something about that line that raised a red flag.

Reading through the other various Boston newspapers of the day—the *Boston Journal*, the *Post*, the *Record*, the *Daily Advertiser*, and the *Traveler*—not one mention turned up of any exploding bean works or any problems at the ball game. The *Journal* noted that an earlier explosion (not at a bean company) in Lowell had claimed another victim. After a burglary in Wrentham, the crooks escaped using a stolen railroad handcar. A seven-year-old drowned in Fall River. A Charlestown woman had been missing for two days. A runaway horse injured two people in Franklin Square when it bolted due to the noise of an elevated train.

There was no ball game on August 12, but it was not because the park was being cleaned of baked bean residue. The team was simply on its way to Detroit.

The *Boston Post* noted many of the same stories as the *Journal* and paid particular credit to Reserve Officer Morse for saving several small children by stopping the runway horse. The *Post* offered a sports page cartoon of the ball game (a 5-1 Boston victory), and depicted four baseballs being lofted off Waddell to various parts of the park, but did not illustrate any explosions, screaming whistles, or rain of beans. A man in Braintree, a hunter, shot himself in the left hand by mistake. John J. Sullivan, a fireman with Ladder 2, caught a 5'4" skate fish off Apple Island. There were any number of stories, but notable by its absence was any account of an exploding baked-bean cauldron.

The *Boston Record* offered a follow-up story regarding an accident at the Philadelphia baseball park, the National League park where the Boston Nationals had been playing against the Phillies. The games there had been called off because of an accident that had taken place on August 8. An altercation between two drunks outside the park caused a number of people to rush to the wall overlooking the street, and as people crushed forward to gawk at the disturbance, the wall collapsed, killing a number of people and causing over 200 to be treated for injuries. At least 12 people died in the collapse or in the days that followed. It must be one of the most serious accidents ever to occur at a major league baseball park.

As a reporter from Philadelphia, Dryden had to be aware of the tragedy. This made the Boston story seem more credible, since this was hardly a time for levity. One would have to believe that Dryden didn't just make up the story of the baked beans in Boston. How can we explain this remarkable story that was remarked upon by no other writer?

In email correspondence, Tim Wiles had written me that he

BILL NOWLIN is VP of SABR and the author of a dozen books on the Red Sox, including 2006's *Day By Day with the Boston Red Sox* and (with Cecilia Tan) *The 50 Greatest Red Sox Games*.

Charles Dryden

NATIONAL BASEBALL HALL OF FAME, COOPERSTOWN, NY

thought it might be a good idea to poll SABR and "see if anyone knows whether Dryden had a mischievous streak." He added, "This might make a nice little article on the pitfalls of repeating what others have written without double-checking."

First, I decided to look around a bit myself, to see what I could learn about Dryden. The very first item I found showed Charles Dryden enshrined in, of all places, the very Hall of Fame where Tim works. He was a 1965 recipient of the J. G. Taylor Spink Award. Dryden was listed as a charter member of the Baseball Writers' Association of America. What more reliable sources could we hope for than Mike Gershman, Tim Wiles, and a Spink Award honoree?

Uh-oh. There it was. In the next sentence, the Hall of Fame bio provides a crucial bit of information about Dryden: "The humorist was often regarded as the master baseball writer of his time."

It turns out Dryden was the one who coined the phrase: "Washington—first in war, first in peace, and last in the American League." He labeled Frank Chance the "Peerless Leader" and called Charles Comiskey "The Old Roman." The Hall of Fame's web site noted of Dryden: "Upon receiving compliments from New York writers on his humor-filled columns, Ring Lardner replied: 'Me, a humorist? Have you guys read any of Charley Dryden's stuff lately? He makes me look like a novice.'"

Further research on Dryden shows that he particularly enjoyed tweaking Rube Waddell. In another story, he claimed that Waddell had once been found taking a bite out of the Washington Monument, but that it was not a serious problem because the Athletics pitcher had rubber teeth. Dryden also informed readers that the reason left-handed pitchers were called southpaws had nothing to do with early 20th-century ballparks being positioned in such a way that home plate was toward the west and the late afternoon sun would therefore not be in the eyes of the batter. The truth, Dryden assured his readers, was a simple one: there was a particular left hander who tried out for the Chicago Cubs and hailed from Southpaw, Illinois. It was as simple as that.

Dryden's account of the August 11, 1903, game reads smoothly enough and contains the expected information about the ball game. Entitled "Prodigal Waddell Pitched and Lost," it starts on page one and continues inside on page five. It is only in the 11th paragraph that the story about the baked beans turns up, seemingly out of nowhere but seamlessly integrated into the account of the day's game. There was an earlier story of a mascot retained for the game by Lave Cross, a "human reservoir" described as "a colored man who can drink ten quarts of water or any other liquid without removing the pail from his lips." Dryden added, "When Cross engaged the reservoir the teams wanted to know why he did not use 'Rube' for a mascot." Cross did not reply. The story continued on to note Waddell's role "once again as chief actor in a baseball tragedy"—and then recounts the story of the exploding steam cauldron of baked beans.

The *Philadelphia Inquirer* failed to notice any explosions, but did note that Boston had now taken five out of six from the 1902 champion Athletics. The game had been the final one of a six-game set, with Philadelphia taking the second game but losing all

Rube Waddell

the others, including this day's 5–1 defeat at the hands of Long Tom Hughes and the Boston Americans. Boston scored twice in the first, once in the second, and coasted on Hughes' seven-hit pitching, the only run for the visitors coming in the eighth inning. The win left Boston at 60–34 on the season. Philadelphia was 54–41, in second place but 6½ games behind.

And after the game, the Athletics—presumably accompanied by Dryden—caught an 8:00 p.m. train which in 36 hours would bring them to Chicago.

Back in 2003, Norman Macht had posted a warning still found today on SABR's web site, in a section of guidelines devoted to BioProject: "A writer's credentials do not guarantee reliability. Fred Lieb's books have errors of fact. Charles Dryden, like other reporter-humorists, made up stuff. Jim Nasium had either a porous memory or fertile imagination." Apparently, we knew it all along, but that such a wildly improbable story was reported as fact by both eminent writers Gershman and Wiles is a lesson in double-checking even primary sources and considering the quality of those sources. And a reminder that baseball research can result in some very entertaining forays.

Thanks to Nicole DiCicco, Clifford Blau, and Tim Wiles. Additional research via ProQuest.

TOM RUANE

Do Some Batters Reach on Errors More Than Others?

On one level, the answer to this question seems obvious: since batters strike out, fly out, and ground out at different rates, and since each of these three ways of making an out have very different associated error rates, batters who ground out in a high percentage of their at-bats should reach base on errors more often than batters who predominantly strike out and fly out. But there still is a host of other potentially interesting issues I want to explore. Are there significant differences even among similar classes of hitters? Are there situational factors that need to be taken into consideration? For example, if there are much lower error rates with no one on, do leadoff batters reach base this way less frequently than cleanup hitters? How big a factor is batter speed? Or whether the batter bats from the right or the left side? Do some parks have much higher errors rates than others, due either to the influence of official scorers or environmental factors such as rocky infields, poor lighting, and unusual wind currents?

This article will attempt to explore these issues, although not necessarily in the order above. Before I begin, however, I must admit to some fuzzy terminology. When I talk about a batter reaching base on an error, I mean some things that are not classified as errors. This includes batters who strike out and reach first because of a wild pitch or passed ball. I include a batter who reaches due to a bad fielder's choice that results in no outs being recorded on the play. In short, any play where no outs are made (except for the cases where the batter or runner gets greedy and is thrown out attempting to take an extra base) and the batter is charged with either a hitless at-bat, sacrifice hit, or sacrifice fly. Note that I am not including catcher's interference in this group.

I examined play-by-play data of games from 1960 to 2004. I did not have play-by-play information for all these games, but I came pretty close.

The Simple Approach

In the simplest terms, if you just look at the number of times a player's outs turn into errors, do some players have much higher error rates than others?

To answer this, I computed how many outs a player was charged with, as well as how many of those resulted in an error. For each year I also generated an expected number of errors, by multiplying the number of outs by the league average of errors per out. I summed all of these, the player's actual and expected errors, for his career and compared them.

What did I find? Well, among players making at least 2,000 outs in their careers from 1960 to 2004, here are the ones who exceeded their expected errors by the greatest percentage:

Batter	Outs	Err	GO%	FO%	SO%	ExErr	ErrF
Derek Jeter	3859	114	47.0	27.9	25.2	66.9	1.705
Otis Nixon	3831	124	51.3	30.6	18.1	73.4	1.689
Manny Mota	2631	93	55.7	32.7	11.6	59.8	1.556
Rey Sanchez	3627	102	51.9	34.2	13.9	66.7	1.529
Mickey Stanley	3855	127	47.9	37.5	14.6	83.5	1.520
Bob Horner	2781	89	37.1	44.5	18.4	58.7	1.516
Rondell White	3276	91	42.7	32.7	24.5	60.6	1.502
Joe Girardi	3131	89	48.9	31.7	19.4	59.3	1.500
Wil Cordero	3131	85	36.9	38.8	24.3	58.5	1.453
Willie McGee	5471	161	53.6	23.8	22.6	111.8	1.440
Stan Javier	3794	102	45.8	32.1	22.1	71.5	1.427
Greg Gross	2743	86	52.8	38.1	9.1	60.5	1.422
Cesar Tovar	4130	126	45.1	45.0	9.9	89.8	1.403
Jose Vizcaino	3816	102	48.5	33.8	17.7	72.8	1.402
Deivi Cruz	2916	71	46.6	39.8	13.5	50.7	1.400
Chad Curtis	3039	77	39.7	38.0	22.2	55.1	1.397
Miguel Tejada	3122	75	41.4	38.9	19.7	53.8	1.394
Gary Disarcina	2876	72	52.2	37.1	10.6	51.9	1.389
Scott Fletcher	4029	108	48.4	38.2	13.4	77.8	1.388
Roberto Clemente	4526	146	54.0	25.4	20.6	105.7	1.381

And the lowest:

Batter	Outs	Err	GO%	FO%	SO%	ExErr	ErrF
Darren Daulton	2792	29	30.6	43.4	26.0	56.2	0.516
Mike Lowell	2264	21	28.5	50.7	20.8	40.5	0.519
Jim Gentile	2169	25	32.7	37.0	30.2	48.2	0.519
Mo Vaughn	3957	37	32.5	31.3	36.1	70.8	0.523
Mike Epstein	2180	25	31.1	39.4	29.6	46.6	0.537
Ernie Whitt	2893	33	38.6	44.4	17.0	57.6	0.573
Bobby Murcer	4967	62	34.3	48.7	16.9	107.0	0.579
Bernie Carbo	2036	26	38.7	31.4	29.9	44.6	0.582
Henry Rodriguez	2272	26	27.8	36.9	35.3	44.1	0.589
Jim Dwyer	2101	26	31.5	49.4	19.1	43.6	0.596
Darrin Fletcher	2918	34	38.1	48.3	13.7	55.5	0.613
Greg Walker	2143	26	36.3	39.5	24.3	42.4	0.613
Carlos Delgado	3656	39	30.3	35.7	34.0	63.5	0.614
Franklin Stubbs	2027	25	27.8	41.3	30.9	40.5	0.617
Sid Bream	2353	30	38.3	42.5	19.1	48.3	0.622
Jason Giambi	3408	37	29.7	43.5	26.9	59.1	0.626
Ken Henderson	3440	48	36.0	41.8	22.2	76.3	0.629
Andy Van Slyke	4222	55	35.6	39.2	25.2	86.5	0.636
Jeromy Burnitz	3617	42	29.8	37.2	33.0	65.8	0.638
Boog Powell	5004	70	39.7	35.8	24.5	108.7	0.644

```
Outs: Number of outs made
Err: Number of times reached on errors
GO%: Percentage of outs that were ground balls
FO%: Percentage of outs that were fly balls
SO%: Percentage of outs that were strikeouts
ExErr: Expected number of errors based on league rates
ErrF: Error factor (Err / ExErr)
```

These are lists of very different types of players. For one thing, the players on the upper list hit a lot more ground balls than those on the lower. Here are the averages of the two groups:

	GO%	FO%	SO%
Lots of Errors	47.4	35.0	17.6
Few Errors	33.4	40.9	25.7

Another thing that seems apparent is that the players on the bottom list tend to be a lot slower than the ones on the top. So it does look as if speed has something to do with the ability to coax errors out of a defense.

Still, there are anomalies. For example, Bob Horner would fit in much better with the players who seldom reach on errors. He's a slow, fly-ball hitter. But instead of being surrounded by Jim Gentile and Mo Vaughn, he is in the company of Willie McGee and Cesar Tovar. So how much of this can be explained by simple randomness?

To find out, I simulated a random distribution of errors and compared these results to what actually happened. This approach is perhaps best shown by example.

The first season we have play-by-play data for Roy McMillan is 1960. He made 315 outs that season. In the National League that year, batters made 31,953 outs and reached on error 728 times, for a rate of .022785 per out. So to simulate a random season, I generated 315 random numbers (one for each out he made) between 0 and 1. If a number was less than .022785, I counted it as an error. I totaled all the simulated errors for that season and then did the same thing for all the seasons we have. When I was done, I had a randomly generated number of "errors" in Roy McMillan's career (or at least that portion of his career for which we have play-by-play data).

I repeated this process 999 times, so that each player had 1,000 simulated careers.

Not surprisingly, the spread we see in the data is not random. The variance of the 835 players with 2,000 or more outs in our database was 201.55; the highest value in the 1,000 random simulations was 86.27. That is, the real-life data beat every one of the 1,000 random simulations, and by a considerable margin. It is therefore extremely unlikely that the players on the lists above got there by luck.

Now I mentioned earlier that this is not too surprising. After all, most errors are made on ground balls and it's common knowledge that there are ground-ball and fly-ball hitters. In the rest of the article we will develop more sophisticated ways of determining the number of times a batter might be expected to reach base on errors.

Do Men on and the Number of Outs Affect Error Rates?

Yes.

Okay, perhaps I should expand on that answer.

What follows is a table with information on the three ways of making outs (groundouts, flyouts and strikeouts) in each of the 24 game situations (where outs go from 0 to 2 and the bases go from empty to full). Since we know that sacrifice bunts and failed fielder's choice are affected by men on and the number of outs (for example, we can't have either with the bases empty), they have been removed:

F S T	Out	GO Total	GO Err	FO Total	FO Err	SO Total	SO Err
- - -	0	39.4	3.96	39.2	0.36	21.4	0.36
- - -	1	39.0	3.84	38.0	0.35	23.0	0.38
- - -	2	38.7	3.86	37.0	0.38	24.3	0.42
X - -	0	42.0	5.33	38.9	0.34	19.0	0.00
X - -	1	41.1	5.09	39.2	0.36	19.7	0.00
X - -	2	39.0	3.36	39.1	0.40	21.9	0.27
- X -	0	41.4	4.17	35.7	0.42	22.9	0.40
- X -	1	38.2	4.59	37.4	0.43	24.4	0.30
- X -	2	38.5	4.11	36.3	0.40	25.1	0.35
X X -	0	42.2	5.65	36.8	0.34	21.1	0.00
X X -	1	39.8	5.78	38.8	0.36	21.4	0.00
X X -	2	38.7	3.78	37.6	0.37	23.7	0.30
- - X	0	36.6	4.82	39.4	0.42	24.0	0.44
- - X	1	36.6	5.60	39.8	0.49	23.6	0.44
- - X	2	39.2	3.87	35.9	0.42	25.0	0.36
X - X	0	41.1	6.48	40.2	0.56	18.7	0.00
X - X	1	41.4	6.50	39.6	0.46	19.0	0.00
X - X	2	39.6	3.56	37.7	0.46	22.7	0.24
- X X	0	37.5	5.07	38.7	0.62	23.8	0.31
- X X	1	36.4	6.24	38.3	0.47	25.3	0.41
- X X	2	37.7	4.10	34.9	0.45	27.3	0.29
X X X	0	38.3	6.77	40.3	0.49	21.5	0.00
X X X	1	39.7	6.73	39.0	0.43	21.3	0.00
X X X	2	37.8	4.23	37.6	0.46	24.6	0.28

The number on the right (under "TOT") shows how frequent the out is in that situation. So with no one on and no one out, the batter is out 39.4% of the time on a groundout, 39.2% of the time on a flyout, and 21.4% of the time on a strikeout.

The number on the right (under "ERR") shows how frequent an error is for that type of play in that situation. So with bases loaded and no one out, a batter will be safe on an error 6.77 % of the time on a groundout, 0.49% of the time on a flyout and never on a strikeout (since the catcher does not have to cleanly field a third strike with first base occupied and less than two out).

The first thing to notice is that the error rates are very different for different types of plays. Not surprisingly, groundouts result in errors around 10 times as often as flyouts, and batters reach base least often on a strikeout, but there are situations (no one on) when the flyout is the least likely play to result in an error.

The next point of interest is that the frequency of plays vary from situation to situation. Strikeouts are at their highest in all situations when there are two outs. Groundouts spike to more than half of all outs when there is either a man on first or a man on first and second with no outs.

Error rates also vary. For groundouts, the error rate goes from a low of 3.36% (man on first and two outs) to a high of 6.73% (bases loaded and one out). Fly-out error rates go from a low of .34% (no outs and a force at second) to a high of .62% (men on second and third and no outs).

Two things are clear from this analysis. First, we should take into account the type of outs a batter makes before declaring that he has a "talent" for reaching on errors. And second, it would be a good idea to consider the context of his outs as well, since expected error rates vary quite a bit from situation to situation.

Do We Need to Consider Park Effects?

I have always wondered whether or not certain parks were more "error-friendly" than others. In addition, I wondered whether parks favored some types of outs over others. To determine this, I looked at each team's rates of errors, groundouts, flyouts, and strikeouts in the 24 game situations in both their home and road parks. Using their road rates, I computed an expected number of errors, groundouts, flyouts, and strikeouts in the home park. I next generated the four factors by dividing the actual home totals by the expected values.

There is certainly a fair amount of noise in the data, but something is going on here. As I did with the players, I also ran 1,000 random simulations. And as before, the spread in the data is not random. The variance of the 1,132 teams in our database was 211.55; the highest value of the 1,000 random simulations was only 91.28. Here are the teams with the highest error factors:

Year	Team	Park	ERR/F	AErr	EErr
1993	COL-N	DEN01	1.766	132	75
1991	ATL-N	ATL01	1.717	132	77
1994	NY-N	NYC17	1.701	71	42
1981	SF-N	SF002	1.684	80	48
1991	BAL-A	BAL11	1.664	93	56
1998	SF-N	SF002	1.659	76	46
2000	BOS-A	BOS07	1.625	87	54
1989	CHI-N	CHI11	1.606	103	64
1969	DET-A	DET04	1.596	104	65
1990	LA-N	LOS03	1.577	117	74
1986	DET-A	DET04	1.570	98	62
2002	CLE-A	CLE08	1.562	92	59
1998	DET-A	DET04	1.553	94	61
2004	COL-N	DEN02	1.545	71	46
1993	BOS-A	BOS07	1.544	107	69
1966	CHI-N	CHI11	1.530	128	84
1996	CHI-N	CHI11	1.497	101	67
Year	Team	Park	ERR/F	AErr	EErr
1988	CHI-N	CHI11	1.492	122	82
1994	COL-N	DEN01	1.472	79	54
1980	CAL-A	ANA01	1.470	96	65

ERR/F: Actual errors in home games divided by expected errors (given road rates)

AErr: Actual errors, home games

EErr: Expected errors, home games (given road rates)

What factors in the games played in these parks that led to significantly higher than normal error rates? Environmental factors could be to blame, but the obvious cause would seem to be the official scorer. Clearly, many error/hit decision made by the scorers are not clear-cut and I'm sure we've all been to baseball games where we thought a decision of theirs was overly harsh or lenient. The teams with the lowest error factors:

Year	Team	Park	ERR/F	AErr	EErr
1981	STL-N	STL09	.567	41	72
1994	MIN-A	MIN03	.590	43	73
1987	BOS-A	BOS07	.638	50	78
1986	CHI-A	CHI10	.641	54	84
1982	PHI-N	PHI12	.644	61	95
1994	ATL-N	ATL01	.651	39	60
1985	CIN-N	CIN08	.655	66	101
1971	KC-A	KAN05	.657	69	105
1993	TOR-A	TOR02	.660	59	89
1975	HOU-N	HOU02	.661	77	116
2002	ANA-A	ANA01	.661	57	86
1993	MON-N	MON02	.664	90	136
1994	STL-N	STL09	.669	39	58
1989	MON-N	MON02	.670	68	102
1963	BAL-A	BAL11	.670	59	88
2001	PHI-N	PHI12	.672	53	79
2004	KC-A	KAN06	.681	67	98
1963	LA-N	LOS03	.682	81	119
1998	BAL-A	BAL12	.690	49	71
1976	KC-A	KAN06	.695	72	104

In reviewing the entire list of teams, I found a few interesting things. For example, look at the Atlanta Braves from 1966 to 1975 (Table 1). I don't know, but I suspect something happened in 1971 to affect the error rates in Fulton County Stadium. From 1966 to 1970, fielders were more than 20% less likely to be charged with an error in Atlanta than they were when the same two teams played in another park. I would love to know who were the official scorers in Atlanta during that decade and if anything changed in 1971 to make their decisions less friendly to the fielders there.

Just about every team's table raises similar questions. Table 2 shows data for the St. Louis Cardinals. What changed around 1997 to make errors more common in Busch Stadium? From 1966 to 1993, that park had lower than average strikeout rates in 17 of the 18 years—what happened around 1994 to make the park more neutral in that regard?

The answers will probably be: "I don't know" or "Nothing," but I do think it's clear we need to take the park into account when determining expected error rates. I also think that, given the variation in much of this data, we need to average those rates over a three-year period.

For the subsequent analysis, I averaged the data for the prior and subsequent seasons if the team played the majority of its home games in the same park, and I weighted the current year twice as heavily as the surrounding ones.

Table 1. Atlanta Braves' actual versus expected errors, 1966–1975

Year	Team	Park	Err/F	GO/F	FO/F	SO/F	AErr	EErr	Min	Max	Exc
1966	ATL-N	ATL01	.752	.914	1.139	.923	70	93	63	133	12
1967	ATL-N	ATL01	.734	1.008	1.059	.889	74	101	73	130	1
1968	ATL-N	ATL01	.853	1.028	.989	.962	61	72	49	101	117
1969	ATL-N	ATL01	.723	1.123	.895	.893	77	107	80	139	0
1970	ATL-N	ATL01	.776	1.147	.836	.984	80	103	73	133	12
1971	ATL-N	ATL01	.966	1.012	1.043	.887	87	90	60	121	409
1972	ATL-N	ATL01	1.395	.998	1.048	.910	93	67	47	90	0
1973	ATL-N	ATL01	1.190	1.023	1.000	.955	90	76	51	100	49
1974	ATL-N	ATL01	.992	1.053	.980	.923	108	109	78	144	484
1975	ATL-N	ATL01	.957	.973	1.021	1.030	104	109	68	146	354

Table 2. St. Louis Cardinals' actual versus expected errors, 1987–2004

Year	Team	Park	Err/F	GO/F	FO/F	SO/F	AErr	EErr	Min	Max	Exc
1987	STL-N	STL09	.827	1.018	.993	.977	76	92	62	121	46
1988	STL-N	STL09	.936	1.015	.988	.983	89	95	69	128	310
1989	STL-N	STL09	.880	1.061	.997	.885	69	78	49	103	161
1990	STL-N	STL09	.977	1.020	1.037	.895	73	75	49	100	462
1991	STL-N	STL09	.766	1.056	1.010	.877	70	91	60	122	9
1992	STL-N	STL09	.810	1.047	.964	.977	62	77	44	109	44
1993	STL-N	STL09	.746	.996	1.040	.934	74	99	71	128	2
1994	STL-N	STL09	.669	1.001	.947	1.093	39	58	34	87	5
1995	STL-N	STL09	.771	1.113	.964	.881	65	84	59	115	16
1996	STL-N	STL09	.784	.937	1.036	1.052	71	91	63	127	13
1997	STL-N	STL09	1.115	.992	1.049	.961	76	68	45	93	178
1998	STL-N	STL09	.935	1.007	1.009	.973	67	72	45	100	315
1999	STL-N	STL09	.994	.970	1.096	.919	86	87	56	122	528
2000	STL-N	STL09	1.145	.925	1.039	1.049	78	68	43	96	129
2001	STL-N	STL09	1.001	1.005	.973	1.024	70	70	44	103	493
2002	STL-N	STL09	1.102	.935	1.045	1.043	74	67	46	94	207
2003	STL-N	STL09	1.199	.992	1.027	.971	69	58	37	79	79
2004	STL-N	STL09	.757	.951	1.035	1.035	61	81	52	107	15

Adjustments

So it looks like we need to adjust the simple approach used at the beginning of the article to take into account the type of outs, situations, and parks a batter hits in. I also wanted to make one more adjustment. Since the handedness of the batter makes a big difference, I wanted to adjust for this in order to see if some players hit balls that were harder to field cleanly, independent of their handedness. So I computed error factors for each league by handedness, and adjusted the players for these factors. After all these adjustments, the players with the highest error factors were quite a bit different than before (see Table 3 and Table 4).

Considering that Bob Horner was the only fly-ball hitter on the earlier list, it is not too surprising that he jumps to the top of the class once we take the types of outs into consideration. One interesting thing about Horner is that his final adjusted-error factor ended up being the same as the one we started out with. He got a big boost (1.516 to 1.687) for being a fly-ball hitter, then saw his rate drop (1.687 to 1.620) because he played in generally error-friendly parks, and then was dropped back to his original rate (1.620 to 1.516) because he's a right-handed hitter.

The column "SPD" is the batter speed, derived using Bill James' speed scores (higher is faster). Notice that speed is also a big fac-

tor. I took the righties, lefties, and switch-hitters and broke each of these groups into 10 sections, sorted by their adjusted error factors. Table 6 shows the average speed scores for the players in each group.

Once again, the spread we see in the data is not random, although the spread is far less now that we've accounted for many of the things causing it. The variance of the 835 players with 2,000 or more outs in our database is now 119.25; the highest value in the 1,000 random simulations was 83.91. It is unlikely (although not as unlikely as before) that the players on those lists above got there by luck.

It does seem, however, that if we are making all of these adjustments to attempt to see if players had different abilities to hit into difficult chances, we might want to remove strikeouts from the picture. We've already looked at strikeout rates and seen how they affect a player's ability to reach on an error, but let's see what happens when we ignore them.

So this time we are ignoring strikeouts, sacrifice attempts, and not treating unsuccessful fielder's choice as errors (since they were handled cleanly). The changes to the leader board are displayed in Table 6; not a tremendous difference, but I do think

Table 3.

Name	B	SPD	Outs	Err	GO%	FO%	SO%	A/Prk	PrkF	HndF	A/Hnd	TErrF
Bob Horner	R	3.2	2781	89	37.1	44.5	18.4	54.9	1.620	1.069	58.7	1.516
Gene Tenace	R	3.4	3390	82	27.2	43.4	29.4	53.0	1.546	1.045	55.4	1.479
Wil Cordero	R	4.9	3131	85	36.9	38.8	24.3	55.6	1.529	1.077	59.8	1.421
Glenn Hubbard	R	4.9	3466	100	35.4	46.1	18.5	66.2	1.510	1.066	70.5	1.417
Ron Kittle	R	3.7	2091	43	24.8	39.6	35.6	29.3	1.470	1.040	30.4	1.413
Willie Crawford	L	5.8	2558	66	39.1	35.1	25.8	52.1	1.267	.911	47.5	1.390
Rusty Greer	L	5.3	2713	61	39.7	39.9	20.5	50.3	1.212	.880	44.3	1.377
Pete Incaviglia	R	4.5	3229	71	29.8	30.7	39.5	49.2	1.444	1.056	51.9	1.367
Todd Helton	L	4.0	2728	59	37.4	42.7	19.9	49.1	1.201	.882	43.3	1.362
Otis Nixon	B	7.8	3831	124	51.3	30.6	18.1	92.5	1.340	.989	91.5	1.355
Robby Thompson	R	6.1	3543	96	35.3	36.8	27.9	66.2	1.450	1.074	71.1	1.350
Greg Gross	L	5.1	2743	86	52.8	38.1	9.1	70.5	1.220	.906	63.8	1.347
Jim Wynn	R	5.7	4991	134	32.6	39.4	28.0	95.6	1.401	1.049	100.3	1.336
Reggie Sanders	R	7.1	4116	92	30.9	34.2	34.9	65.0	1.415	1.059	68.8	1.336
Glenn Davis	R	4.1	2799	69	35.7	42.4	21.9	48.7	1.416	1.063	51.8	1.333
Dick Schofield	R	6.2	3445	89	37.2	42.9	19.9	63.6	1.400	1.052	66.8	1.332
Rondell White	R	5.4	3276	91	42.7	32.7	24.5	64.8	1.405	1.057	68.5	1.329
Dave Hollins	B	4.8	2511	57	35.8	36.8	27.4	46.0	1.240	.948	43.6	1.309
Eddie Bressoud	R	5.5	2235	57	32.2	40.5	27.2	42.5	1.342	1.028	43.7	1.305
Kevin McReynolds	R	5.7	4064	102	32.8	49.8	17.4	73.4	1.389	1.068	78.4	1.301

Table 4.

Name	B	SPD	Outs	Err	GO%	FO%	SO%	A/Prk	PrkF	HndF	A/Hnd	TErrF
Mike Lowell	R	4.1	2264	21	28.5	50.7	20.8	32.0	.657	1.052	33.7	.624
Mo Vaughn	L	3.2	3957	37	32.5	31.3	36.1	65.6	.564	.873	57.3	.646
Ernie Whitt	L	3.1	2893	33	38.6	44.4	17.0	55.5	.595	.906	50.2	.657
Jason Varitek	B	3.4	2019	24	36.5	35.0	28.5	37.7	.637	.955	36.0	.667
Jim Gentile	L	2.9	2169	25	32.7	37.0	30.2	39.9	.626	.937	37.4	.668
Ken Henderson	B	5.0	3440	48	36.0	41.8	22.2	70.6	.680	1.002	70.7	.679
Bernie Carbo	L	4.0	2036	26	38.7	31.4	29.9	42.2	.617	.907	38.2	.680
Felix Fermin	R	4.5	2164	44	62.6	30.6	6.8	60.8	.723	1.057	64.3	.684
Rick Dempsey	R	2.9	3704	53	36.1	44.1	19.9	72.6	.730	1.056	76.7	.691
Preston Wilson	R	5.6	2169	28	33.6	29.6	36.8	38.3	.730	1.054	40.4	.693
Larry Herndon	R	6.2	3613	58	41.0	37.1	21.9	79.3	.732	1.049	83.2	.697
Boog Powell	L	2.6	5004	70	39.7	35.8	24.5	109.2	.641	.912	99.5	.703
Lee Thomas	L	4.8	2466	36	38.8	45.4	15.8	54.7	.658	.935	51.2	.703
Greg Brock	L	4.1	2452	32	40.2	40.7	19.1	51.1	.627	.891	45.5	.704
Dick Groat	R	5.0	3170	74	52.8	36.7	10.5	100.2	.738	1.048	105.0	.705
Tim Foli	R	5.3	4750	87	47.6	44.0	8.4	116.7	.745	1.050	122.6	.710
Sid Bream	L	3.7	2353	30	38.3	42.5	19.1	48.8	.614	.862	42.1	.713
Jose Hernandez	R	5.2	3215	44	35.1	24.7	40.2	58.3	.755	1.053	61.4	.717
Jody Davis	R	2.4	2765	40	34.9	39.4	25.8	52.4	.764	1.065	55.8	.717
Bobby Murcer	L	5.2	4967	62	34.3	48.7	16.9	93.9	.660	.912	85.7	.724

HndF: Individual handedness factor
A/Hnd: Expected number of errors adjusted by handedness
TErrF: Total error factor (Err / A/Hnd)

Table 5. Average speed scores, by group

Type	#	1	2	3	4	5	6	7	8	9	10
Right	46	5.39	5.20	4.81	4.87	4.74	4.66	4.86	4.45	4.70	4.49
Switch	11	6.86	6.42	5.71	6.45	5.52	5.95	5.86	5.60	4.55	5.25
Left	25	6.10	5.63	5.58	5.39	5.50	4.95	5.11	4.50	4.26	4.10

#: Size of each group (leftover players added to the last group).
1: Group with highest adjusted error factors
2: Group with second-highest adjusted error factors, etc.

Table 6.

Name	B	SPD	Outs	Err	GO%	FO%	A/Prk	PrkF	A/Hnd	TErrF
Gene Tenace	R	3.4	2371	81	38.0	62.0	46.2	1.755	48.9	1.655
Bob Horner	R	3.2	2268	87	45.4	54.6	50.5	1.723	55.0	1.581
Glenn Hubbard	R	4.9	2756	92	42.0	58.0	57.2	1.608	62.3	1.478
Rusty Greer	L	5.3	2152	58	49.7	50.3	45.8	1.268	39.6	1.465
Wil Cordero	R	4.9	2358	79	48.5	51.5	50.3	1.571	55.0	1.436
Rondell White	R	5.4	2467	90	56.5	43.5	58.9	1.528	63.2	1.424
Reggie Sanders	R	7.1	2664	86	47.2	52.8	56.3	1.529	60.7	1.417
Otis Nixon	B	7.8	3070	112	61.8	38.2	83.0	1.350	79.7	1.406
Jim Wynn	R	5.7	3565	123	44.8	55.2	83.6	1.472	89.9	1.368
Alex Rodriguez	R	6.2	2815	85	49.9	50.1	56.9	1.494	62.3	1.365
Robby Thompson	R	6.1	2457	82	46.9	53.1	54.6	1.501	60.2	1.363
Greg Vaughn	R	5.5	3169	90	41.7	58.3	61.7	1.459	67.3	1.337
Jeff Blauser	R	5.4	2439	83	47.3	52.7	57.3	1.448	62.7	1.323
Todd Helton	L	4.0	2184	52	46.7	53.3	45.7	1.137	39.5	1.315
Johnny Bench	R	3.7	4415	139	45.1	54.9	98.5	1.411	106.5	1.305
Jack Clark	R	4.6	3662	121	45.4	54.6	85.1	1.422	92.7	1.305
Vada Pinson	L	7.0	5358	156	49.2	50.8	133.8	1.166	119.9	1.302
Glenn Davis	R	4.1	2180	63	45.6	54.4	44.4	1.420	48.4	1.301
Greg Gross	L	5.1	2453	74	57.4	42.6	64.2	1.153	57.0	1.297
Gary Gaetti	R	4.1	5173	153	47.1	52.9	110.1	1.389	118.3	1.293

Table 7.

Name	B	SPD	Outs	Err	GO%	FO%	A/Prk	PrkF	A/Hnd	TErrF
Tim Foli	R	5.3	4182	70	50.1	49.9	100.6	.696	108.0	.648
Mo Vaughn	L	3.2	2528	32	50.9	49.1	57.8	.554	49.2	.651
Rick Dempsey	R	2.9	2905	45	43.8	56.2	63.1	.713	68.0	.662
Larry Herndon	R	6.2	2788	52	51.9	48.1	72.2	.720	77.4	.672
Dick Groat	R	5.0	2784	65	58.2	41.8	88.5	.735	94.1	.691
Joe Orsulak	L	5.9	2754	39	50.8	49.2	66.3	.588	55.9	.697
Ernie Whitt	L	3.1	2382	31	46.1	53.9	50.3	.617	44.4	.699
Jody Davis	R	2.4	2035	36	46.5	53.5	47.1	.764	51.3	.702
Rich Aurilia	R	4.4	2311	34	41.4	58.6	45.1	.754	48.2	.706
Boog Powell	L	2.6	3752	63	52.2	47.8	98.0	.643	88.7	.710
Manny Sanguillen	R	4.4	3270	68	53.6	46.4	87.6	.776	94.4	.721
Luis Alicea	B	6.4	2361	31	44.2	55.8	44.7	.693	42.8	.724
Jose Lind	R	5.6	2403	47	55.8	44.2	58.5	.804	64.6	.728
Derrel Thomas	R	6.5	2941	57	51.2	48.8	72.1	.791	77.4	.736
Bobby Murcer	L	5.2	4109	58	41.1	58.9	86.0	.674	78.1	.742
Dick Green	R	4.5	2284	44	51.6	48.4	56.0	.785	59.2	.743
Frank Taveras	R	7.3	2556	53	55.4	44.6	66.0	.803	70.9	.747
Alan Ashby	B	2.4	2533	46	57.3	42.7	63.3	.726	61.4	.749
Eric Young	R	6.7	3783	71	52.2	47.8	88.2	.805	94.6	.750
Ed Kirkpatrick	L	4.5	2164	35	48.4	51.6	50.9	.687	46.5	.753

this focuses more clearly on what we are trying to look at. Some players dropped off the list because removing strikeouts brought them below the 2,000–out minimum for inclusion.

Table 7 shows the players with the lowest error rates with these plays removed. Tim Foli, with a very low strikeout rate, moves to the top of this list, and Felix Fermin would have been in third place if he had still met the 2,000 out requirement.

We shouldn't let all of these adjustments obscure the fact that right-handed ground-ball hitters generally reach base on errors a lot more than lefty fly-ball hitters. Despite the final results above, Derek Jeter still reaches base a lot more often than any player on these adjusted lists, and one could argue that the most significant list of players we presented in this article is the first, totally unadjusted, one.

Still, I wanted to go through these contortions to see if I could identify two groups of players: one whose batted balls tended to be difficult to handle and one whose outs posed much less of a challenge. Much like the differences in ballpark error rates presented above, I don't know if Gene Tenace, Bob Horner, and Glenn Hubbard really hit scorching groundballs or whether Mo Vaughn didn't. Perhaps people who have watched the players on these two lists play more than I have can comment on this. I do know that these differences are unlikely to occur by chance. Even after taking into consideration a host of things that might account for these differences (with the notable exception of batter speed), there still seems to be some significant differences in how difficult each batter is to retire on his outs.

What About Pitchers?

I realize that the title of this article mentions only batters, but I figured it would be an oversight to conclude this piece without a discussion of which pitchers gave up more than their share of errors. This is probably more interesting to current researchers than what I've been talking about so far, in light of recent work (most notably by Voros McCracken and Tom Tippett) on the subject of how much influence pitchers have over the successful disposition of balls in play.

Before getting too far into this, it should be obvious that one big thing pitchers can do to minimize errors is to strike out as many hitters as they can. Error rates on strikeouts are extremely low, as are errors on fly balls. So we should see a wide disparity between error rates behind different types of pitchers and, at least before any adjustments are made, we do.

Pitchers with the highest error factors are listed in Table 8. As you might expect, the top list is dominated by ground-ball pitchers, and the bottom list is filled with those who primarily get their outs in the air or by strikeouts. Adjusting for type, situation, park, and handedness mixes things up a bit (see Table 9).

Table 8. Highest and lowest error factors, pitchers

Highest factors	Outs	Err	GO%	FO%	SO%	ExErr	ErrF
Hal Woodeshick	2077	86	56.0	23.4	20.5	50.1	1.715
Bob Locker	2568	91	55.6	21.9	22.5	55.8	1.631
Roger McDowell	3034	99	59.9	22.8	17.3	61.2	1.618
Frank Linzy	2371	83	60.4	24.5	15.1	53.1	1.562
Kent Tekulve	4188	138	54.7	26.7	18.6	89.3	1.546
Rick Honeycutt	6251	195	52.5	30.9	16.6	128.0	1.523
Atlee Hammaker	3157	100	46.5	34.0	19.5	66.0	1.514
Rick Camp	2720	88	53.5	31.5	15.0	58.2	1.512
Mike Fetters	2059	56	46.6	28.2	25.2	37.3	1.500
Randy Jones	5616	185	57.6	29.4	13.1	123.7	1.495
Ted Abernathy	2619	85	51.8	24.9	23.3	57.6	1.475
Andy Hassler	3219	101	51.0	29.5	19.6	69.4	1.456
Jack Aker	2153	68	52.4	28.8	18.8	47.0	1.446
Kip Wells	2324	58	43.7	30.6	25.6	40.5	1.433
Mike Hampton	5762	153	50.1	28.3	21.6	107.0	1.430
Steve Trout	4272	127	55.7	29.0	15.4	89.2	1.424
S. Schoeneweis	2038	50	47.8	32.8	19.3	35.2	1.422
Matt Clement	3376	86	41.9	27.7	30.5	60.7	1.417
Jason Grimsley	2569	65	50.0	26.6	23.4	46.0	1.412
Al Jackson	4002	136	51.0	30.8	18.1	96.9	1.403

Lowest factors	Outs	Err	GO%	FO%	SO%	ExErr	ErrF
Eddie Guardado	2165	17	23.9	46.1	30.0	38.1	.447
Jaret Wright	2178	20	38.0	35.9	26.1	38.0	.526
Eric Milton	3495	33	25.4	49.6	25.1	60.9	.542
Jeff Brantley	2497	28	30.0	40.9	29.2	49.8	.562
Robert Person	2610	28	25.7	44.7	29.6	48.2	.581
Jeff Reardon	3335	40	24.6	49.1	26.3	68.2	.587
Dick Radatz	2039	26	24.1	39.4	36.5	44.2	.589
Don Gullett	4016	53	32.4	44.9	22.8	89.6	.591
Bob Buhl	3976	58	43.2	40.3	16.4	97.2	.597
Pat Jarvis	3521	47	38.3	41.3	20.4	77.9	.603
O. Hernandez	2561	27	29.8	42.8	27.5	44.7	.604
D. Eckersley	9644	121	30.0	45.1	24.9	199.6	.606
Luis Tiant	10137	134	29.9	46.2	23.8	220.7	.607
Sid Fernandez	5491	69	20.4	47.9	31.7	112.0	.616
Denny McLain	5499	74	31.6	45.0	23.3	119.1	.621
Randy Wolf	3017	34	30.9	40.4	28.7	54.2	.627
Art Mahaffey	2891	45	31.4	46.5	22.1	71.5	.630
Mark Gardner	5094	62	32.9	42.4	24.7	98.1	.632
Gary Nolan	4905	69	33.3	45.5	21.2	108.9	.634
Jim Palmer	11416	162	35.4	45.3	19.4	244.9	.661

```
Outs: Number of outs made
Err: Number of times reached on errors
GO%: Percentage of outs that were ground balls
FO%: Percentage of outs that were fly balls
SO%: Percentage of outs that were strikeouts
ExErr: Expected number of errors based on league rates
ErrF: Error factor (Err ÷ ExErr)
```

Two things concern me about this methodology when used with pitchers instead of hitters. First, while a batter puts balls in play against a variety of defenses during the course of a season, a pitcher is stuck (or blessed) with much the same defense in every game. The other important thing to remember is that the pitcher himself is also part of his defense and could be a significant factor in both errors on sacrifice attempts as well as the incidence of strikeout victims reaching base.

So it's unclear whether Dave McNally's ability to minimize errors is really a skill we should attribute to him or to Mark Belanger, the shortstop for many of his starts. Pitchers move from team to team, and team defenses also change, sometimes dramatically, over time, but these concerns are still there and, at least to me, muddy the water in a way they didn't for the batters.

Conclusion

It shouldn't be a surprise to anyone that this article raises many questions and comes up with relatively few answers. It does provide some data to back up what most of us already knew: grounders produce more errors than flyouts, righties reach on errors more often than lefties, the speed of a batter affects error rates, and so on. But I feel that the questions it raises are far more interesting than these "answers," and I hope that this article stimulates interest in this somewhat obscure topic and encourages people to investigate some of these open questions. What caused error rates to suddenly drop or rise in certain parks? What caused the fluctuations in some parks' ground-out, fly-out or strikeout factors? Why were Bob Horner's outs so much harder to field cleanly than Mo Vaughn's? Hopefully, this article is a first small step toward answering some of these kinds of questions.

Table 9. Highest and lowest error factors, pitchers, adjusted for type, situation, park, and handedness

Highest factors	B	Outs	Err	GO%	FO%	SO%	A/Prk	PrkF	HndF	A/Hnd	TErrF
Al Hrabosky	L	2111	55	28.1	45.9	26.0	33.6	1.636	1.036	34.8	1.579
Scott Sanders	R	2012	48	32.4	36.2	31.4	33.7	1.422	.992	33.5	1.434
Ramon Ortiz	R	2592	55	38.0	39.3	22.8	40.6	1.354	.972	39.5	1.393
Balor Moore	L	2023	55	38.0	38.1	23.9	38.4	1.434	1.031	39.6	1.390
Jason Johnson	R	2908	64	37.1	40.7	22.1	48.3	1.324	.969	46.8	1.367
Tim Wakefield	R	6008	138	34.1	41.9	24.0	104.5	1.321	.972	101.5	1.360
Mark Leiter	R	3450	80	34.5	39.6	25.9	60.0	1.332	.980	58.9	1.359
Eddie Solomon	R	2086	61	43.0	40.8	16.2	46.7	1.307	.977	45.6	1.338
Matt Clement	R	3376	86	41.9	27.7	30.5	66.2	1.300	.992	65.6	1.311
Atlee Hammaker	L	3157	100	46.5	34.0	19.5	73.6	1.359	1.047	77.1	1.298
Ron Robinson	R	2311	54	37.1	42.4	20.5	43.0	1.257	.974	41.8	1.291
Jerry Johnson	R	2249	67	43.8	34.4	21.7	53.2	1.261	.979	52.0	1.288
Bruce Dal Canton	R	2707	78	44.5	37.6	17.9	62.4	1.250	.976	60.9	1.281
Dave Morehead	R	2399	59	36.8	37.1	26.1	47.4	1.244	.972	46.1	1.279
Mike Fetters	R	2059	56	46.6	28.2	25.2	44.8	1.251	.980	43.9	1.276
Paul Byrd	R	2649	54	35.4	43.8	20.8	43.0	1.257	.987	42.4	1.274
Eric Plunk	R	3341	63	29.0	38.7	32.4	50.5	1.248	.983	49.6	1.269
Tim Worrell	R	2664	59	35.1	38.4	26.5	47.5	1.243	.981	46.5	1.268
Larry Sherry	R	2044	57	38.7	35.2	26.0	46.0	1.239	.979	45.0	1.266
Reggie Cleveland	R	5300	145	41.7	40.8	17.5	117.1	1.239	.986	115.5	1.256

Lowest factors	B	Outs	Err	GO%	FO%	SO%	A/Prk	PrkF	HndF	A/Hnd	TErrF
Jaret Wright	R	2178	20	38.0	35.9	26.1	38.8	.515	.974	37.8	.529
Bob Buhl	R	3976	58	43.2	40.3	16.4	99.8	.581	.990	98.7	.587
Eddie Guardado	L	2165	17	23.9	46.1	30.0	26.6	.639	1.081	28.8	.591
Dave McNally	L	7841	120	41.3	39.4	19.3	174.5	.688	1.062	185.4	.647
Ron Taylor	R	2313	36	39.6	40.3	20.0	55.8	.646	.987	55.0	.654
Rolando Arrojo	R	2003	27	42.7	31.7	25.6	42.6	.634	.969	41.3	.654
Hal Brown	R	2011	32	40.4	45.9	13.7	49.5	.647	.973	48.2	.664
Armando Reynoso	R	3077	46	41.9	40.1	18.0	69.7	.660	.989	68.9	.668
Pete Smith	R	2966	41	39.1	39.3	21.6	62.7	.654	.972	60.9	.673
Sidney Ponson	R	3754	45	42.1	36.5	21.4	69.2	.650	.964	66.7	.674
John Butcher	R	2398	38	48.0	36.9	15.1	56.2	.676	.975	54.8	.694
Jamey Wright	R	3175	55	50.6	30.4	18.9	80.1	.686	.988	79.2	.695
C. C. Sabathia	L	2218	27	33.4	39.6	27.1	35.9	.752	1.068	38.3	.704
Milt Pappas	R	8116	123	41.3	40.1	18.6	178.2	.690	.979	174.4	.705
Eric Milton	L	3495	33	25.4	49.6	25.1	42.7	.773	1.091	46.6	.708
Masato Yoshii	R	2166	30	38.8	40.6	20.6	42.6	.703	.992	42.3	.709
Bob Milacki	R	2299	33	41.9	41.2	16.8	47.5	.694	.980	46.6	.709
Pat Jarvis	R	3521	47	38.3	41.3	20.4	67.1	.700	.984	66.0	.712
Dick Selma	R	2418	36	39.9	32.0	28.2	51.2	.703	.982	50.3	.715
Mike Mussina	R	8199	98	35.5	36.9	27.5	140.8	.696	.974	137.1	.715

The Hawaiian All-Stars and the Harlem Globetrotters
A 1948 Barnstorming Tour

In 1946, the West Coast Negro Baseball League was organized to exhibit black baseball to the Pacific region. The teams included the Portland Rosebuds (owned by Jesse Owens), Oakland Larks, San Diego Tigers, Los Angeles White Sox, San Francisco Sea Lions, and Seattle Steelheads. The "Steelies," named after the salmon runs, were actually the Harlem Globetrotter baseball team, but were renamed to appeal to the local crowds. The Globetrotters were formed as a barnstorming baseball team in 1944 by Abe Saperstein, who also owned the Globetrotters basketball team and was part-owner of the Birmingham Black Barons.

The teams were to play 110 games in the Pacific Coast League parks while the white teams were traveling. The Steelheads also were scheduled to play in Tacoma, Bremerton, Spokane, and Bellingham, Washington, to expand their appeal. But a big blow was dealt to the fledging league when catcher Paul Hardy jumped from the Chicago American Giants to become the player-manager of the Steelheads, and, as a result, a ban was placed on Negro players playing in Seattle. The league folded in July, and the Steelheads again became the Globetrotters and resumed barnstorming, traveling with the Havana La Palomas throughout the Midwest. In the late fall, Saperstein created "Abe Saperstein's Negro All-Stars," which combined players from the Globetrotters and other Negro teams, including Dan Bankhead, Mike Berry, Sherwood Brewer, Piper Davis, Luke Easter, Paul Hardy, Herb Simpson, and Goose Tatum. They played against local teams in Hawaii, among other places, winning 13 successive games.

This trip set the stage for the barnstorming tour of the Globetrotters and the Hawaiian All-Stars in 1948. This was an important tour in a number of ways. It took place one year after Jackie Robinson's debut with the Brooklyn Dodgers and represented an integrated tour of black and Asian-Pacific players. For players of Japanese ancestry from Hawaii, which had been attacked in 1941 by Japan, the trip enabled them to make a statement about their ethnic acculturation and American citizenship. As Joel Franks has said, baseball "offered some Hawaiians opportunities to show, in Hawaii as well as the American mainland ..., that baseball belongs to no single region, race, ethnic group, or

nationality." In addition, the multinational racial makeup of the teams provided an excellent display of Hawaiian aloha, a valuable trait to display on the mainland for the developing tourist trade and the emerging movement for statehood. Obviously, the tour was as much exhibition as competition. As the won-lost records in 1946 and 1948 attest, the Globetrotters were superior to the Hawaiian All-Stars, but the semi-pro island players acquitted themselves well and succeeded in promoting Hawaii as a unique combination of exotic and American qualities. In the pictures taken as they toured the cities where they played, they appear as smiling, barefoot young men wearing aloha shirts, happy to be given the opportunity to experience mainland America and to have its inhabitants experience them.

The Players

Nine players from the 1946 Steelies played on the 1948 barnstorming team: Paul Hardy, catcher-manager; Johnny Cogdell, rhp; Rogers Pierre, rhp; Sherwood Brewer, 2b; Ulysses Redd, ss; Herb Simpson, 1b; Eugene Hardin, utility; Zell Miles, rf; and Howard Gay, cf. Sherwood Brewer was signed by the Globetrotters after the war and played with Luke Easter and Lester Lockett for manager Paul Hardy. A fast runner, he raced against Jesse Owens in promotional exhibitions at some Negro league games. He moved to the Indianapolis Clowns in 1949 and then to the Monarchs in 1953, where he played alongside shortstop Ernie Banks and for Buck O'Neil as manager, ending his Negro league career in 1955.

Another important player was Ulysses Redd, who played for the Birmingham Black Barons in 1940. After war service, he played for the Cincinnati Crescents, Steelies, and the Globetrotters. Following his last year with the Chicago American Giants in 1952, he returned to the Globetrotters as their bus driver.

Four of the Globetrotters had ties with the Harlem Globetrotter basketball team. Pitcher Joe Bankhead played guard in 1947–48; outfielder Sam "Boom Boom" Wheeler played guard for the Trotters and the Harlem Magicians from 1946 to 1959; and pitcher Othello Strong played from 1949 to 1952. Third baseman Parnell Woods, who was a key member of the 1945 championship Cleveland Buckeyes and an all-star from 1939 to 1942, was also the business manager for the Trotters for 24 years.

Before the tour began on June 13, the Globetrotters had already played 53 games and won 47. In their most recent series they went 10–2 vs. Satchel Paige's Kansas City Stars, 7–1 vs. Cincinnati Crescents (also owned by Saperstein), and 2-0 vs. the

FRANK ARDOLINO is a professor of English at the University of Hawaii, who has written a number of articles on Hawaiian baseball istory. He is currently working on the presentation of the Reverse of the Curse of the Bambino in films.

L to R: Hawaiian All-Stars Bill Yasui, Dick Kitamura, James Wasa, Collie Souza

semi-pro champs Golden Coors. The *Los Angeles Times* claimed that they were "generally conceded to be the greatest Negro aggregation in the land."

The tour was organized by Hawaii promoter Mackay Yanagisawa of Sports Enterprises, who had put in an unsuccessful bid to have an Hawaii team in the PCL, and Abe Saperstein. Yanagisawa was known as the "Shogun of Sports" for his many sports enterprises. He was the founder of the Hula, Pro, and Aloha Bowls, and in 1997 he was inducted into the Hawaii Sports Hall of Fame.

Fifteen top senior players from the semi-pro Hawaii Baseball League were chosen to participate in the barnstorming tour: Ernest "Russian" Cabral, p; Matsuo "Lefty" Higuchi, p; Jyun "Curly" Hirota, c; Larry Kamishima, 3b; Dick Kitamura, ss; Harry Kitamura, p; Kats Kojima, lf; Crispin Mancao, p; Masa Morita, p; Jun Muramoto, cf; Clarence Neves, inf; George Rodrigues, mgr—util.; Collie Souza 1b; Jimmy "Porky" Wasa mgr—2b; Bill Yasui inf. After the barnstorming tour, Dick Kitamura and Cris Moncao were invited to play for the Globetrotters, respectively, in the 1949 and 1950 seasons. In addition, pitcher-outfielder "Russian" Cabral, who pitched in many of the games and got key hits in their victories, was signed by the Chicago Cubs for a tryout, which, however, did not result in a major league career.

These players were chosen from the teams of the Hawaiian League, which was formed in 1925 and organized according to a quasi-ethnic basis with the six original teams loosely representing Hawaiians, Chinese, Caucasians, Filipinos, Portuguese, and Japanese. The Japanese team was the most restrictive ethnically, and to ease wartime tensions their name, Asahis, meaning "rising sun," was changed to the Athletics. In addition, Jimmy Wasa was paid $900 a season to switch from the Athletics to the Braves (Portuguese). He played for the Braves for seven years, and, as he observed, he provided a good example of ethnic cooperation by allowing "people to find out about the other person." Wasa and some of the Honolulu League players had gained invaluable experience competing against major leaguers who were stationed in Honolulu during the war.

The most prominent player on the all-stars was Jyun Hirota, who was recruited for the Tokyo Giants in 1952 by Wally Yonamine, a star athlete from Hawaii who was inducted into the Japanese Baseball Hall of Fame in 1994. As the starting catcher for the Giants, Hirota won four World Series in 1952, 1953, 1954, and 1955. When he returned to Hawaii in 1956, he coached at the University of Hawaii, and in 1970 he became the farm team manager of the Japanese Kintetsu Buffaloes, whom he led to their first championship in 23 years.

Another important player was Crispin Mancao, who, in 1998

at the age of 84, was honored as an "ageless wonder," the oldest Super Seniors softball player in Honolulu. Despite his diminutive size, 5'5", 140 lbs., he was known for his moving fastball, and when he was 46 he served as a relief pitcher for the PCL Hawaii Islanders in 1961, their first year in Hawaii. He also coached baseball at local high schools and at the University of Hawaii for head coach Dick Kitamura, his barnstorming teammate.

This team followed in the tradition of other squads from Hawaii, including the six-month, 130-game tour in 1935 of U.S. and Canada; and the National Baseball Congress tournaments in Cuba in 1940 and on the mainland in 1947. In addition, the Asahis, the most successful team of the Hawaii Baseball League, had traveled periodically to Asia since 1915, and the Hawaiian Chinese University baseball team had toured the mainland six years in a row starting in 1910.

The Games

According to Mr. Wasa's records, the Hawaii All-Stars played 79 games, both scheduled and unscheduled, in two months, in 16 states: California, Oregon, Washington, Idaho, Utah, Colorado, Kansas, South Dakota, Indiana, Michigan, Minnesota, Ohio, West Virginia, Illinois, Pennsylvania, New York, and British Columbia. They won 45 games, compiling a record of 20-30 against the Globetrotters and 25-4 against local teams. They played before crowds generally ranging from 500 to 5,000 and at four major league stadiums: Wrigley Field, Shibe Park, Forbes Field, and Yankee Stadium. Their biggest thrill was playing in Yankee Stadium before 20,000 fans and touching the lockers of Gehrig and Ruth. Their final game on August 11 at the Polo Grounds was rained out after three innings of a scoreless game with the San Juan All Stars.

The squad left for Los Angeles by Pan American clipper at 4:30 p.m. Friday on June 11 and played their first game on June 13 at Riverside, CA, which they lost 8-5. In the second game on June 14 at Wrigley Field, CA, the Globetrotters won 10-6 before 5,000 fans. Dick Kitamura, the Hawaii shortstop was injured in a race around the bases against Jesse Owens, which also involved one of his teammates and two Globetrotters. He fell down rounding second and was spiked in the hand by Owens, who was too close to avoid him. Kitamura was unable to play for the rest of the tour, but he served as scorekeeper. As a result, the All-Stars were forced to use manager George Rodrigues as a utility player. After the game, Rodrigues promised his team would get better once they lost their nervousness about playing on the mainland against the Globetrotters. On June 20, in Oakland, they split a doubleheader, losing 18-2 and winning the second game 7-6. In the fourth inning of the first game, Herb Simpson broke his leg sliding into third base. Between games Jesse Owens made an appeal—which netted $365—to the crowd for donations to send Ollie Matson, San Francisco high school runner and future NFL great, to the Olympic tryouts.

On July 13 in Yakima, Washington, the All-Stars won their most lopsided victory, 16-7, over the Trotters. Three days later in Spokane at Ferris Field, in the most exciting game of the tour, they beat the Globetrotters, 10-8, on a two-run homer with two out in the bottom of the ninth after the Trotters had tied it in the top of the inning with two runs. On August 6, at Forbes Field, the Globetrotters won, 15-7, before a crowd of 1,736. Before the game, Jesse Owens raced against a horse and lost at the tape. At Yankee Stadium on August 8, they lost to the Globetrotters, 7-4, in the first game of a doubleheader. In the second game, the Philadelphia Stars topped the N.Y. Cubans, 4-3. Jesse Owens in another exhibition ran around the bases in 0:13.2. Their final game on August 11 at the Polo Grounds was rained out after three innings of a scoreless game with the San Juan All Stars.

The Hawaii players considered this trip to be a dream come through. They got to play baseball across the U.S. and in Canada against the Globetrotters. They enjoyed touring the cities they played in and welcomed the attention of fans, who were very receptive to them. At the same time, they found the grind of playing so many games in succession exhausting. The Globetrotters provided them with a bus and a driver, and they slept on the bus most of the time, staying at hotels only when they had to wash their uniforms. They were not paid for playing such an exhausting schedule, and received a minimal allowance for food. In addition, a major disappointment occurred after the tour was over. The team expected to play in the National Baseball Congress tournament in Wichita, Kansas, but the Hawaii commissioner of baseball did not support their entry. This was particularly galling because many of the local teams they beat handily on the tour were scheduled to play. Nevertheless, as Jimmy Wasa has told me, the All-Stars were young and withstood the rigors of the tour, and, although he would not repeat the experience without a salary if he had the opportunity to do so today, he and his teammates were very proud to represent Hawaii in this unique barnstorming experience with a celebrated professional team.

The author would like to thank Jimmy Wasa for providing memories and materials which were invaluable in writing this article.

The Best and Worst Batteries
Comparing ERAs 1960–2004

Sometimes a pitcher and a catcher (battery) come together as a fully charged duo outperforming all other battery combinations for either player. In some cases the result of this pairing has been a full point or more below both the pitcher's and the catcher's individual ERA. On the other hand, the battery can fall a little short on electricity and the result is a pairing of a full point worse than either's ERA. A study was undertaken to ascertain which batteries were the best and which ones were the worst using comparative ERAs as the measure on both a seasonal and a career basis.

Methodology

Using Retrosheet "Event Files" for the years 1960-2004, the Earned Run Average for every battery combination (BERA) was computed by counting every inning-out and every earned run attributable to the battery. The ERA for the pitchers (PERA) was then tabulated for all of their catchers and the same was done for the catchers paired with all of their pitchers (CERA), for each season and in total for the data period (identified as career). For each of the specific battery combinations, their BERA was subtracted from both the pitcher's and the catcher's ERAs. The resultant above/below numbers were then averaged to determine which batteries performed better or worse than both player's individual season or career ERA.

Some Numbers

There were a total of 55,938 different battery combinations in the data set of the forty-five years analyzed. In the career (total) summary group there were 36,060 such pairings involving 3,768 different pitchers and 780 different catchers. Because some of these pairings were only for ⅓ of an inning while others were for more than a thousand innings, a minimum inning of pairing was established. The criteria used for the analysis was 75 innings per year (seasonal) or 250 innings (career) paired as a battery. In addition, the battery's seasonal or career innings could not exceed 75% of the pitcher's total innings for the season or career nor could the comparative batteries be below 75 innings per year (or 250

innings career). This criteria was used so that there would be a meaningful comparison with other match-ups and that the one or two season anomalies would not be included. These minimums reduced the number of battery combinations to 2,039 (seasonal) and 1,093 (career), which meant that the pair generally worked together for about a half of a season or for two to three years.

The data period represented 1,605,600⅔ total defensive half innings and 690,938 earned runs for a baseline ERA of 3.87. The National League during this period had an ERA of 3.76 with 331,013 earned runs in 791,738 innings that involved 2,589 different pitchers and 539 different catchers. The American League had an ERA of 3.98 with 359,925 earned runs in 813,952⅔ innings using 2,752 different pitchers and 548 different catchers. There were 38,954 batteries where the pitcher was right handed for a BERA of 3.90 and there were 16,984 batteries involving a left-handed pitcher who had a BERA of 3.94.

The single season high for most innings paired belonged to Wilbur Wood and Ed Hermann of the White Sox in 1972 when they joined for 353⅓ innings. Their BERA was 2.50 just slightly better than Wilbur's seasonal 2.51 PERA. Five batteries (out of 55,951) had 300+ innings in a year while 407 had 200+ innings and 725 had just ⅓ of an inning. The highest number of career innings paired belonged to Bill Freehan and Mickey Lolich with 2,331⅓ Gary Carter and Steve Rogers came in second with 1,982⅓. Forty-nine batteries (out of 36,063) had 1000+ innings together in their career; 329 batteries had 500+ innings and 470 teamed up for only ⅓ of an inning.

The Best Batteries

Who were the best batteries using this Combo Earned Run Average methodology? Taking just the pitchers' career ERA compared to the specific battery's ERA found that 12 batteries had a BERA of two or more runs better in the data set. For the catchers' career ERA bumped against the specific battery's ERA the results showed just one battery that performed better by two or more runs. By averaging the two above/below ERA comparisons, the study identified 52 batteries that were at least one full point better. Who were these phenomenal batteries?

First, we'll look at the career batteries (BERA) compared to just the pitchers' numbers (PERA). The very best duo was pitcher John Farrell and catcher Andy Allanson. In over 439 innings together they had a BERA of 3.36 compared to Farrell's career of 6.59 in 259 other inning pairings which is a difference of −3.23, or more

CHUCK ROSCIAM is a retired Navy Captain with 43 years active service. A SABR Member since 1992, he also was an amateur catcher for over 40 years and the creator of www.baseballcatchers.com and www.tripleplays.sabr.org.

than three runs better. Coming in second place was the team of Ryan Dempster and Mike Redmond who had a BERA-minus-PERA of two plus runs better at −2.76 in 410 innings. Table 1 shows the Top Ten in this analysis.

By comparing the battery's ERA to the catcher's earned run average (CERA), the top ten list has a complete turnover (See Table 2). The very best pairing was with pitcher Kevin Brown and catcher Charles Johnson for a BERA of 2.22 with a differential of −2.26 or two runs better than Johnson's career CERA of 4.49. Second place belonged to the tandem of Jose Rijo and Jeff Reed with a −2.11 differential.

The last step in the Best Combo Earned Run Average approach is the averaging of the two previous comparisons. This produces the best of both perspectives (BERA is better than both the PERA and the CERA). See Table 3 for the Top Ten Career Rankings and Table 4 for the Ten Best Seasons.

The very best career pairing—the two guys with the best performance together—were Kevin Brown and Charles Johnson. They came together for 352 innings and produced a BERA of 2.22, which on average was nearly two full runs below their individual earned run averages (PERA = 3.32 and CERA = 4.49). Coming in at a very close second in the averaging ranking were the twosome of Jose Rijo and Jeff Reed whose differential was −1.95 with a BERA of 2.24.

In the Best Combo ERA for a Season the winners were pitcher Felipe Lira and catcher Brad Ausmus. In 1996, while playing for Detroit they had a BERA of 3.14 in 106 innings which was, on average, −3.19 better than their individual ERA's that year. They were one of only two seasonal batteries in the qualifying 2,039 pairings that had on average three or more runs better than any other pairings.

The lowest BERA for a season (minimum of 75 innings paired) was recorded by Bob Gibson and Johnny Edwards in 1968 with St. Louis for a phenomenal 0.89 in 91 innings. Gibson's PERA that year was 1.12. Gibson teamed up with catcher Tim McCarver that same year to capture second place in the BERA ranking with a 1.22. Mike Torrez and Gene Tenace came in third with a BERA of 1.26.

The lowest BERA for a career belongs to Vida Blue and Dave Duncan who notched 1.74 in 362 innings compared to Blue's career PERA of 3.45 with other catchers which he attained in 2,981⅓ innings. The Blue-Duncan duo headed a list of three batteries out of the 1,093 qualifying teammates that all had a BERA of less than 2.00.

Who was the duet with over 1,000 innings together that had the best differential over the long haul? That honor goes to the team of Pedro Martinez and Jason Varitek who, in 1,133 innings, had an average differential of -1.80 when they posted a BERA of 2.34. Forty-seven other pairings had 1,000+ innings together and 46 of them had an average differential below their individual numbers. Only one tandem had a BERA higher than their career numbers but they were less than one run above.

Table 1. BERA Better Than Pitcher's Earned Run Average (PERA)

Pitcher	Catcher	BERA	PERA	B-P	B Inn	P Inn
John Farrell	Andy Alanson	3.36	6.59	-3.23	439.3	259.3
Ryan Dempster	Mike Redmond	3.38	6.14	-2.76	410.0	574.7
Steve Kline	Thurman Munson	2.43	4.84	-2.41	492.0	258.3
Ron Bryant	Dave Rader	2.87	5.18	-2.31	458.3	458.7
Mike Bielecki	Damon Berryhill	2.47	4.78	-2.31	317.3	913.7
Chris Knapp	Brian Downing	3.92	6.21	-2.29	321.7	282.7
Dave Frost	Brian Downing	2.98	5.27	-2.28	280.7	270.0
Cory Lidle	Ramon Hernandez	3.09	5.22	-2.13	315.0	652.3
Matt Keough	Jim Essian	2.62	4.70	-2.08	299.3	890.7
Tim Lollar	Terry Kennedy	3.55	5.62	-2.08	589.0	317.0

Table 2. BERA Better Than Catcher's Earned Run Average (CERA)

Pitcher	Catcher	BERA	CERA	B-C	B Inn	C Inn
Kevin Brown	Charles Johnson	2.22	4.49	-2.26	352.3	9231.0
Jose Rijo	Jeff Reed	2.24	4.35	-2.11	325.3	7362.7
Pedro Martinez	Jason Varitek	2.34	4.37	-2.03	1133.3	5242.3
Kevin Appier	Brent Mayne	2.59	4.51	-1.93	522.0	8369.3
Doug Drabek	Don Slaught	2.29	4.16	-1.87	319.0	9329.0
Gaylord Perry	Ray Fosse	1.82	3.64	-1.82	306.7	6781.0
Kenny Rogers	A.J. Hinch	3.01	4.82	-1.81	322.7	2285.3
Randy Johnson	Damian Miller	2.38	4.15	-1.77	733.3	4945.7
Greg Maddux	Eddie Perez	2.50	4.26	-1.76	832.3	2720.0
Bartolo Colon	Einar Diaz	3.42	5.14	-1.72	554.7	4328.0

The Worst Batteries

And now what about those guys who should never have been brought together? Who were the worst batteries, both in a season or in a career? First, we'll start with the seasonal pairings that were almost dead batteries. Comparing the duo's BERA to the pitcher's season (PERA) the bottom of the barrel belongs to pitcher Steve Sparks and catcher Brandon Inge who, while playing for Detroit in 2002, posted a differential (PERA-minus-BERA) of +3.74 or almost four runs worse than Sparks's seasonal ERA of 3.24. Coming in at a close second was the battery of Charlie Hough and Don Slaught with a BERA of 5.81 compared to Hough's PERA of 2.57 which he notched for the Rangers in 1986.

The other seasonal perspective is CERA-minus-BERA or how well (or poorly) the tandem did in comparison to the catcher's ERA is also held by the Sparks-Inge duo. While playing for the Tigers in 2002 the two showed no electricity at all when they had a differential of +2.61 or two and a half runs worse than the catcher's season. Thirteen other batteries (out of the qualifying 2,039) had a differential of two runs or more above CERA.

When the two differentials are averaged, the worst seasonal battery again was Steve Sparks and Brandon Inge who should have been kept apart on the 2002 Tigers' playing field. Their +2.73 average differential in 105⅔ innings was the worst out of the qualifying pairings that had a minimum of 75 innings together. Table 8 shows the seasonal bottom five near-dead batteries.

Looking at the career worst, the PERA-minus-BERA leaders were Tippy Martinez and Rick Dempsey who, in 516⅓ innings,

had a 2.79 worse ERA than Martinez's career 1.73 without Dempsey. Coming in second place was the duo of Greg Minton and Bob Brenly whose differential was +2.16. In the CERA-minus-BERA analysis, the worst was pitcher Kirk McCaskill and backstop Ron Karkovice who posted a +1.25 differential above Karkovice's career CERA of 3.68. Willie Blair and Brad Ausmus with a differential of +1.21 came in a very close second place. The very worst career battery, when both the PERA and CERA are considered is the team of Greg Minton and Bob Brenly. They posted a 1.23 higher BERA than either's career numbers. Tables 5, 6, and 7 give the lowdown on the five bottom dwellers for all three perspectives.

The highest BERA for a season (minimum of 75 innings paired) was recorded by pitcher Brian Bohanon and catcher Henry Blanco who had a horrible 7.17 in 85⅓ innings in 1999 with the Colorado Rockies. Bohanon's PERA that year with all other backstops was 5.63 or one and a half runs better. Second place in the seasonal highest BERA is held by the duo of Jaime Navarro and catcher Dave Nilsson (MIL 1993) who posted 7.74. These two batteries headed a list of twenty batteries that all had a BERA greater than 6.00 and all twenty had BERAs above the pitcher's ERA that year.

The highest BERA for a career (minimum of 250 innings together) belongs to pitcher Scott Erickson and catcher Charles Johnson who notched 5.32 in 264 innings together, compared to Erickson's career PERA of 4.43 with other catchers. Coming in second was the team of Paul Abbott and Dan Wilson who posted a BERA of 5.30. They were just two of the four pairings with BERAs greater than 5.00 in 1,093 qualifying career batteries.

Table 3. Average of BERA to both PERA and CERA, career best

Pitcher	Catcher	BERA	B-P	B-C	AVG	B Inn	PC Inn
Kevin Brown	Charles Johnson	2.22	-1.10	-2.26	-1.99	352.3	12061.7
Jose Rijo	Jeff Reed	2.24	-1.20	-2.11	-1.95	325.0	8917.7
Doug Drabek	Don Slaught	2.29	-1.66	-1.87	-1.83	319.0	11545.0
Kevin Appier	Brent Mayne	2.59	-1.44	-1.93	-1.83	522.0	10442.7
Pedro Martinez	Jason Varitek	2.34	-0.72	-2.03	-1.79	1133.3	6406.0
Jose Guzman	Ivan Rodriguez	2.77	-1.72	-1.71	-1.71	314.7	14722.7
Vida Blue	Dave Duncan	1.74	-1.71	-1.71	-1.71	362.0	9916.7
Frank Tanana	Terry Humphrey	2.05	-1.77	-1.60	-1.70	373.0	6367.0
Gaylord Perry	Ray Fosse	1.82	-1.36	-1.82	-1.63	306.7	11824.7
Kenny Rogers	A.J. Hinch	3.01	-1.43	-1.81	-1.62	322.7	4629.3

Table 4. Average of BERA to both PERA and CERA, seasonal best

Pitcher	Catcher	Year	Tm	BERA	B-P	B-C	AVG	B Inn
Felipe Lira	Brad Ausmus	1996	DET	3.14	-4.88	-2.90	-3.19	106.0
Bruce Hurst	Rich Gedman	1987	BOS	2.51	-2.96	-3.13	-3.07	82.3
George Stone	Bob Tillman	1970	ATL	1.55	-3.63	-2.80	-2.98	75.3
Mike Hampton	Brent Mayne	2001	COL	2.82	-4.31	-2.39	-2.97	76.7
Kenny Rogers	Geno Petralli	1993	TEX	2.75	-2.57	-3.15	-2.94	91.7
Dick Ellsworth	Sammy Taylor	1961	CHN	2.27	-2.82	-2.77	-2.79	75.3
Kirk Rueter	Brian Johnson	1997	SFN	2.44	-2.16	-2.92	-2.73	77.3
Don Sutton	Jeff Torborg	1970	LAN	1.99	-3.07	-2.40	-2.65	77.0
Jim Slaton	Charlie Moore	1975	MIL	3.29	-3.76	-2.16	-2.59	134.0
Jeff Suppan	Hector Ortiz	2000	KCA	3.58	2.19	-2.94	-2.57	78.0

Hall Of Famers

In the data period there were 19 seasonal pairings of Hall Of Famers and seven career match-ups. Only two seasonal pairings and four career pairings met the criteria. The best season was recorded by the battery of Carlton Fisk and Tom Seaver while with the Chicago White Sox in 1984 who had a BERA-minus-PERA÷CERA of −2.29 in 130⅔ innings. The only other seasonal qualifier was the duo of Whitey Ford and Yogi Berra who in 1960 posted a differential of −1.17 for the New York Yankees. The best career differential belongs to Carlton Fisk and Dennis Eckersley with −0.88 in 468 innings when they had a BERA of 2.90. The worst career performance was by the Johnny Bench and Tom Seaver battery who posted a differential of −0.26 or just slightly better than their individual ERAs on average.

Summary

Using comparative earned run averages for all batteries provided an easy measure to gauge the very best and worst pairings in the data period (1960–2004). The duo of Kevin Brown and Charles Johnson were slightly superior to any other career match-ups. Together they never had a BERA higher than any other pairing for either player. That's saying something given that Johnson had 187 different battery mates and Brown had 23. The same could not be said for the various worst batteries that separately had decent ERAs, but together they were a bad combination. Perhaps more attention should be paid to the dynamics of battery pairing. Certainly this study shows that sometimes a pitcher and a catcher have a certain spark as a team while other batteries should have been disconnected.

Notes

Retrosheet *Event Files* is the source material for the years 1960–1992 and 2000-2004. David Smith provided the *Event Files* for 1993–1999.

Special thanks to SABR members Jim Charlton, David Smith, Tom Ruane, Clifford Blau, Keith Karcher, and to West Point Mathematics Professor Mike Huber for their critique and suggestions. Also thanks to Craig Wright, Keith Woolner and Tom Hanrahan whose research on the subject opened the door for further investigation.

Both the pitchers' earned run averages (PERA) and the catchers' earned run averages (CERA) do *not* include the specific battery's earned run average (BERA) components.

This study does not purport that there is any statistical significance between individual catcher's ERAs and other backstops on the same team, only that some measure of difference exists. Furthermore, like all small sample sizes, there is the possibility of random noise, but the specific criteria was used to wipe out as much noise as possible.

Table 5. BERA worse than pitcher's earned run average (PERA)

Pitcher	Catcher	BERA	PERA	B-P	B Inn	P Inn
Tippy Martinez	Rick Dempsey	4.52	1.73	+2.79	516.3	317.7
Greg Minton	Bob Brenly	4.72	2.56	+2.16	282.3	848.3
Bobby Thigpen	Carlton Fisk	4.51	2.53	+1.97	259.7	309.0
Sparky Lyle	Thurman Munson	4.04	2.10	+1.93	559.7	830.7
Ron Perranoski	Johnny Roseboro	3.57	1.76	+1.82	667.3	507.3

Table 6. BERA worse than catcher's earned run average (CERA)

Pitcher	Catcher	BERA	CERA	B-C	B Inn	C Inn
Kirk McCaskill	Ron Karkovice	4.93	3.68	+1.25	324.7	6648.0
Willie Blair	Brad Ausmus	5.11	3.90	+1.21	318.7	11443.0
Bobby Jones	Mike Piazza	4.71	3.54	+1.17	275.0	11752.7
Larry Sherry	Johnny Roseboro	4.27	3.14	+1.13	291.0	9639.7
Jose Lima	Tony Eusebio	4.59	3.49	+1.09	263.0	3768.3

Table 7. Average of BERA to both PERA and CERA, career worst

Pitcher	Catcher	BERA	B-P	B-C	AVG	B Inn	PC Inn
Greg Minton	Bob Brenly	4.72	+2.16	+1.07	+1.23	282.3	5926.7
Kirk McCaskill	Ron Karkovice	4.93	+1.01	+1.25	+1.21	324.7	8052.3
Willie Blair	Brad Ausmus	5.11	+0.10	+1.21	+1.12	318.7	12398.3
Larry Sherry	Johnny Roseboro	4.27	+0.78	+1.13	+1.12	291.0	10049.3
Bobby Jones	Mike Piazza	4.71	+0.44	+1.17	+1.10	275.0	12996.3

Table 8. Average of BERA to both PERA and CERA, seasonal worst

Pitcher	Catcher	Year	Tm	BERA	B-P	B-C	AVG	B Inn
Steve Sparks	Brandon Inge	2002	DET	6.98	+3.74	+2.61	+2.73	105.7
Joaquin Andujar	Darrell Porter	1985	SLN	5.40	+2.53	+2.61	+2.59	81.7
Jim Slaton	Darrell Porter	1975	MIL	6.51	+2.95	+2.38	+2.45	83.0
Mike Oquist	A.J. Hinch	1998	OAK	6.86	+0.65	+2.56	+2.40	99.7
Dan Spillner	Ron Hassey	1980	CLE	6.83	+2.76	+2.25	+2.30	114.7

JOURNAL CORRECTIONS

BRJ 33

In the article on Sadaharu Oh the table on page 53 shows that Oh had a BA of .320 or better 0 times and yet had a BA of .340 or better twice. The correct number for .320 or better is ten (10).

In the article on Why It's So Hard to Hit .400, the author notes that the following corrections should be made:
1. In the second paragraph, the last sentence should end in sacrifices, not strikeouts.
2. Equation 3 should read $SLG = (1 - KAVG) \times IPSLG$
3. The x-axis label in Figure 1 is missing. It starts in 1875 and proceeds to 2005 in five-year increments for the minor ticks and 10 year increments for the major ticks.

BRJ 32

In the chart on page 45, Jim Tobin is listed with a 58 CGOBS streak in 1922. The value of 58 CGOBS streak, which began on April 29 through July 11, was derived by Herm Krabbenhoft's from the "official" day-by-day (DBD) records on file at the Hall of Fame Library. Trent McCotter discovered that there was an error in the DBD records. While the DBD indicates that Tobin (as a pinch hitter) had 0 at bats, 0 hits, 0 walks, and 0 hit by pitches on July 4, Trent found that Tobin actually had one at bat according to the box score of the game. So Tobin's CGOBS streak apparently ended at 51. However, upon further examination, Trent found that Tobin's batting line for the second game of a double header on May 27 had been entered after the game on October 1 instead of after the first game on May 27. In that second May 27 game, Tobin was 1-for-4. Thus, Tobin's CGOBS streak (April 29 through July 3) actually was 52. Trent also found another 50-game CGOBS that was previously undetected: Cleveland's Tris Speaker, June 17 through August 7, first game, 1926. Speaker went 0-for-2 on August 7, second game, before being removed; he went on to reach safely in the next 23 straight games, making it 73 out of 74.

ROAD TRIPS

Norman Macht notes that the box score in the 26-inning game article was reproduced from the *Oakland Tribune*. It contains an error; Ivy Olson should have the nine assists; Bernie Neis had 0 that day.

TNP 25

Jerry Holub notes that in the article "Ty Cobb, Master Thief" the attendance in Cleveland for the game of June 15, 1928 is estimated at up to 85,000. Since the Indians played the game in League Park, and had not yet moved to the much larger Municipal Stadium, this statement is in error.

On page 16 of the article on the Nugent era, the statement is made that Chuck Klein holds the franchise single-season scoring record of 158 runs and the NL assists record for one season of 44. Billy Hamilton holds the Phillies, NL, and ML record for runs scored in a season with 192 in 1894, and Klein's assist record is the post-1900 NL mark. On page 18, the correct number of Phillies victories between 1938 and 1942 is 225 games, not 185.
In the description of the Sept. 3, 1939 game page 55, it states that Selkirk swung at the first wide pitch. In fact, Selkirk was on third; Dahlgren was the batter.

On page 68 of the Carl Erskine article the Dodger pitcher recalls talking about his first game with writer Charlie Park on July 23, 1948. However, his first game took place two days later. On page 70 the article misstates that Erskine pitched in game 6. He pitched in games 4 and 5.

On page 108 in the second column Hoss Radbourn's record should be 27-12 for his last season in Boston, not for his last four seasons. In his five seasons in Boston and his swan song in Cincinnati, Hoss completed 216 of the 225 games he started.

On page 120 of the article on Point Men, a reader points out that the Royals did not have the best record by an expansion team. Buffalo in 1879 had a .590 record in its first year as the NL expanded from six to eight teams.

Photo above from *The Sporting News*, December 21, 1939.